Electronic Money Flows

Electronic Money Flows

The Molding of a New Financial Order

edited by
Elinor Harris Solomon
The George Washington University

Kluwer Academic Publishers
Boston / Dordrecht / London

Distributors for North America:
Kluwer Academic Publishers
101 Philip Drive
Assinippi Park
Norwell, Massachusetts 02061 USA

Distributors for all other countries:
Kluwer Academic Publishers Group
Distribution Centre
Post Office Box 322
3300 AH Dordrecht, THE NETHERLANDS

Library of Congress Cataloging-in-Publication Data

Electronic money flows: the molding of a new financial order/edited
   by Elinor Harris Solomon.
      p.   cm.
   Includes bibliographical references and index.
   ISBN 0−7923−9134−9
   1. Electronic funds transfers.   I. Solomon, Elinor Harris.
HG1710.E47   1991
332.1′028—dc20   90−20523
                                                CIP

Printed in the United States of America.

This book is dedicated with great respect and gratitude to Dr. Gottfried Haberler, one of the most influential economists of the 20th century. Dr. Haberler's writings and guidance for 60 years have profoundly influenced both economic thought and the direction of contemporary public policy. Prominent among Dr. Haberler's many fundamental contributions has been his definitive analysis of the nature of dynamic processes and innovation, with which this book is concerned.

E.H.S.

Contents

Contributing Authors

Gottfried Haberler
Resident Scholar at American Enterprise Institute and Professor of Economics
  and Galen L. Stone Professor of International Trade Emeritus, Harvard
  University
1150 Seventeenth Street, N.W.
Washington, D.C. 20036

C. Dianne Martin
Professor, School of Engineering and Applied Science
Department of Electrical Engineering and Computer Science
The George Washington University
Washington, D.C. 20052

Linda K.S. Moore
President, L.K.S. Moore & Co., Inc.
Electronic Banking International
P.O. Box 1889
Venice, CA 90294–1889

Yoshiharu Oritani
Manager
Research Division II
Institute for Monetary and Economic Studies
The Bank of Japan
Tokyo, 100–91, CPO Box 203, Japan

Kenneth Robinson, Esq.
Senior Legal Adviser to the Chairman
Federal Communications Commission
1919 M Street, N.W.
Washington, D.C. 20554

Thomas D. Simpson
Associate Director
Division of Research and Statistics
Board of Governors of the Federal Reserve System
Washington, D.C. 20551

Elinor Harris Solomon
Professor of Economics
The Department of Economics
The George Washington University
Washington, D.C. 20052

Thomas H. Solomon
Post Doctoral Fellow
Center for Research in Nonlinear Dynamics
Department of Physics
University of Texas at Austin
Austin, TX 78712

Fred W. Weingarten
Executive Director
Computing Research Association
1625 Massachusetts Ave., N.W. (#110)
Washington, D.C. 20036−2212

Preface

Electronic Money Flows describes the far-reaching present changes under-
way in payments and capital markets. Electronic payment forms are in the
process of molding a new financial regime—largely shared and interdependent—throughout the world.

Our earlier *Electronic Funds Transfers and Payments* (Kluwer, 1987)
looked at the new money technology in its initial phases of development
and in broad focus. Then, as now, the contributors came from many
different disciplines. The synthesis of their diverse views laid out the
background for the electronic payments revolution to come, and the great
benefits but also risks for segmented sectors of society.

The old questions have not gone away; new ones have been added to
the agenda. For example, what is the nature of money today amidst an
array of computer-based options? What money and turnover concepts
are appropriate to the electronic age? What are the effects of high-speed
money flows on markets, volatility, money control, even the business
cycle? Is the financial system more prone to instability but also to faster
correction, given the swift movement of money and payments? At the
same time, is privacy imperiled by the ubiquitous computer-linked webs
that move both information and money?

This second book is thus companion to *Electronic Funds Transfers and
Payments* and expands upon it. Contributors discuss the expectations that
have and have not come to fruition, together with the new issues of the past
four years. New theoretical approaches are developed, while the insights
and lessons to be gleaned from history are set forth. Explanations for the
policy puzzles are posed. Possible policy implications are suggested.
Choices and strategies for vendors and users are analyzed within a context
of the always present tradeoffs. The benefits to and concerns of the average
citizen are addressed.

The Format of the Book

Electronic Money Flows focuses on ongoing change in an area already affecting everybody, expert and man-in-the-street alike. It is therefore designed for the ordinary citizen as well as practitioner in the new technology, be he or she banker, attorney, operations specialist, engineer, or student.

Since the contributors come from many disciplines, the book's use, we hope, will also be multidisciplinary. It is crafted to cut across a diverse mix of college classes and business occupations: economic, financial, legal, technical, and scientific. Each chapter presents a different set of issues and policy concerns. Each can be read separately, according to interest, or as part of the whole collection of contributed chapters. Each chapter adds further coloration to the more complete story of how the latest economic revolution is affecting the way the economy works and societies interact.

Money and payments concepts and some basic elementary monetary theory, appropriate to the electronic age, are set forth in part I. Payments media choices are presented for the years ahead, with microeconomic theory relevant to the ultimate market selection. Vendor and supplier considerations, too, are evaluated.

Part II analyzes stability, business cycle theory and control, and macroeconomic policy choices in systems dominated by electronic payments. Some lessons from the past and theoretical models for the future are set forth.

Part III deals with issues of global cooperation and competition in a now seamless 24-hour web of money and capital flows. The nature of electronic networks and the evolving new mechanisms are the focus. Part IV underscores the societal benefits and progress toward the electronic society yet to come as the present young computer-literate among us come of age. It flags the concerns of society as well, and the adequacy of legal protections underscoring the technology and its rapid current dispersion.

Acknowledgments

As before, I have been most fortunate in the experience and diversity of the group of authors. To all I owe a very special debt. The contributors are actively involved in hands-on issues and in the many unknowns generated by technological change. Each is a leader in the field. Yet each brings a different perspective: business cycle theorist, central banker, attorney, consultant to technology users, academic.

This book taps also the skills of contributors from the "hard" sciences, physics, electrical engineering, computer science. One can scarcely make any sense out of present technical developments without such help. In this effort I have been very lucky. A great part of the excitement and fun of this second book, for me, was this interaction with concerned and imaginative experts from the multiple diverse disciplines, who raised important questions and provided fresh perspectives.

I especially want to thank Professors Bryan Boulier, Anthony Yezer, and other George Washington University colleagues for their help and support. I appreciate the assistance of many within the Federal Reserve System, especially Jeffrey Marquardt, Edward Ettin, Stephen Rhoades, Donald Savage, David Humphrey, and George Juncker. Attorneys Donald I. Baker and Karen Grimm have tutored me in the legal nuances as well as the complexities of electronic payments in practical application. My George Washington University students have provided insights and encouragement, as have Dr. Eleanor Hadley, Dr. Penelope Hartland-Thunberg, and Barbara Johnston and the kind scholars of the American Enterprise Institute. I appreciate the help in many different ways of Jennifer Lin and Eva Skryjova of our Economics Department and Derric Ward of George Washington University's Computer Science Department. Finally, once again I want to acknowledge the patience and invaluable assistance of our editor Zachary Rolnik, of the Kluwer organization, and of my long-suffering husband.

INTRODUCTION

The electronic financial links, sending payments mostly at the speed of light, are growing exponentially. This book examines the economic and global implications of a virtually instantaneous binding together of people, money, markets, and nations. Its focus is the heightened payments flows. The approach is multifaceted as it must be when money, technology, and telecommunications become fused into one economic and social force.

We expand in this book upon the various kinds of money and payments and the surprisingly diverse implications of the new. That which constitutes an acceptable medium of exchange ranges from the commonplace physical and accounting money to the space-age variety of computerized money pulses devoid of any tangible financial institution interface. The vision of the future spelled out in the last book has become reality now, with the exponential proliferation of dedicated nets and electronic financial links around the world.

Part I, Money and Payments, deals with the story's background. It picks up where the last book left off, with the work of Paul Henderson and Linda Moore. The new technology requires some basic rethinking about the nature of money. The modern alchemy succeeds where the old failed. The ancients of the middle ages were not able to turn lead into gold. But the

Solomon, E.H., (ed.), *Electronic Money Flows*.
© 1991 Kluwer Academic Publishers. ISBN 0–7923–9134–9. All rights reserved.

medium of electronics converts magnetized elementary particles (bits) stored in computer memory into money-like value. Messages to transfer money can take the form of photons moving at the speed of light on satellite, microwave relay, or fiber optic threads; or they can move in only slightly more clumsy fashion at the speed of electricity, when the medium of telephone wires become the means of payments transmission chosen by telecommunications firms.

Under these circumstances, some updating of money concepts would seem to be in order, to fill in gaps in the saga of how and why the new money technology is creating a revolution in the way we conduct a payments business. Part I provides a start to this difficult task, and suggests some specific money updating in order to encompass the reality of virtually instantaneous money flows.

Chapter 1, "Money: Image and Reality," sets the stage for the book. The slant is institutional and microeconomic. We look at the different kinds of money, beginning with the Federal Reserve System's conventional "M" categories as measured and commonly used. The focus shifts then to the other electronic money forms, such as "daylight" money, bank-linked electronic money, and information-based money flows without systematic bank settlement arrangements. In the extreme, the latter can become a kind of electronic barter.

The concept of continuous money and continuous money flow is developed for later use in the book. Money flows are unpredictable in a milieu where computerized trading tools may drastically turn up (or down) the effective velocity parameter within seconds. It only stands to reason that there will be system and perhaps macroeconomic effects. Moreover, when money is several layers removed from the reserve base, and often settled not in reserves but in other forms of electronic money or barter, money control becomes further thrust off target.

While large dollar payments are almost entirely electronic, the small payments retain (for the time being) much of their traditional character. There are reasons for this lag at the cash end of the spectrum. There may be ways also to remedy the situation to the consumer's satisfaction, so as to speed the way toward the oft-predicted cashless, checkless society.

Linda Moore (President, L.K.S. Moore & Co., Inc.) addresses these particular questions in chapter 2. In "Money in the Third Millineum," Moore describes the way that money or liquid assets may be most rationally allocated as between cash, deposits, and prepaid cards such as the "smart card." There are many technical possibilities, and a host of cost and benefit decisions for vendors, users, and producers to consider. These are laid out for the first time here by a leading money technology expert with extensive background at the Federal Reserve Bank of New York (Special Assistant for Operations) and most recently as international electronic banking consultant.

Moore's microeconomic analysis provides underlying theory and new insights. The chapter discusses also the varied menu of specific payments forms made possible by the technology. Some are in use abroad, in Japan, France, and other countries on the Continent. Moore looks at the prepaid media already available and in use around the world, and the various smart cards of different gradations of memory, convenience, multiuse capability, and cost. Finally, Moore discusses how vendors can help consumers maximize their utility, find a market for their product, and entice the retail sector more swiftly into the most cost-efficient payments mode. Chapter 2 provides perspective about what money is and can be in the years to come.

Part II, Stability and the Business Cycle, shifts gears to the macroeconomic. Something unusual but clearly significant has happened to the money control process in the past decade. At least in part, the puzzle appears related to changes produced by the money flows speeds, that is, by the system's greater current ability to move money. Perhaps fundamental changes have developed within the business cycle process, too. The greatest business cycle theoretician of our day, Dr. Gottfried Haberler, addresses these critical matters. His chapter encompasses not only the present but the historical view, the lessons to be learned from the Great Depression in the modern interconnected—and hopefully more enlightened—world.

The dynamics of change enters into the outcome and always has in the business cycle control sense. The dynamic model of cumulative change, with its time lags and perspective of the endogenous forces that move markets, was the subject of Dr. Gottfried Haberler's pioneering work, *Prosperity and Depression* (1937). That book remains to this day a powerful and relevant model of business cycle movements and transitions at the turning points from growth downward to recession.

In his new work, *What Happened to the Business Cycle?*, Dr. Haberler —my distinguished and kind professor to whom generations of students have turned for wise counsel—re-examines the same questions. Dr. Haberler, Resident Scholar at the American Enterprise Institute and Professor of Economics Emeritus of Harvard University, inquires into the nature of today's business cycle. He asks whether we finally are back in (inflationary) recession, due to war in the Persian Gulf, after almost eight years of unprecedented expansion. Such a recession is not likely to be of the magnitude of the Great Depression, however. True, there have been some scary stock exchange crashes, in 1987 and 1989–1990, but that they did not bring on a recession suggests that monetary management in the seven leading industrial countries has greatly improved.

Dr. Haberler looks to the fundamentals behind the main policy mistakes that produced the world-shaking Great Depression of the 1930s. The record of economic misjudgments then was horrendous. They ranged from severe monetary contraction to inappropriate tax increases and tariff barriers, which served only to export our depression around the world. When the economy did begin to pick up in 1937, the Federal Reserve overreacted once again to cause a new and extremely vicious recession.

It is inconceivable to Dr. Haberler that such mistakes will be made again by any of the leading industrialized countries, a member of the Group of Seven or the Group of Ten. Monetary management has been much better in the 1980s and, hopefully, the 1990s. Financial experts have better cooperated around the world—for example, to curb the stock market slides. Flexible exchange rates have also helped countries lessen any impact of a financial crash upon the real economy and control inflation.

All this effectively rules out any economic contraction coming anywhere near the Great Depression, except in case of some catastrophic event such as war. The question of the fundamental nature of the business cycle remains, however. Dr. Haberler thinks that perhaps the German word *Konjunkturschwankungen* is a better term. It easily translates into "business fluctuations," a good substitute for business cycles because the phrase suggests variety rather than uniformity.

Dr. Thomas H. Solomon, now post-doctoral fellow at the Center for Nonlinear Dynamics (University of Texas), and I follow up on this general theme: the nature of economic fluctuations. The experiments on fluids dynamics ("chaotic advection") conducted at the Haverford College Laboratory (T.H. Solomon and J.P. Gollub) have provided many useful insights and tools for examination of economic control mechanisms. The question of what electronic money speeds may do to the underlying money control process is a challenging one.

In *Money Stability and Control: The Perverse Effects of Feedback Loops*, we look at feedback mechanisms in money control systems, both before and after the advent of electronic funds transfers (EFT). The role of time lags always has been important in thwarting short-term money control efforts, as highlighted by Milton Friedman. But especially interesting is the "quantum leap" introduced by electronics into the already difficult money control process.

In order to gauge this effect, the money flows parameter is varied in the model. The ability of EFT to move money faster (that is, to raise the system's "saturation level") increases the evidence of any unstable short-run money movements. A shift to targets with swift implementation possibilities (for example, the Fed funds rate) reduces potential volatility that arises from this particular source. Market-based targets can also help "decouple" any destabilizing feedback links between interest rates and money.

Part III concerns The Seamless Global Mesh, and the interdependence that follows. The perspective is that of two key central bankers on opposite sides of the globe. Dr. Thomas Simpson (Federal Reserve Board) and Dr. Yoshiharu Oritani (Bank of Japan) analyze the flow of money and capital in a seamless 24-hour web. Oritani focuses on payments nets, Simpson on the broader capital markets mesh.

Both make policy proposals on how best to promote efficiency and safeguard system integrity at the same time. Oritani suggests the forging of tighter links between central banks directly, in guarantee of payments finalty. Simpson stresses the need for eventual simultaneous settlement and multilateral payments netting across instruments. The latter approach will reduce the gross payments flows and market volatility as well as minimize risks: systemic, settlement, and counter-party. However, neither proposal is easy to implement. For one thing, there are tradeoffs and choices to be made between often conflicting goals of efficiency and system stability, a theme noted also in chapter 8 of this book and the subject of recent judicial dispute. The problem of persuading present holders of payments subsidies to part with them is also a recurrent refrain, noted by Solomon, Moore, Robinson, and Henderson (1987).

In chapter 5, "Globalization of Payments Network and Risks," Dr. Oritani, Manager of the Institute for Monetary and Economic Studies at the Bank of Japan, addresses the global flows of money across a variety of private and central-bank-sponsored links. Oritani has an outstanding knowledge of payments issues to match his economic theory skills. He looks at technological underpinnings of the global flow and the kinds of forms the now rapidly proliferating global nets might take. One form is the inhouse transnational network, linked to the central bank wire (such as Fedwire). Another is the independent proprietary corporate or financial international system without tangible direct bank interface (such as noted in chapter 1).

Oritani analyzes the familiar questions of risk, especially systemic risk, with innovative solutions. The remedy, he believes, is both payments finality—which only an independent central bank can provide—and interglobal central bank cooperation. The central banks should act also as lender of last resort to prevent international financial disorders from rippling from one country to another halfway around the globe.

Dr. Haberler has just noted (chapter 3) the effectiveness of more limited forms of cooperation on several occasions—in October 1987 and 1989, to stem the New York Stock Exchange decline, and in March 1990 to ease the tensions in the Tokyo exchanges. Oritani goes still farther in this direction. He observes that a global network of central banks could minimize systemic risk, for several reasons. First, the central banking network could facilitate a cross-border funds transfer with finality; it could also provide a quick extension of credit whenever central banks might want to play the role of lender of last resort. Of great importance, however, is the assurance of independent central banks and their continued credibility.

Dr. Thomas Simpson, Associate Director of the Research Division of the Federal Reserve Board, addresses the "24-hour seamless web" of money and capital flows. Simpson's "Trends in Global Securities Markets," chapter 6, raises important and fundamental new issues. Dr. Simpson for over a decade has been a pioneer in financial markets innovation, and he highlights for us here the great international payments changes. Simpson observes, as does Oritani, the present high degree of interdependence among national financial markets. The impact of electronics upon these exchanges, and upon capital flows generally, is analyzed carefully. The present forms of market-making systems in national capital markets are explained, and the desirable attributes of a market system discussed.

The necessary reforms are set forth, including simultaneous settlement and standardization within trading systems in leading financial centers. The barriers to such reforms are indicated also: among them, a continued preference for paper by some holders of securities and a rather natural unwillingness to give up float by those who would end up losing (brokers, possibly). Multilateral clearing house settlement would reduce unnecessary payments "churning" and increase payments efficiency by a great deal. A collateralization of risk by the clearing house would reduce the necessary liquidity required for clearing and raise customer confidence in the system.

Balanced against advantages are the costs of risk control, in particular curbing the "moral hazard" incentives that accompany the mutualization of risk. The familiar refrain is echoed: there are no easy solutions here. Someone or something is bound to object to reforms in the transition to a fully electronic society.

Part IV—Money and Society: Technology and the World Ahead—concerns the societal impacts. The protective role of the law is examined also, in its often futile effort to keep up with the moving target of rapid technological change.

There is both eagerness and reluctance to adopt the new technology, by the ordinary consumer user. The demographics and age of the user is a divisive factor. The lags noted in the last book remain; however, consumer resistance should not continue much beyond the next decade. The computer-literate young are growing up, as indicated by electronic telecommunications expert Kenneth Robinson (Senior Legal Adviser to the Chairman, Federal Communications Commission). Robinson's chapter 7, "Information Services, Demographics, and Dynamics of Change," shows that the benefits of the new money technology are beginning to be more fully realized by the new generation coming of age and into economic power on their own; many have even tutored their elders in the United States and Japan. The advantages—for example, of teleshopping—are not lost on the increasingly more numerous working women among us either.

But the legal system is presently ill-equipped to cope with this transition, which may be abrupt. The substitution of judges for regulators as all-powerful decision makers at the conflict resolution level is not a satisfactory approach, Robinson believes. Problems with the AT&T divestiture are illustrative of the greater difficulties yet to come. Regulators shun their traditional role as providers of guidance to the market and relinquish authority to those perhaps less well able to do the job.

"Conflicts: Banks, Consumers, and the Law" (chapter 8) examines the role now thrust upon litigators that was once the realm of the central bank in the payments arena. I analyze the problems and conflicts faced by those of the diverse industry and marketing elements who must offer the expensive new technology jointly. The retail payments world today is a far cry from the homogeneous bank-dominated one of the past.

In part this new diversity breeds competition, new services, and modes of delivery, and is much to be desired. But it also causes some severe conflicts and internal payments strains to flare. The role of the Federal Reserve, Federal Communications Commission, and Antitrust Division is at question. Private litigators must resolve conflicts engendered by an uncertain melange of joint arrangements, put together by sometimes uncomfortable groups of payments partners with different outlooks and industry backgrounds. Many are newcomers, coming from the technology rather than payments background. Their eclectic views can tend to make bankers uneasy. Is a greater central banking presence perhaps a good idea under these circumstances? One is struck powerfully with the commonality of this dilemma today at both the retail electronic payments area (part IV) and in the global arena (part III).

In chapter 9, the spectrum is broadened further by consideration of the technology and societal questions in "The Less-Cash/Less-Check Society: Banking in the Information Age." The technology is explained for the layman by two of the most influential and leading authors in the field. This great revolution offers enormous benefits to mankind; it also suggests personal risks. The societal risks involve financial security and personal privacy. These are of a quite different nature than those noted in parts II (system instability) or III (systemic or settlement, among others).

Chapter 9 reviews the role and ability of the law to safeguard citizens from such threats. The legal and operational gaps and difficulties in keeping up with the moving target are specified very clearly. The threat of "big brother" hovering above us all, potentially able to pull the strings, is dealt with. In this final chapter Professor Dianne Martin (of the George Washington University Electrical Engineering and Computer Science Department) and Dr. Fred Weingarten (then Project Director of the Congressional Office of Technology Assessment) look at the societal impacts in a spellbinding way one does not soon forget.

Common Themes

Each contributor indicates very clearly his/her conclusions, and it would be repetitive to include them here. But many common themes pervade the writings in this book. The emphasis throughout is on information and money flows, instantaneous, continuous, and global. Finance, telecommunications, and distribution modes are fused.[1] Institutions evolve, coalesce, and change in a process akin to Darwin's survival of the fittest. Vendors are caught in the middle, many unprepared. The underlying dynamics of the economic process changes, affecting the nature of theoretical models and the practicality of established public policies.

All contributors observe that the pace of the new technology is breathtaking; all contributors note that the benefits are enormous and are beginning to be taken for granted, at least in the large-dollar payments modes that move markets. However, many observe that present statutes protecting individuals and property are inadequate (Weingarten and Martin, Robinson). The establishment of elaborate financial data bases can threaten privacy. The language of the law does not clearly cover funds movement by electronic pulses. The regulators, in leaving the natural forces of technology to the market, have stepped back, while some confusion has been left in their wake. Those uncertainties will be clarified ultimately both by the market and the legal system in cases of any market failure (Robinson, Simpson, Oritani, Solomon). In the interim we have difficulties.

The legal system worries that it is overburdened. Supplier firms are saddled with extra costs and market uncertainties. The newcomers decry the persistence of market power in the hands of established payments providers. The banks and their regulators fret as outside firms—expert in the technology but unknowing in the finer payments issues—wrest a measure of control over the payments system (Moore, Martin and Weingarten, Solomon).

Bank management can decrease vulnerability and recapture market share through strategic, futuristic electronic banking plans (Moore, Martin and Weingarten). The marketing potential for attractive and multipurpose cash substitutes such as the smart card seems great. Home banking and teleshopping are likely to catapult in use. Consumer preferences are of interest to vendors, as are the costs and benefits of particular strategies (Robinson, Moore). Everyone agrees that in their own best interest consumers ought to become more informed and vocal. To a degree this is happening, possibly suddenly, as the younger technology-oriented members of our society ascend to positions of spending power (Robinson).

Given the speed of communications and payments flows, the banding together of nations as well as diverse industry groups is a common theme. The glue of the new technology is impressive. It spans national borders, and obliterates the industry and state branching constraints. Vendors everywhere scramble to enter, and it is in user interest that they do so. The high costs and risks of the electronic ventures necessitate cooperation among vendors, within and between customary markets (Solomon) as well as political borders (Haberler, Oritani, Simpson).

But despite the high degree of cooperation, the conflicts do not cease. Rather, competition may become more rather than less intense (Solomon, Moore, Oritani, Martin). The useful and diverse strategies pulling participants apart practically assure the eruption of disagreement, while providing a healthy and new injection of ideas and technology within systems. We see the difficult competition/cooperation paradigm (first proposed by attorney Donald Baker) at work at the global level (Oritani and Simpson). We see the balancing act required by this paradigm also at the financial retail and telecommunications systems level (Robinson and Solomon).

To help smooth out disagreements or resolve them before they fester too badly, most contributors urge a more visible, albeit restrained, public presence. For nations, continuing international cooperation is seen as a safeguard, designed to insure not only against systemic risk (Oritani) but also the onslaught of any severe depression or collapse later (Haberler). Initiatives toward better standardization of payments formats are important and in progress, within an international capital markets framework. The international effort to standardize financial capital market trading systems has been impressive (Simpson). Impressive also has been the speed and strength of central banking cooperation, given financial emergencies (Haberler and Oritani).

However, rules too rigid may not help. Policy restraint and flexibility may be the key, especially in the presence of high-speed and often erratic money velocity and money flows (T. and E. Solomon). Federal Reserve efforts to push a money (or any) control policy too hard may be self-defeating given the perverse feedback effects as enhanced by present electronic flows speeds. The role of the market and its "feel" in central bank terminology is thrust again to center stage. The sense of *déjà vu* amidst the new is remarkable.

A common theme relates to the need for updating of money and payments concepts (Moore, Robinson, E. Solomon, T. Solomon). The Federal Reserve is urged to provide researchers with faster and more complete access to data, flaws and all. Especially in the approach of nonlinear dynamic modeling, which seems appropriate to the present fast-moving money era, a lot of current data points are essential. For this particular use data should be frequent, raw (not adjusted or smoothed) and preferably supplied computer to computer to save the painstaking effort of data transfer from magnetic tape or hard copy. The computer makes possible the analysis of such data in quite new and potentially revealing ways.

In conclusion, all contributors extoll the staggering benefits of the new technology in money and payments, while pinpointing deficiencies and questions. All agree there is no turning back, that the pace of society's acceptance is likely to accelerate in the next decade. All are equally certain that there is a lot of work to be done; none of us is sure about the answers.

We have tried in this book to define more precisely the parameters of electronic money flows and their pervasive impacts. We have worked on new conceptual and theoretical approaches, with promising results. We have discussed some important questions—economic, legal, and social—that merit a public policy forum and open debate. Too much of what is going on now to resolve issues is behind closed doors. Worse, there is too much public apathy about concerns of vital interest. This book, we hope, will generate interest, research, a further continued interdisciplinary mesh of skills, and peer review.

Note

1. This fusion between finance, telecommunications, and distribution networks was the focus of the innovative First Conference of the Institute for Posts and Telecommunications Policy, held in Tokyo, Japan, on March 15–16, 1990. I have been grateful for the opportunity to share new ideas and participate in this international forum sponsored by the IPTP.

I ELECTRONIC MONEY AND PAYMENTS

The concept of a checkless, cashless society is far from fruition. Part I presents the background behind the successes and lags, the microeconomic focus. The switch to electronic delivery modes is a fait accompli for large financial payments. The reasons are obvious: efficiency, relative safety, and, most important, speed. Electronic money can move very fast; it can buy financial assets around the world several times over in one day. Chapter 1, "Today's Money: Image and Reality," focuses on the nature of this important money form.

In analysis of money flows, the conventional money forms, the Federal Reserve "M's," seem incomplete; the Fed's M's represent only a part of the money value which today provides payment for goods and services, especially at the large-dollar and global end of the scale. Other "value" acceptable by sellers is excluded from the formal M's because it is short-lived, incapable of measurement, or a payments value form that does not quite fit the usual money criteria in a textbook sense. Quite novel is the concept of "money" flowing at the speed of light or electricity, possibly commingled with other financial information. The manner of settlement can be unusual also: deposit money or Fed funds but also future claims to goods, electronic barter, or other information flows.

Quite obviously, this technological feat affects the quantity and velocity of effective money—the continuous money flows available for spending throughout a 24-hour day, through the entire economic and financial pipeline.

Chapter 1 provides some underlying concepts and theory about the money flow continuum available for purchases throughout the day. We compare discrete (end of period) and continuous concepts, and consider in more detail the expanded information-based component. The matching velocity concepts, discrete (gross national product (GNP)-based) and continuous, are added and compared. The possible breakdown of "money" generated by the new electronic instruments into traditional and electronic money grouping, M_E, is considered. The derived money flows function, which cojoins all money value and its continuous turnover rate, is developed in basic form for later theoretical analysis (chapter 4).

The policy implications of the new money-like forms are considerable. As the cost drops of forging telecommunications links across oceans, the swift-moving, information-based money expands, and flows can rise unpredictably in times of market flux. But erratic money flow velocities, and the electronic-based shifts from money types bearing different requirements, may doom any rigid Fed money control effort. The multiple layers of money forms perched upon a rather narrow reserve base add to the money control difficulties. So also does the fact that while many payments forms may be settled in Fed funds or bank deposits, other types of the new money may clear in electronic barter forms. A portion of the cloud of electronic money moving in geosync orbit in the form of virtually weightless photons may have severed altogether the links to the measurable reserve base.

But while electronic networks have captured the large dollar payments, the technology at the other end of the payments scale has thus far failed to penetrate the marketplace. Linda Moore's innovative "Money in the Third Millennium" analyzes these new prepaid money forms, at the low-value portion of the spectrum. In chapter 2, Moore brings to the book her wide central banking and practical business experience, as Special Assistant for Operations at the Federal Reserve Bank of New York and technology consultant, here and overseas. Moore describes the smart card and coin, and other innovative prepaid media, and the requirements for their eventual market acceptance and supply feasibility. An analytical framework evaluates the microeconomic preferences of users, payor and payee. Moore also provides a useful glossary that translates the new high tech terms for the interested reader.

Consumers can choose to hold traditional payments media for transactions, bank deposits, or cash. The intrinsic worth of the privacy or convenience of holding cash is balanced against the benefits of holding funds on deposit at a bank. Deposits yield a positive value to the consumer in terms of interest paid and security—or the mitigation of a negative value such as service fees or interest charges, in the case of an overdraft.

But a prepaid payments medium adds a third dimension to the payments media decision. Once existing payments networks have maximized transaction efficiencies represented by the tradeoff between cash and bank deposits, new and fairly unique benefits may come from the addition of this third dimension.

The preference of the payor is based on the evaluation of the costs and benefits associated with his/her choice. The payee, however, has a quite different tradeoff, and can and often does specify the form as well as the time of a payment. Obviously important also is the availability of payments media, government and private, and their relative production costs. Given demand for the new media and their costs of production, Moore develops a business opportunity evaluation matrix that sets forth the tradeoffs and other business specifics. Considered in tandem with the microeconomics, the analysis is both valuable theoretically and potentially very useful to users and suppliers.

Moore gives particular attention to the smart card, with computer chips for information storage and processing. Among the simplest is the French payphone card, which contains a memory chip that can store and decrement value. More complex are the integrated circuit (IC) cards, or read/write cards that can store and process information as well as compute value. Of particular interest are the "contactless cards," which hold a computer chip sealed inside a plastic card along with wires that run though the card and serve as antennae.

Multi-service smart cards in an "open" environment (one not limited to a particular group setting such as Club Med or the U.S. Armed Forces) suggest broad market appeal, once vendors identify the appropriate technologies and techniques. However, as home banking has shown, marketing can be difficult for a multiservice card. Security requirements in an open environment of this type, too, are somewhat more difficult but can be overcome through encryption or other still newer techniques.

Whatever the specifics of the scheme may be, Moore points out the importance of a clearing mechanism. Owners of prepaid cards should be able easily to redeem cards and receive reimbursement for any unused value still in the card. One benefit of a variable-value coin or a prepaid card is the possible capture of productive funds, which might otherwise lie idle in piggy banks or old cards. If the clearing mechanism can capture and invest inventoried value, productive uses of this savings are made possible.

1 TODAY'S MONEY: IMAGE AND REALITY

Elinor Harris Solomon

The new technology conjures up some basic rethinking about the nature of money. The modern alchemy succeeds where the old failed. The ancients of the middle ages were not able to turn lead into gold. But the medium of electronics turns magnetized elementary particles (bits) stored in computer memory into money-like value. Messages to transfer money can take the form of photons moving at the speed of light on satellite, microwave relay, or fiber optic threads; or they can move as electron flows when telephone wires become the chosen means of payments transmission.

Under these new circumstances wrought by the technology, what is money? Money still can be defined as a form of value generally acceptable in payment of goods and services. It ought also to serve as a unit of account and a medium for storing value effectively. The textbook definition of money need not change much. Much of what we see is a simple extension of the conventional money forms, flowing at higher speed and often blended in (or "bundled" with) other information or services.

Given these attributes, the new money is often difficult to measure precisely or even to identify. The new electronic value forms have not quite succeeded in the universal acceptability required of money; in this primitive sense perhaps they are still in part a barter value form. One transfers

Solomon, E.H., (ed.), *Electronic Money Flows*.

15

deposits for value credits on electronic net or on chip-imbued smart card. The concepts of electronic money and electronic barter blur. Often blurred also in the newest electronic money forms is the demarcation between underlying money—which may be slim, even nonexistent in the formal sense—and turnover of the value that serves as money. What we see is effective money flow in the aggregate.

In the electronic age, money first consists, as always, of physical cash or deposits. But to this familiar money must be added the more ethereal and information-based money flow, as first developed by Paul Henderson (1987). Money-like value is in motion and continuously available for purchase of goods and services throughout the day. The flow represents all money—whether manifest in physical form or as memory on a computer chip—times the rate of its continuous use. Money flow is a curious mixture of electronic turnover speed plus a not-so-little dash of good old-fashioned "float"—the latter being the payments subsidy about which users and purveyors of the new money technology are subtly locked in conflict.

In this introductory chapter, we first analyze each kind of money. We look at the ways in which the familiar and electronic-based concepts may differ, often considerably. Of interest is money velocity, or how often the money is "turned over" during a given period, both from discrete (end of time period) and continuous viewpoint. The chapter concludes with the more comprehensive concept of money flows in a continuum, as background explanation for other theory and policy discussion throughout this book.

Money Today

A new grouping of money types emerges. They are depicted in figure 1–1 below. First is *conventional money* (A): cash, deposits, and other components of the Federal Reserve M1, M2, M3, and L aggregates, ranging from narrow to broadest conventional (M) money. The transactions (M1) and some M2 money is backed in part by the reserve base, or deposit liabilities at a Federal Reserve Bank (the so-called Fed funds) and cash in vault (R in figure 1–1). The Fed's conventional M's are discrete and point-in-time concepts, and are measured as of end of day. They often appear as settlement balances for the electronic money flows, including those on most retail nets (ACH or debit/POS—point of sale—card) and wholesale (large dollar) systems.

Second (B) is the electronic *daylight money*. This potential money form can be created from "intraday" overdrafts, a type of daylight electronic

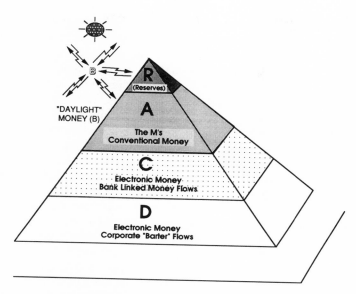

Figure 1–1. The Shape of Money Today
Note: See tables 1–1 through 1–3 for explanation of electronic money.

float. In theory such float can give rise to matching bank customer credits and short-lived daylight money. The creation process can occur like clock-work at the time when payors send out funds on Fedwire electronically in the morning. But the transitory "intraday" Fed reserve credits (and the matching customer deposit accounts) must inevitably self-destruct when funds are collected at end of day, only to arise again like the sun the next morning (on business days).

The other two groups, C and D, in figure 1–1 represent *electronic money* in somewhat more durable form since their expected lifespan can theoretically extend beyond the daylight hours. This money consists of any one of a number of different types, but essentially it represents electronic value.

This value served up as payment for goods and services is frequently comingled with other information flows in broad-scale economies of scope. The messages that make the flows possible often move on joint venture net or dedicated private wire to payee (Electronic Data Interchange, or EDI) via satellite and with the speed of light. They are settled in no particular proscribed way: perhaps deposit money, Fed funds, electronic claims to goods (barter), even other information flows.

Although existing in ephemeral form on electronic nets during the day, a good part of this information-based intangible "money" is netted out ("settled") still by means of old-fashioned accounting money, such as bank deposits. There usually are no formal reserve requirements. The designated "clearing bank" which settles in deposits makes informal and generally nonsupervised arrangements with system members and agents about the prudent level of private balance requirements.

If that particular value-based money retains regular (say, end-of-day) settlement links via conventional banking modes, it can be construed still to fit within the conventional money system, at least come settlement time. It becomes a third money type, where links with conventional money forms have been not entirely but only partially erased by electronics. We call such electronic money the *"bank-linked money flows"* (C, on figure 1–1).

For example, money may flow on retail electronic nets such as debit card or automated clearing house (ACH), for transfer to the merchant seller, the owner of the fast-food franchise or the gasoline station. What is being transferred is the conventional bank deposit. The electronic money retains a very firm bank link. To take another example, the money-like values flowing on the private large dollar net, CHIPS, are gross electronic flows that move a lot of markets during the day. But they are netted out (or settled) at end of day in Fed funds. In these cases of "bank-linked money flows" the links with conventional money forms have not been severed but merely altered in rather significant ways.

Any money flowing on these bank-linked electronic nets is traceable, albeit often with a lag; debit/credit card companies and the trade press provide yearly data and comparative estimates (VISA and *Nilson Report*, for example). At least for now, customers make the transfer from conventional money holdings—although this may not necessarily continue when prepaid media and home banking modes become more popular. For the moment, there is at least some backing, albeit attenuated, in conventional reserves.

No one, however, can extract the precise money flows values from the "bundled" corporate information flows data. For want of a better name, we call this fourth and most elusive kind of electronic money value the *"corporate 'barter' flows"* (group D in figure 1–1).

Corporate barter flows move comingled to other parts of the nation and world on private electronic nets or via electronic data exchange (EDI) modes. They may be settled in other electronic money credits to other nets, or in goods or claims to goods (barter modes). Informal commodity standards (oil, airline ticket credits and debits) exist for some; these may provide for eventual "net net" monetary settlement at some future time in order to retain a satisfactory unit of account and workability. But for many, links to the banks may be severed entirely in any fixed or definite manner. Bank and reserve ties, if they exist at all, may be far removed in this most modern but rapidly growing class of money-like value we have dubbed the electronic barter flow.

In the complex skein there are "interfirm" and "intrafirm" barter flows to consider, of which some replace conventional money forms in their national and transnational links. Much of the information is and will remain proprietary, hence difficult to analyze.

Money: Conventional and Short-Lived ("Daylight")

Let's examine each type of money shown in figure 1–1 in somewhat more detail. First is the conventional money M's.

Conventional Money

Conventional money (A) includes all the money commonly contained in the Fed's money aggregates (M1, M2, M3, and L). Most still are backed in part by the reserve funds (R) shown on the consolidated Fed end-of-day balance sheet as deposit liabilities against a Federal Reserve Bank. These Fed deposit liabilities owed to member DI's enter, along with cash in bank vaults, into the monetary base. They are used to calculate the base money multiplier which is widely followed. They support M1 and, to lesser degree, much of the broader cumulative money aggregates, and require no further elaboration.[1]

Daylight Money and Credits

More interesting for this discussion are the nonphysical electronic forms. They are irrevocably part of the dawning of the information age and the computer-generated speed of money flows. Daylight money owes its existence to the new technology, and to the speed with which messages to transfer money ownership can travel. Daylight money arises from electronic float, officially called the "intraday overdrafts" or credits.

The presence of this float in alarming amounts is due, quite simply, to the inability of legal payments forms such as the Fed's Regulation J to run apace with technological change in payments forms. Its generation and present large supply are stimulated by the fact that such float is generally free, made available at zero cost to holder.

In the United States two large wholesale ("large dollar payment") systems now exist. The first is Fedwire which transfers Fed funds (or deposit liabilities at a Fed bank) and bookentry securities transactions. The second is the privately owned and operated CHIPS system which links 141 U.S. depository institutions and U.S. branches of foreign-based institutions. CHIPS handles mostly international dollar transactions.[2] Payments on these two large dollar electronic systems permit the creation of the short-lived daylight "proxy money." Each net works a little differently.

With respect to Fedwire, there is presently a mismatch between outward funds transfers (typically early in the day) and collection (late in the day). The Fed's long-standing Reg J requires that all funds sent out on Fedwire be "good" funds. For these transfers the payment is considered irrevocable and final, irrespective of what happens to the fortunes of the sendor.

When a depository institution (DI) makes a payment over Fedwire, it instructs its Federal Reserve bank to transfer funds from its own account to that of another institution. All Fed member depository institutions (DI's) must maintain a positive balance in their reserve accounts at the "close of the business day." During the course of the day the reserve balances of some DI's may be negative, however, and the running of an overdraft (below the permitted "cap") incurs no penalty, either interest charge or otherwise.

New reserve balances are encouraged by their zero cost to be created intraday as a form of electronic float; they represent desirable shadow bank reserves available for customer daylight use for a time. With no "price" on the free credits, their supply becomes stretched to the fullest extent possible. In this process something that is of value to people is created automatically and given away for nothing. Payors are encouraged to send out their funds early and on a gross flows basis, for that will maximize the free daylight reserves available to them. (For suggested remedies see Humphrey (1987) and Federal Reserve staff (1989).[3])

The intraday overdraft behaves like the float of the paper-based world. It has the capability (not necessarily used) to extend the effective money supply for a brief time. Some purchases of goods or services can be made by presenting the daylight money. However, the hour of its eventual demise is more predictable than in the case of ordinary commercial bank or Reserve Bank float. Snowstorms and check delivery delays affect not at all

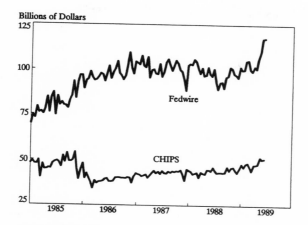

Figure 1–2. Fedwire and CHIPS Overdrafts
Note: For individual institutions, overdrafts are measured as biweekly averages of their daily peak overdrafts. Aggregate overdrafts are the sum of these individual biweekly averages.
Source: Federal Reserve Bank of Kansas City, *Economic Review* (Sept./Oct. 1989); Board of Governors of the Federal Reserve System.

its lifespan, assuming the electronic net is not "down." Intraday credits make possible the creation of money and credit during the day for a very predictable period of hours. At end of day the electronic overdraft will terminate.

The amounts are far from trivial. As shown in figure 1–2 from Van Hoose and Sellon (1989), peak overdrafts on Fedwire amounted to $118 billion and on CHIPS to about $52 billion (daily average) in 1989. This intraday money and credit, however large, are ephemeral. Like Cinderella's finery at the ball, the life span of the daylight overdrafts is very brief. However, their advantage is considerable: they are able to be resurrected in one giant cloud come dawn (or its banking equivalent, 10 a.m.), as surely on business days as the sun must rise. In the interim by moonlight, user banks can borrow funds in the Fed funds market overnight, at the going Fed funds rate of interest. This privilege enables users to bridge the nighttime shortfall. Figures 1–3A and 1–3B depict this constant creation, destruction, and reincarnation process around the clock.

Given such predictability, is there any present significant use of the massive intraday funds? As far as anyone knows, not for a precise interest

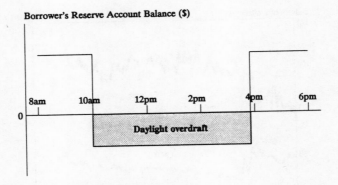

Figure 1–3A. Creation of a Daylight Overdraft
Source: Federal Reserve Bank of Kansas City, *Economic Review* (Sept./Oct. 1989); Board of Governors of the Federal Reserve System.

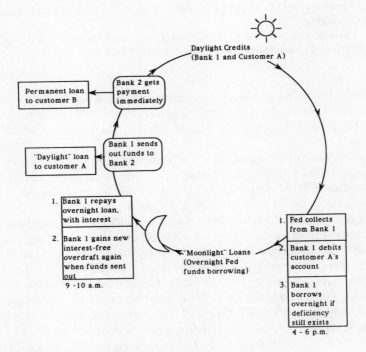

Figure 1–3B. The Fedwire Credit Cycle: Day into Night

fee, at least. No organized intraday credit market is in place, where momentary Fed overdrafts can be bought and sold formally during the daylight hours of their existence. Indeed the Fed is careful not to encourage any such market from developing for that would only increase its worries about potential Fed daylight exposure—that is, the credit and systemic risks implied. Instead, the intraday Fed funds are apparently given away "free" to certain good bank customers, as part of the ongoing customer relationship or as implicit payment for noninterest-bearing demand deposits. The informal overlines thus become the basis for customer purchases and informal daylight money creation.

However, since their life span is destined to be cut off sharply at end of day, the daylight Fed overdrafts cannot be used to cover deficient bank reserve positions. The multiplier effects normally associated with Fed funds use are therefore curtailed. Multiple money creation is not possible; the daylight money creation must be simply on a one-on-one basis. During their brief life the transitory intraday Fed funds must function more like ordinary money incapable of supporting other money, rather than as kingly "high-powered" reserve money.

Nor can the intraday reserves be easily used for arbitrage or other 'round-the-world exchange operations which may require continued back-up by permanent rather than intermittent funds. Their life is lopped off too abruptly for these kinds of operations. However, the intraday Fed funds can act as an ordinary daylight credit line, granted briefly to payor banks who then may pass that credit on to their own corporate or respondent bank customer. Perhaps the funds will serve as cover for funds the customer has sent out already but for which it has no current cash backing.

Since intraday credits on Fedwire comprise a sizeable amount of money (a daily average peak of $118 billion), they logically cannot be ignored. Their trend since 1985 was shown in figure 1–2. Peak Fedwire overdrafts consistently exceed end-of-day reserve balances, and in June 1989 were approximately twice as large as the underlying reserve balances (figure 1–4A). They are concentrated among a few large clearing banks, who by now could suffer real pain from any abrupt removal (figure 1–4B). Open for discussion has been the possible pricing at minimal levels of any Fed funds overdrafts over a certain cap (Federal Reserve Staff, May 1989). But there are practical difficulties in implementing the plan. It seems no easier to remove this embedded subsidy at wholesale than at retail on credit card or check float (Henderson (1987) and chapter 8 of this book).[4] For quite obvious reasons, users are unwilling to give up float whether electronic or check, which yields positive benefits such as interest return at zero cost.

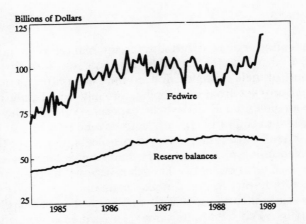

Figure 1–4A. Fedwire Overdrafts Compared to Reserve Balances
Note: Overdrafts are defined in figure 1–2. Reserve balances are average end-of-day balances measured over a two-week reserve maintenance period.

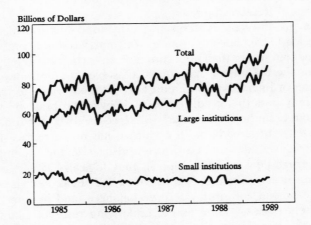

Figure 1–4B. Funds Overdrafts by Size of Institution
Note: Overdrafts are cross-system overdrafts on Fedwire and CHIPS. Cross-system funds overdrafts are the combined overdrafts on the two wire systems at a given time of day. This measure differs from the measure of peak overdrafts used in figure 1–2. For more details see Belton (1987). Large institutions include U.S. banks with more than $10 billion in assets and U.S. agencies and branches of foreign banks. Small institutions include banks under $10 billion in assets and nonbank financial institutions.
Source: Federal Reserve Bank of Kansas City, *Economic Review* (Sept./Oct. 1989); Board of Governors of the Federal Reserve System.

Electronic Money: Bank-Linked and Barter Forms

Still more difficult to grasp in concept or verify in scope or use is the purely information-based money form. Yet it is probably the fastest growing of all money. Included here are groups C as shown in figure 1–1 (the bank-linked money flows) and D (the information barter flows).

For the scientifically curious, the money messages consist of electrons (negatively charged elementary particles) when transmitted over telephone lines. However, their physical manifestation is the even tinier photon (the elementary light particle) when money information travels by microwave relay, fiber optics, or satellite. The light-beam route is the most cost-effective way of transmitting money across long distances. For this purpose the satellite and fiber optic links proliferate.

Paul Revere and his beacon of light live on. Its "one if by land and two if by sea" message becomes the one/two bit code of computer machine language. The massless photon flow of light replaces the lantern's beam as message conveyor across oceans and within nations, too.

The facts of economic life now get a bit more complicated, though. The electronic money flows can be part of broader kinds of confidential and proprietary corporate information all "bundled together." There is no way to unbundle the money-like information from that sent along within other corporate message flows on a transponder portion of the satellite; and neither the Fed nor public would have any right to obtain the private information if such unravelling of data skeins were possible.

Such money is continuous not intermittent, and less predictable than daylight money in creation, timing, and future scope. Unlike the daylight group we have little information on amount or flow. The size of flows is private information, published infrequently (say, once a year) and without any mandatory requirements or surveillance. The money exists as quite intangible information flows. Much of it moves on private satellite or nonbank links outside the banking system altogether.

Yet messages transmitting such information-based "value" are used just like any other money in payment for goods and services. They can contribute to the volatility of financial asset prices. Such money "buys" financial assets at wholesale, futures, and options of financial assets and commodities; it hedges private traders and investors against risk, flows around the world on private wires currently built and in the process of construction and expansion.

This form of money value can move silently on satellite 22,000 miles up in the sky,[5] with transmission effected by corporations and banks in solo

(Chase, GM, Geico) or as part of broader joint ventures comprised of bank and nonbank partners alike (AT&T, Discover, Prodigy, PULSE). It is true, you do have to pay in real money eventually. But that eventuality may be stretched out, depending on how the final payments netting occurs—whether through bank-linked (C) money or information barter strategies of a variety of ingenious types (the D money of figure 1–1).

It is sometimes difficult to separate out the two. Many electronic nets such as financial futures and commodity options retain bank links on a stretched-out basis while also employing barter or "swap" techniques. However, for purposes of simplification of the discussion, we have divided electronic money flows into the two general categories.

Bank-Linked Money Flows (C)

Group C money is one level removed from deposit money. It is not deposit money, but settlement is in deposit money or cash. It may be delivered on electronic nets such as VISA and MasterCard—or the automated teller machine (ATM) systems—and settled once a day in conventional money. Flows of money (debit card systems) and credits (credit card systems) intermingle on the same net, which also provides the instant cash (VISA/ PLUS). This may give rise to some confusion by users as to whether they are getting a line of credit (the credit card portion), instant cash (the ATM), or an instant bank debit. But there is no doubt that the bank links are present.

VISA, for example, settles in deposit accounts at a variety of conveniently located Fed member banks (originally, the Bank of America). The bank link can generate a partial deposit trail as customer payors eventually draw down bank accounts for end-of-month payment. Many point-of-sale (POS) nets will have a similar deposit match, as retail customers' accounts are debited and merchant accounts credited at time of purchase. Or, in retail POS the clearing often will be through the increasingly competitive although largely Fed-operated automated clearing houses (ACH's). The so-called ACH-POS is now popular in fast-food restaurants, convenience stores, and supermarkets. Surprisingly, most ACH's settle in bank deposits rather than Fed funds.

At retail, therefore, the customer's deposits still provide the final monetary backing, and typically enter into the conventional M's as a money form for recording purposes. But at wholesale (for large dollar transfers), this grafting of electronic and conventional money M's is not necessarily the case anymore.

In large dollar transactions "net net" balances may be settled in Fed funds (e.g., CHIPS). They may be settled in deposits at a clearing bank (the Options Clearing Corporation). There are other instances where settlement appears, at least in part, to be in commodities or barter, or other electronic money or electronic claims to future assets (the Chicago Mercantile Exchange). An extensive New York Fed Bank literature on the subject devotes separate volumes to each class of major wholesale bank-linked net and the manner of their operations: the timing, manner of clearing, and other specifics.[6] But nothing much is available about the details of the still more complex and purer corporate barter flows.

The Corporate Barter Flows (D)

An old-new corporate barter form emerges as Group D money. It reflects the influence of the new proprietary nets, which serve to transmit money *interfirm* and *intrafirm*. Corporate barter flows may serve the needs of different firms as buyers and sellers interact in payment with one another (the "interfirm flows"). Or they may cross oceans within the corporate infrastructure so as to place buy-and-sell orders with speed, or to distribute products and parts electronically within the infrastructure (the "intrafirm flows").

The corporate links need not necessarily be elaborate. An electronic message form of rising popularity is corporate electronic data interchange (EDI). EDI has the important characteristic that it transmits financial and accounting or corporate distribution information jointly with the money/value flows. EDI effectively utilizes "economies of scope," where one message flow can serve a number of different ends. The American Banker's *1990 Technology Review* shows operations bankers as predicting that EDI will be widely accepted within five years, hence more widely used as an efficient value transfer—interfirm (between those with close trading ties) as well as intrafirm.

As you get farther and farther away from the reserve base and from the money that passes through banks, it becomes harder to track down the "money." This is especially true if there is bundling of a lot of different kinds of corporate information or settlement in some kind of commodity account (oil or futures, for example). The value of an aggregate flows gross becomes supported by a dwindling reserve and money base relative to the expanded electronic blob as a whole. Like the creatures beyond the time warp of Arthur Clarke's *A Space Odyssey: 2001*, the physical links may be severed altogether for the Group D money forms.

Electronic Barter Flows: Nonbank Generation

The Congress presumably could extend the control powers of the Fed from the bank holding company sphere to the nonbank companies that offer the bank-like services or accept a form of consumer value akin to deposits (the Money Market Mutual Funds or the Sears Discover card). But that prospect appears not presently in the cards, although the nonbanks have entered retail electronic funds transfer (EFT) in full force, i.e., IBM and Sears' joint venture into home-banking via PRODIGY.

The high-tech sectors promise to be increasingly competitive with the banks, who in the initial phases at least provide the payments linkup. AT&T has converted its phone card to more generalized use; its plans are to supply electronic data information (EDI) services for corporations, with bank linkup for eventual clearing through the ACH system. Other telecommunications firms here or around the world may follow. Such wholesale entrants may have no need to use the United States' automated clearing house (ACH) or CHIPS net. Plenty of new proprietary payments links currently are in process of construction. The telecommunications nets and their nonbank masters will then be positioned to wrest control of a portion of the payments system, outside the Federal Reserve realm of influence. The banks worry quite a lot about this prospect.

There are many straws in the wind. The smart card, or integrated circuit (IC) card as known in Japan and Europe, may foreshadow a lesser dependence upon cash and a greater turnover of money bits stored in memory but originally "downloaded" from deposits. Citicorp's proposed Enhanced Telephone (promptly dubbed ET) contains a slot with which the smart card can be charged up at home from the user's bank account. Or, the transfer may come from reserve balances, if it is the central bank that "charges up" the card, or if the customer converts cash into smart card balances as a matter of greater convenience or utility.

What happens to the smart card money beyond that point as it darts around, in pursuit of its function as a medium of exchange, is anyone's guess. We may see money or other assets being down-loaded onto smart cards from other electronic money forms owned by nonbanks, such as telecommunications firms with advanced technology.[7] There is much interest in such ventures in Europe and Japan as, of course, there is in the United States. Newly developed is a "smart" Japanese prepaid coin with memory and chip technology. Such a coin, too, may initially be charged up from a central bank or from elsewhere within the banking system. But once the money moves onto the chip, the tracking of money balances becomes difficult, without invasion of personal privacy.

Around the world, the ethereal money nets may "speak" privately to one another (Moore, 1987). Through terminals at merchant location, or through home personal computer (PC), they may interconnect to transfer "value" balances without tangible monetary interface. Retail barter flows then may rise dramatically, too, apace with the corporate.

Money Turnover: Stock and Flow Concepts

All the value-based money contained therein may zoom around outside the banking system entirely, passed on directly from one electronic net to another net, its physical content consisting of magnetized electrons (see Martin and Weingarten, chapter 9).

The *rate of use* of an originally fixed money quantity will rise when based on the initial deposit's chargeup onto, say, the wholesale electronic net. That fact affects greatly the effective money flows available for spending on either real goods or capital markets assets. A more efficient use of cash, or inventoried value within prepaid media, will also increase the effective money turnover (Moore, chapter 2).

It is not fanciful to consider that the practical macro effect of heavier money flows of all types can be considerable. To determine the money stock in the manner of the M aggregates seems not to be the whole story. For macro analysis we want to know how often that money, whatever it in fact may be in physical content, turns over in payment for goods and services. It makes a big difference whether money holders stuff their cash inside mattresses, dig holes in the ground for their gold, leave smart card balances intact on the card, or zap funds around the world many times a day.

The velocity concept has been around for a long time. It helped to explain why mercantilist Spain, with all its gold, produced an inflation-rife society. The Spaniards would not have suffered ruinous upward price volatility, so the anti-mercantilist theory of Hume and later Adam Smith went, had they fashioned the gold plundered from the New World into goblets or religious ornaments. The stolen gold would not then have entered into the money economy in competition for a limited amount of real goods. So it is with the electronic money. Velocity or the rate of money use matters. The new money is able to turn over at electronic speeds. The effects on long-run price stability may be considerable when effective money, money times its continuous rate of use, is elastic. But it is difficult to determine the rate of money velocity when turnover is considered to be continuous. The published data have not kept pace with electronic realities.

Money Stock (Discrete) Turnover

The Fed's three V's, corresponding to the three M's, are computed as a simple ratio between average end-of-period money stock and the gross national product for that period. The GNP velocity of M2, for example, shows us how many times average M2 money stock went into GNP for the quarter or year.

However, that simple discrete ratio of GNP velocity masks the continuum of money flows throughout the day which must produce much higher turnover rates. Money is used not just to purchase final goods and services such as GNP but to purchase goods and services at all stages of production and thoughout the lifetime of a financial asset. In the Fisher "equation of exchange" money times its rate of use (on the buyers' side) must equal transactions for all purposes times the average price at which they are exchanged.[8]

When you look at all the transactions, including those in the financial markets, it seems appropriate to consider money turnover as continuous throughout the day, not frozen as of a discrete point in time. Since it includes the often heavy intraday turnover, such a continuous rate must be much higher than the discrete GNP velocity, depending upon the nature of bank business and its location. For the big New York clearing banks with much wholesale and international business, the continuous transactions turnover rate may be as high as 100 or 1,000 times a day for M1 transaction flows. For country banks with retail or middle-market orientation, the M1 money may turn over at a rate of once a day or less.

The Continuous Turnover Concept

The GNP-based concept of velocity as of end-of-day average is, of course, a stock not flow concept, and cannot be expected to show any multiple intraday flows between payors and payees. The published data on bank debits better capture the idea of a continuous money turnover process.[9] However, while bank deposits data may be quite comprehensive at retail (for small dollar flows), they are not very inclusive in an electronic-based wholesale payments world. Many intraday electronic money movements fail to be reflected in deposits turnover. They fall into the class of information-based message flows. The Fed's dollar value of transactions data does include the electronic nets where data are available (for instance, Fedwire and CHIPS) and hence better capture the gross payments flows. Unfortunately, these data are not available publicly on any frequent or current basis, probably because of construction and data estimation difficulties.[10]

Money Flows: Concept and Reality

The notion of payments combines all money of whatever type, however, and the velocity of each. What matters for real goods price changes, or financial markets volatility, is the total mesh of money and its turnover, i.e., all the money flows available for expenditure. Payments can be considered as a *discrete* and netted MV-based concept relative to final GNP, in a series of snapshot cameos captured at end-of-day intervals. Or, we may observe the whole *flow of money continuum* for the purchase of all transactions (including financial assets) throughout the day.

Table 1–1 provides a comparison of discrete and continuous concepts, with terminology we shall need later in this book. Table 1–2 looks in more detail at the conventional M's and the expanded M_E. The latter includes any information-based component without a Fed M counterpart. For convenience, we call the aggregate money whole, M4.

The Discrete Money Concept

The discrete approach is the traditional one on which all money and banking students, and Fed employees of at least earlier generations (including this author) have been weaned. The concept is both easy to grasp and capable of measurement. One can multiply the GNP-based V by its companion M, in order to get a discrete view of average money stock times the number of times it turns over for the purchase of final demand goods and services.

The Fed publishes data on the three M's—M1, M2, and M3—plus the liquid near-money L such as T-bills and large bank CD's. We thus can construct easily the related V's—V1, V2, V3—along with companion money multipliers, once the GNP for the period is known. A GNP-based V reflects the number of times the companion (average) money stock "turns over" in payment for GNP final goods and services within the time period.

Table 1–1. Money and Money Flows Concepts: Paper-Based and Electronic

Paper-Based Discrete		Electronic-Based Continuous	
M	Money stock; the M's (point in time) M3 plus L	M4	All money, A − D The M's plus value-based electronic M_E (net of double counting)
V	Rate of money stock use (velocity) For GNP/time period	V4 = gamma V (γ)	Rate of all money (M4) use (velocity) for all transactions/ time period
MV	Payments through the M's M stock × GNP-based V	MV fl = phi ϕ	Flows of all money through time (continuous) Higher flow speeds than MV since unmeasured but very active electronic nets flows included

Note: For comparisons with chapter 4 in this book the following relationships are considered to be applicable:

M4 = all money in broadest form, the money stock aggregates and any electronic money (M_E). M_E is electronic money-like value, transmitted on electronic nets during the day and available for the purchase of goods and especially financial services but not entered in any way into the Fed Ms.

V4 = gamma V, γ = rate of use (velocity) of all this money in all markets, not just final GNP markets.

MV fl = phi = M4 × gamma V, or ϕ = all the money flows, information-based and conventional M, for the purchase of all goods and financial and other services, during the specified time period.

Also closely watched is the rate of turnover of base money, the velocity of deposits at a Federal Reserve Bank (the Fed funds).

One recognizes easily the MV = PT of quantity theory as expressed in the equation of exchange of Irving Fisher, later converted to a more narrow income-based concept in the Marshallian version as follows:

1. $MV = PT$, or all money times its rate of use must equal all money transactions times the average market price at which those transactions are conducted.

Let $K = 1/V$, where K is represented as money demand (a simple reciprocal of V in the Cambridge version). Further, let Y (or GNP) be substituted for T, as of any given time period, so that $MV = PY$.

2. Then, $M = KPY$ (Cambridge cash balance approach), i.e., money supply equals money demand (K), a function of income times the average price of goods and services within income or GNP.

Table 1–2. Comparisons of the Fed and Electronic-based M's

The M's (Federal Reserve)		*The Expanded M*s*
M1	Transactions money	M1*	= M1
	Cash, checkable deposits OCD's, travellers checks		plus smart card or smart coins as electronic cash substitute
M2	Near money (small) plus M1	M2*	Retail, small electronic + M2
M3	Broad money (large) plus M2	M3*	Wholesale and institution, large $ nets + M3 High turnover rate
L	Short-term liquid assets plus M3	L*	Liquid assets such as T bills or foreign currency exchange + L Very high turnover
M_E	New M: All electronic-based M* components (shown to the right of this table) which do not have an M money counterpart		
B	Physical barter forms Goods swapping "Moonlighting" for services Exchange of services Transactions in the underground economy	B*	All barter, physical + electronic Commodity nets Dedicated wire exchange by corporations Electronic data interchange (EDI) with bundled money flows

Note: Conceptually, conventional A money corresponds to the published M's. The Group B daylight money of figure 1–1 has a counterpart in electronic money, M_E. Group C money, the money transferred by electronic nets but cleared in conventional money and deposits (bank-linked money flows), finds a counterpart in all the kinds of M's, including electronic M. Group D money, the purely information-based money, finds its probable counterpart in the wholly electronic barter money, with some M3 and L spillover. See matrix of table 1–3 for further explanation of this conceptual arrangement.

The Fed's GNP-based V is defined as GNP/M.

Thus, substituting for V in equations 1 and 2,

3. $M \times (GNP/M) = P \times GNP$.

The M's will cancel out and we are left with the truism that GNP as expressed in dollar terms must equal GNP times the average dollar price at which the GNP components trade within the time period. The focus is price stability and the role of money growth. The Federal Reserve February 1990 *Monetary Policy Report to Congress* tells us, for example, that while M1 grew only 1/2 percent in 1989, M1 velocity continued the upward trend that resumed in 1987. Transactions money did not grow very much in 1989, and possibly shrank in real terms when corrected for price changes. But there existed a higher rate of use of the narrow M1 money that was available.[11] This information, while of interest, does not give us a very comprehensive view of continuous money flows during the period, nor of the forces propelling changes in prices of goods and financial assets. We turn elsewhere.

The Continuous Concept: Money Flows

One may think now of money flows as continuous in time, used and useable throughout the day and around the world. Money flows in concept represents the full value of payments transactions throughout the day, year, or other time period, specified in terms of dollars or other currency (see Henderson, 1987).

The Fed's dollar transactions data come closest to such a money flows concept. However, such data have the real disadvantage that they are only infrequently published; the latest available to me in January 1990 was for the year 1987. Once available, such data have the second disadvantage that they must exclude at least some proprietary value-based information transferred on electronic nets. Any intercorporate payments flowing with other proprietary corporate information such as billing and ordering cannot be unbundled at all for the outsider.

Thus, we can obtain (belatedly) most dollar flows data for the conventional money forms as shown earlier in figure 1–1 (group A), with the caveat that not much is known about cash transfers in the underground economy. Some portion of the electronic-based money-value flows enters into the dollar transactions data. CHIPS money flows are apparently included. But great chunks flowing on the private corporate or retail nets are missing because estimates are impossible. Double counting is another serious difficulty. The problem is that the flows may hop from net to net, showing up in the data with each stop of the journey.

Whatever the gaps (or spurious double counting) may be, the size of such daily flows is quite obviously staggering. Fed dollar transactions data reveal that on an average *day* in 1987 (latest data available) the amounts transferred were about equal to one-third the entire GNP for the year. In order to gain some idea of relative size, figure 1–5 depicts some rudimentary stock and flow relationships. Data size and relationships are drawn from the *Federal Reserve Bulletin* (Belton, Humphrey, Marquardt, and Gelfand, November 1987).

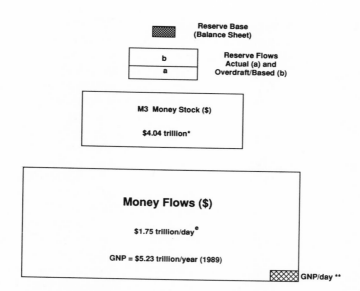

Figure 1–5.   Money and Reserve Contrasts: Stock and Flows*
Averages of daily figures, M3, 1989.**
eMoney flows extrapolated based on 1987 data (Federal Reserve).

Fed staff data (May 1989) are most illuminating, as have been my discussions with Dr. Jeffrey Marquardt, one of that study's co-authors, and Dr. Donald Savage. The importance of the briefly cloned intraday reserve base as well as the speed with which the whole base turns over are quite startling. The Fed funds market is very active, in part due to the new possibilities for hedging and trader avoidance of market risk from interest rate changes. On average, some $605 billion typically flowed on Fedwire per day. The turnover ratio in 1988:Q2 for Fed funds on Fedwire was 6.26. This means that balance-sheet reserves at Reserve Banks plus Fed funds overdrafts together had a daily transactions velocity of over 6. Fed funds moving on Fedwire were running at multiples about 17 times the actual base of permanent end-of-day Fed balance sheet reserves. A lot of ephemeral money and reserves exist, therefore, for variable time periods, perched on a narrow Fed Bank deposit liability base.

Our teaching of the conventional money multiplier analysis can seem quite inadequate under present circumstances. The conventional M1 to (discrete) base money multiplier shows a ratio of about 2.7. If turnover of the conventional M money were to be transactions based (continuous), the reality would be many times greater. Were we to add the money-information flows, the effective multiples to permanent base money would be enhanced further and rising still.

Of course, any higher real velocity need not necessarily be inflationary in their effects upon consumer prices. Surely in our complex society the number of transactions required to produce final GNP or a given final real sector product—say, a house or automobile—might be enhanced. The complexity of financial markets makes profitable, and often requires, numbers of additional payments steps. Irving Fisher (1911) regarded this greater complexity of society, too, as a technological change required to be taken into consideration in evaluation of the relationships between money and prices. The great change in payments habits is an important part of the story; with credit cards fewer checks may be drawn and payment consolidated into monthly payments. On the other hand, more media for using cash may exist (vending machines, parking meters, and the like). Whatever, the relationships between money and reserve base, and doubtless prices, too, have been altered in significant terms.

Table 1–3 attempts to place these complicated relationships in some sort of "ballpark" comparative (but not true empirical) framework. In order to achieve long-run price stability and sustained economic growth, the Fed works to achieve operating and intermediate targets in layered fashion. Legal reserves constitute the money base.[12] Now, there exist layers upon layers through which the money control mechanisms must filter, some real, some accounting in nature, some electron-based. All move, potentially, within the financial economy in one interconnected but somewhat murky mass, the largest with the speed of light. The effective "money multiplier" (that is, the relationship between money base and money) gets watered down as we back away from the conventional M's into the realm of the space-age money. It is not surprising that the Fed might have difficulties in money control under these circumstances.

The Future: Back to the Past?

Meanwhile, effective money, which buys goods and services of all types, consists of conventional money and electronic money (M_E) times its continuous rate of use. From the fusion of the two, the combined money flows concept is derived. As we move farther and farther away from conventional money to the money possibilities of the future, the fusion of the old M and V becomes more likely.

Table 1–3. The Money/Loan Creation Process: Effective Multipliers

	Multipliers, m^* (End of 1989)
A. Money stock concept	
M1 stock to reserve base stock	2.8
M2 stock to reserve base stock	11.5
M3 stock to reserve base stock	14.2
L stock to reserve base stock	17.0
B stock (cash) is hidden reserves	n.a.
B. Money flow concept	
M1 fl to reserve base stock	25–40
M2 fl to reserve base stock	
M3 fl to reserve base stock	40–100
L fl to reserve base stock	
Electronic money $C = M_e$	100–500
Electronic money $D = M_i$	No measurable base connection; m = some very large multiple up to infinity

$^*m$ = money multiplier, where $M = m \times B$, which indicates how much the money supply (M) changes for a given change in the monetary base (B). The multiplier, m, is usually cast in terms of M1.

Sources: Part A (money stock multipliers), Federal Reserve.
Part B (money flows multipliers), best educated guess, based on available *Federal Reserve Bulletin* and staff data (November 1987, May 1989, 1990).

In the hypothetical extreme, there may be no M or monetary base, merely continuous turnover in the money flows total. The money multiplier for the value sector then shifts up to infinity. But this becomes nonsense. Substituted instead, by necessity, is a new payments standard for that particular value segment, based on commodities or electronic barter. In this scenario, credits are provided based on the full faith and credit (or power) of the buyer. Instead of gold, there will be oil or financial futures as "quasi-monetary" backing for that sector of society's new money. In place of required reserves will be the buyer's general reputation or his stores of commodities, present or future.

The electronic net—which holds the commodity credits and settles transactions—may be self-regulated and subject to review of the final marketplace. The new system may well be Pareto optimal for society, given the awesome power and efficiencies of the new technology. The kind of electronic commodity barter that users want may be tailored to the bundled flow requirements of corporate users—or to those of households that will want to use home terminals or Minitel for a variety of purposes.

Business suppliers of such money-like value may act judiciously, in the manner of the successful 16th century goldsmith who knew how much reserves to keep on hand to meet any cash outflows—an early type of fractional reserve banking. Such suppliers may function wisely in the manner of the correspondent banker who holds reserves for others and makes loans to respondents as a "lender of last resort." Or the nonbank suppliers may enter the banking system through charter or purchase and endure regulation voluntarily.

Given all the possibilities, the future attenuation of Fed control over money may not be a problem. Other, more effective means of macro control may be substituted. But one cannot be sure. We cannot know who or what will hold the power. We shudder to think of international aggressors, say, in the Middle East, holding that payments power along with any misbegotten oil (see Haberler, chapter 3). A return to different forms of central bank influence and control is another way to go (see Oritani, chapter 5). Newfound ways exist to adapt to the difficulties imposed by the electronic payments regime. They have much to recommend them.

The Monetary Control Problem

In the textbook sense, the Fed is thought able to control money supply through links between policy tools, reserve base, and money. Through open-market operations or loans to member banks at the "discount window," the Fed can create (or destroy) member bank deposits at the Reserve Banks. The Federal Reserve defines Reserve Bank deposits and cash in vault as legal reserves. When the Fed creates new reserves through, for example, open market purchases, the banks can create new money in multiple amounts depending upon the average reserve requirements against deposits (or money multiplier).

However, in the post-EFT money flows focus, the links are much attenuated and more erratic. Personal savings and small personal money market deposit accounts bear no reserve requirements, yet are quickly convertible to cash, a source of reserve drain. The intraday credits passed down from banks to their good deposit customers for daylight use *are* Fed funds but are transitory and not under Fed control since they arise by mismatch between payments and collection times. Presumably if the size of the intraday money were fairly predictable, the Fed could offset their presence through matched open-market sales early in the day and matched purchases late in the day.

But the *velocity* or rate of use of the money base is also given an electronic boost, on a fairly permanent basis given continuous measurement of Fed funds transactions. That enhanced rate of use as between banks trading in the Fed funds market seems to be almost as important as a rise in aggregate balance sheet (discrete) reserves; any "heating up" of continuous base velocity can have a great deal of relevance in the money control equation. In the same way, any sharp rise in deposits turnover can have important implications not only for money control but also system stability, in the presence of electronic money speeds and time lags in money control implementation (see chapter 4).

The Layers Between Reserve Base and Money

The broader electronic value flows, as bundled message units, portend to be the most troublesome of all from the control viewpoint. No one knows how big they are. Sometimes we know something about the size of the settlement balances. They may be settled in the money base directly—in Fed funds or reserves (CHIPS). However, more typically net settlement is effected through regular bank deposit transfers (VISA or ACH flows), or in other electronic funds or goods outside the banking system entirely (proprietary corporate nets or EDI, for example). The deposit settlement mode reflects an attenuation of the control links; money gets to be settled in other money, rather far removed from Federal Reserve control. The corporate EDI or other barter-like electronic settlement modes still farther up the line can portend a severing altogether of the links between base reserves and money in any meaningful policy-related sense.

This all suggests a serious blow to Fed money control capabilities. The known (published) money velocity has been variable, in the short run at least (Greenspan, 1990). Many unknowns are present. Very important is which money form consumers, both household and businesses, will see fit to choose in payment for goods and services. Also important is the money supplier consumers will see fit to favor, bank or nonbank, financial or nonfinancial corporate. The answer to that question may influence greatly the relative size of the measurable M aggregates relative to the non-measurable and/or unsupported value-based electronic money forms.

The earlier EFT forms used an electronic *delivery* mode but did not alter the money backing much nor take electronic money out from the conventional M's. Credit cards are not "plastic money" as commonly known around the world but merely a line of credit for which the bank deposits (M1 and M2) reflect the backing and ultimate payment form. Electronic money use at point-of-sale (POS) may result in electronic money transfer,

Table 1-4. The Fit: Electronic Money and the Conventional M's

The M's (Fed Res)	Smart Card/Coin M_{EB}	Daylight Money (B) M_D	Bank-Linked Flows (C) M_{EB}	Corporate Barter Flows (D) M_{EC}
M1	X		X	
M2	X		X	
M3			X	X
L			X	X
M_E	X	X	X	X

Note: M_D is the intraday money created between banker and customer through the daylight overdraft opportunities (B money). M_{EB} is the electronic money flowing on the nets that clear in bank money, mostly the retail nets plus CHIPS (C money). M_{EC} is the corporate barter flow money which does not retain bank links, almost wholly M_E or value-based new money in nature. But the other nets, in addition to their M component, must also give rise to the new electronic money in some degree. The X's in this matrix indicate the kinds of money likely best to match the electronic money instruments, both conventional (the Fed M's) and value-based new M_E.

M1 through L aggregates are defined in accordance with Federal Reserve practice but are not additive; the different money forms are kept separate. M_E is our added money value category, the residual information-based money flowing on electronic nets which by definition does not have a conventional M counterpart.

but usually only from one bank account to another, normally M1 initially. The automated teller machine (ATM) provides a faster means of delivering cash (M1) to the customer from his bank account, M1 or M2. However, a nonbank supplier can send around the information-based money without the constraint of reserve requirements subject to the Fed's control. Also, that money may not wind up in any of the M's subject to the Fed's targeting, but rather in value-based money, M_E (see tables 1-1 and 1-2).

The Grid of Money Options

We are seeing a proliferation of the difficult to control nonbank electronic modes. A smart card may originally be "charged up" from the user's M1 or M2 deposit account. However, what happens to the money from that time forward, that is, its rate of use or velocity as it careens from buyer to seller, is essentially a private matter. Table 1-4 sets forth a matrix of these possible end results for money form, depending upon electronic instrument of choice.

The "money" delivered over a variety of electronic nets—large and small dollar, wholesale and retail—scatters into a variety of money permutations, depending upon user needs and wishes (see vertical axis on the grid). Reliability, cost, and quality are of overriding importance in money users' decisions to select one money mode over another, conventional M1 or electronic (M_E) money modes, for example. Another grid may be developed to set all the factors for electronics and paper against one another (Moore, 1987).

The tradeoff between possible lower cost and quality, the "tailoring" of money flows potential to special corporate needs, will also determine the extent to which the proprietary corporate telecommunications nets will continue to proliferate as a specialized money form. It will also affect the rate of use of such information-based nets, the money velocity of theory which affects the money flows supply available for use in both real goods and financial markets. As the information-based wholesale (and retail) nets proliferate, the proportion of money in the value-based M_E mode must also rise.

We don't know too much about user reactions to the new money. Recent (1990) surveys in Japan (International Posts and Telecommunications Policy, Furukawa) and in the United States (Federal Reserve Board, Eliehausen) are important. Demographics and the rise in computer literacy suggest the switch from conventional to electronic payments forms will be accelerated as the young from among our society reach positions of income or power (see Robinson, chapter 7). Corporations find the private telecommunications links to be useful, perhaps in part because of the very lack of constraints combined with speed and private control, but most especially because of efficiency and low cost of electronic data interchange (EDI) with which the flows are likely bundled.

As the cost of forging telecommunications across oceans drops dramatically, nonbank-generated money forms increasingly grow more cost effective.[13] This rising cost advantage suggests the future rapid growth of the presently most uncontrollable money form of all, the information-based money totally outside the familiar Fed M's. But theory suggests that if money flows velocity rises above a certain critical level, the system may show instability (see chapter 4). At the same time, interdependence between central banks is heightened along, perhaps, with competitive conflicts (as described in Oritani's chapter 5). Given Simpson's seamless electronic web of international money and capital flows (chapter 6), we are all in one global joint venture with its benefits and pitfalls. This paradox is similar in some respect to the more limited retail joint venture benefits and difficulties highlighted in chapter 8.

The Present Money/Money Base Pyramid

There is another irony in this situation. The new images conjure up the old, those that predated and hastened the development of the Fed system. Prior to 1913 the reserve "pyramiding" within the banking system was thought to be contributory to the recurrent panics of the time. Money tended to be layered upon a deficient reserve and gold base. The big city banks held reserves of cash and gold. The smaller respondent banks held reserves in the form of central reserve city bank deposits, at one or more layers removed. In case of recurrent bank panics, the big city correspondents often did not have enough reserves of gold both to satisfy their own cash-short customers and also those of the dependent country respondents.

This could happen with prepaid cards, too, which, while backed by deposits, are able to be transferred in split seconds into cash (assuming the physical cash exists on hand). If the central bank issues the "smart cards" for the DI customers, this problem may be mitigated since the initial backup will be reserves directly subject to the central bank's control. The modern tool of open-market operations goes far toward removing the threat within a country of the reserve shortfall that existed in a pre-Federal Reserve environment. It is easier to manufacture Fed funds as reserve backing than create gold out of thin air. Still there has to be concern. The pre-Fed pyramiding of history pales in the face of that arising in the electronic age.

In figure 1–6 a base of Fed deposit liabilities shows up as cash assets on the books of the DI's. The pyramid of figure 1–1 is inverted. The reserve base supports the conventional money A one layer up. The short-lived "intraday" money (B) exists only during the sunlight hours, as an unintended offshoot of the ordinary money and reserve creation process. B money is shown as an exploding and imploding cloud to the left. Phantom though it may be, this chunk of overdraft money is useful to bank customers who probably count on it as a more or less permanently embedded daylight form of asset subsidy.

Less fragile and much more durable, despite its ethereal nature, is the C value money perched still higher up from the overburdened base. Group C bank-linked electronic money maintains some contact with the Fed through the system arrangements to provide settlement in simple deposit accounts at the clearing bank in the manner of the pre-Fed big city correspondent. But Group D barter flows may settle in other value flows or commodities credits and debits. Corporate purveyors of such ghost-like money floating around in the ether may have managed to sever all the Fed and money control links. Furthermore, we can't even know what is up

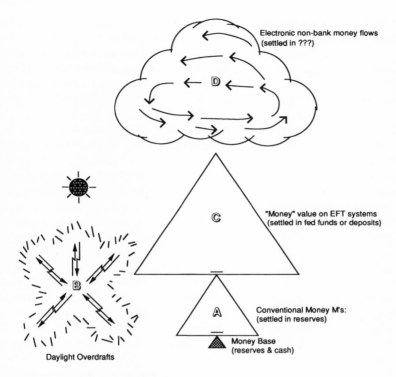

Figure 1–6. The Money/Reserve Link

there, looming somewhere in the ether, let alone the rate at which it may turn over.

The futuristic image sticks. Some unknown money mass hovers, migrates swiftly, and just as swiftly mutates into other money or near-money forms. Innovative new techniques spawned in the computer age make possible the agile movement from money into financial assets, present and future, based on very small price and interest rate differentials present and expected. In the central banking realm, the transfer to the world of science fiction seems not an unsuitable analogy.

The Control Implications

The control implications, however, are less dramatic. Successful central bankers have always functioned according to the "feel of the market." The

Fed in some sense has followed this course ever since electronic money became a difficult reality mostly beyond its control grasp. The Fed has focused on the market end-products of the money and quasi-money churning up the line. The Fed funds rate has been one such focus. The role of the money aggregates has been downgraded, the role of interest rates and underlying market forces upgraded in an information-based policy shift.

Such steps were inevitable. The post-EFT money flows gross has been much higher than the pre-EFT gross, relative to controllable reserve base. The broad M money turnover has been more variable. The money flows continuum has been both higher and less predictable. The degree of money pyramiding atop a small real reserve base is unprecedented. Sometimes the settlement net is netted down the line, in quasi-money or barter. Indeed the banking and deposit link may be gone altogether for some electronic money forms. The Fed has adapted to the reality of new money forms and flows. It has done what it had to do keep its grip on macro policy and financial markets.

One can hardly quarrel with the policy flexibility and relative success of the past few years. In the sense of data availabilities, the research-seeking public, however, has been less well served. It deserves more up-to-date information on dollar transactions and money flows, to the extent that data, however flawed, are or can be made available. With some explanation of the serious inadequacies and problems, those conducting monetary research can form their own conclusions and make their own mistakes. The proper money and money theory concepts also need a thorough overhaul and peer review in light of current technological realities.

Acknowledgments

In preparation of this chapter I am most indebted to Anthony M. Yezer, Bryan Boulier, and other colleagues at the Economics Department of George Washington University; to Jeffrey Marquardt, Edward Ettin, Donald Savage, and Stephen Rhoades of the Federal Reserve Board, George Juncker of the New York Federal Reserve Bank, Linda Moore (L.K.S. Moore, Inc.), Dr. Ruth McDiarmid (N.I.H.), and Dianne Martin (George Washington University). The notion of high money and reserve flows multiples was expressed first by Jeffrey Marquardt at lectures before my Monetary Theory and New Money Technology classes at George Washington University. I alone, of course, am to blame for any errors in fact, interpretation, or possible oversimplification of this complex material.

Notes

1. See Board of Governors of the Federal Reserve System, *The Federal Reserve System—Purposes and Functions* (1984); tables 1.20 and 1.21 (Aggregate Reserves and Monetary Base; Money Stock), *Federal Reserve Bulletin* (1990, monthly); latest monthly and biweekly figures are available from the Board's H.3 (502) and H.6 (508) releases.

2. For full explanation see Federal Reserve Bank of Kansas City (September/October 1989); Board of Governors of the Federal Reserve System, *Federal Reserve Bulletin* (November 1987); Federal Reserve Bank of New York, *Quarterly Review* (Winter 1987–1988) and *A Study of Large Dollar Payment Flows Through CHIPS and Fedwire* (December 1987).

3. On CHIPS things work in somewhat different fashion. CHIPS maintains a "pot" of Fed funds, a deposit account at the New York Fed. All CHIPS players start the day with a zero balance. But net debit and credit positions are built up as messages to transfer funds flow within the net. Participants who send and receive payment messages are recorded as being in a net debit or credit position relative to other participants. At this point prior to end-of-day collection, we see provisional information-based money being transferred between participants. Some CHIPS members (those in net debit positions) owe money during the day to other CHIPS members (those in net credit positions).

4. The total Fedwire overdrafts at the five large DI's whose total overdrafts exceed their cap account for about 40 percent of the aggregate Reserve Banks' direct credit risks resulting from daylight overdrafts, and are major clearing banks.

5. Federal Reserve Bank of New York (February, March, August, and April 1989b,c,d,e); *American Banker*, February 8, 1990, February 13, 1990; Yoshiharu Oritani, Institute for Post and Telecommunications Policy, Ministry of Posts and Telecommunications, First IPTP Conference on Networks and Society (March 15, 1990).

6. See New York Federal Reserve Bank (1989a,b,d,e, February, March, April, July) for details of settlement procedures, on each different kind of wholesale net.

7. For a fuller description of retail payments systems and the options, A. Furukawa, *Retail Banking and Consumer Choice in Japan* and E. Solomon, *Financial Sector Innovation: The Consumer Impact* in Proceedings, First IPTP Conference on Networks and Society, March 15–16, 1990. See Eliehausen, Board of Governors of the Federal Reserve System (April 1990), for the survey on United States consumer choices.

8. I. Fisher, *The Purchasing Power of Money*, 1911; D. Laidler, *The Demand for Money: Theories, Evidence, and Problems*, 1985, pp. 44–47.

9. Federal Reserve Board of Governors, *Federal Reserve Bulletin*, table 1.22, and Federal Reserve Statistical Release, G.6, "Debits and Deposit Turnover at Commercial Banks."

10. Henderson (1987); Belton, Gelfand, Humphrey, and Marquardt, "Daylight Overdrafts and Payments System Risk," *Federal Reserve Bulletin*, November 1987; *Economic Review*, Federal Reserve Bank of Kansas City, September/October 1989.

11. M2 and M3 velocity also rose in 1989 although at a much slower rate than M1 velocity, as one might expect given the rise in M2 and M3 aggregates in real terms.

12. See Wallich (1984) for the first policy analysis along these lines. Governor Wallich stressed there the need for more work on the money demand function shifts in the new environment.

13. Discussed at the First IPTP Conference on Networks and Society by Oritani (1990) and by Furukawa (1990). The seminal work was that of Humphrey (1983) and Humphrey and Berger (1990). Also see Oritani in this book.

References

American Banker, 1989 and 1990.

American Banker, 1990. *1990 Technology Review* (January).

Becketti, Sean, and Gordon H. Sellon, Jr. 1989. "Has Financial Market Volatility Increased?" *Economic Review*, Federal Reserve Bank of Kansas City (June).

Belton, Terrence M., Gelfand, M., Humphrey, D. and Marquardt, J. 1987. "Daylight Overdrafts and Payments System Risk." *Federal Reserve Bulletin* (November).

Board of Governors of the Federal Reserve System. 1990. *Monetary Policy Report to Congress* (February 20).

Board of Governors of the Federal Reserve System. 1990. *1990 Monetary Policy Objectives: Midyear Review of the Federal Reserve Board* (July 18).

Elliehausen, Gregory E., and John D. Wolken. 1990. *Financial Service Markets for Small and Medium-Sized Businesses*. Washington, DC: Board of Governors of the Federal Reserve System (April).

Federal Reserve Bank of New York. 1987. *A Study of Large-Dollar Payment Flows Through CHIPS and Fedwire* (December).

Federal Reserve Bank of New York. 1987–1988. "Large Dollar Payment Flows from New York." *Quarterly Review* (Winter).

Federal Reserve Bank of New York. 1989a. *The Chicago Mercantile Exchange* (July).

Federal Reserve Bank of New York. 1989b. *Clearing and Settling the Euro-Securities Market: Euro-Clear and Cedel* (March).

Federal Reserve Bank of New York. 1989c. *The Federal Reserve Wire Transfer Network* (August).

Federal Reserve Bank of New York. 1989d. *An Overview of the Operations of the Options Clearing Corporation* (April).

Federal Reserve Bank of New York. 1989e. *Trading of Foreign Currency Options and Futures in Philadelphia* (February).

Federal Reserve Bank of Kansas City. 1988. *Financial Market Volatility*. Symposium, August 17–19.

Federal Reserve System, Staff. 1989. *Proposals for Modifying the Payments System Risk Reduction Policy* (May).

Fisher, Irving. 1911. *The Purchasing Power of Money*. New York: MacMillan.

Fortune, Peter. 1989. "An Assessment of Financial Market Volatility: Bills, Bonds, and Stocks." *New England Economic Review*, Federal Reserve Bank of Boston (November/December).

Furukawa, Akira. 1990. *Retail Banking and Consumer Choice in Japan*. Paper prepared for the First IPTP Conference on Networks and Society, March 15–16.

Greenspan, Alan. 1990. "1990 Monetary Policy Objectives." Statements before the Committee on Banking, Housing, and Urban Affairs, U.S. Senate, July 18 and February 20.

Hallman, Jeffrey J., Richard D. Porter, and David H. Small. 1989. *M2 per Unit of Potential GNP as an Anchor for the Price Level.* Staff Study 157, Board of Governors of the Federal Reserve System, April.

Henderson, Paul B., Jr. 1987. "Modern Money." In E. Solomon, ed., *Electronic Funds Transfers and Payments: The Public Policy Issues.* Boston: Kluwer.

Humphrey, David B. 1984. *The U.S. Payments System: Costs, Pricing, Competition and Risk.* Monograph 1984–1/2. New York: New York University.

Humphrey, David B. 1987. "Payments System Risk, Market Failure, and Public Policy." In E. Solomon, ed., *Electronic Funds Transfers and Payments: The Public Policy Issues.* Boston: Kluwer.

Humphrey, David B., and Allen N. Berger. 1990. "Market Failure and Resource Use: Economic Incentives to Use Different Payments Instruments." In David B. Humphrey, ed., *The U.S. Payment System: Efficiency, Risk and the Role of the Federal Reserve System.* Boston: Kluwer.

Moore, Linda K.S. 1987. "Payments and the Economic Transactions Chain." In E. Solomon, ed., *Electronic Funds Transfers and Payments: The Public Policy Issues.* Boston: Kluwer.

Oritani, Yoshiharu. 1990. *Financial Networks and the Financial System: The Japanese Experience.* Paper prepared for the First IPTP Conference on Networks and Society, March 15.

Solomon, Elinor H. 1990. *Financial Sector Innovation: The Consumer Impact.* Paper prepared for the First IPTP Conference on Networks and Society, March 15–16.

VanHoose, David D., and Gordon H. Sellon, Jr. 1989. "Daylight Overdrafts, Payments System Risk, and Public Policy." *Economic Review*, Federal Reserve Bank of Kansas City (September/October).

Wallich, Henry C. 1984. "Recent Techniques of Monetary Policy." *Economic Review*, Federal Reserve Bank of Kansas City (May).

2 MONEY IN THE THIRD MILLENIUM

Linda K.S. Moore

The concept of money as a medium of exchange and as a store of value no doubt predates written history. Each society and each era create their own form of money. Shells, obols, dollars, European Currency Units—all hold a place in history as a unit of measure to represent value and facilitate commerce. The Information Age, the era of the computer, is increasingly represented by electronic money.

Computers have revolutionized the way we work and play; it is not surprising that this same technology has been harnessed to improve the efficiency of our payments system. In two decades it has become common practice to send money around the country or around the world by an electronic transfer of funds.[1]

Electronic banking has also influenced the man on the street. He may get money from a cash machine on the corner, or pay bills electronically, with a touch-tone phone or home computer. He is unaware perhaps how electronic networks have made it easier for him to cash a check at a supermarket or buy gas with the same card he uses in his automated teller machine.

Electronic payments predominate for higher value payments. As the technology has improved, the range of value for payments handled by electronic banking has increased.[2] Payments in the $5 to $10 range are now

Solomon, E.H., (ed.), *Electronic Money Flows.*

considered economically feasible in the on-line payments networks in use in the United States. It is possible that, over time, the cost of these transactions will be so low that even very small values will be handled economically by existing electronic networks. It is also possible that the customer will carry a network in his pocket, and that a low-cost, low-tech application of computer technology will handle the volume of small payments in a way that is separate from but compatible with the existing on-line networks.

The computer technology which has been so successfully applied to high value payments is being reworked by the banking community for applications at the low end of the payments spectrum. At present, it appears that the technology to be used will be a form of prepaid card issued by banks and businesses to their customers. If these cards are successfully implemented, consumer demand for coin and currency could drop, while bank deposits to back these prepaid media would rise. If the effect of high-tech electronic banking has been to churn funds without noticeably changing the measurement of $M1^3$, the influence of low tech changes may be measurable and even significant.

Although cash transactions represent not more than one-half of 1 percent of value, they represent about 83 percent of all transactions.[4] Furthermore, coin and currency in circulation are a significant part of our monetary base. In 1987, all "transferable" bank deposits, that is, primarily demand deposit accounts for which there are reserve requirements, amounted to $547 billion. Coin and currency totalled $198 billion.[5]

This chapter is about a shift in applied technology in the payment system which could be important to the way we manage cash in the third millenium.

The Role of Coin and Currency in the U.S. Economy

Recent estimates for payment transactions in the United States suggest that there are 360 billion payments annually. Of these, one-sixth are bank-facilitated. Sixty billion payments by check, debit or credit card, wire transfer, or automated clearing house transfer can be counted with reasonable accuracy, leaving an estimated 300 billion in cash payments annually.[6]

Additional estimates give 75 percent of total payments a value of $2.00 or less, or 270 billion payments mostly in coins and dollar bills.[7] The U.S. Department of the Treasury estimates that the average value of currency in circulation is $10, and that this amount has not changed in 50 years.[8] This further confirms that cash payments are concentrated below $10 and that

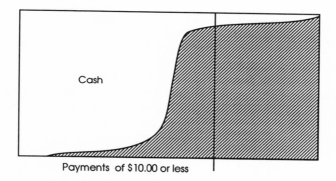

Figure 2–1. Cash versus Bank-Facilitated Payments Media as a Percentage of Total Transactions

Americans are using other payments media for purchases over $10. In the last decade, the number of coins in circulation has increased from 450 per person to over 600,[9] and increased wear and tear on the dollar bill has decreased its life span from 22 months to six.[10] With general statistics such as these in mind, we can guess that a significant number—perhaps 30 billion—of the nearly 90 billion payments over $2.00 must fall in the $2.00 to $10.00 range.

Although precise statistics do not exist, estimates made by different industry experts at different times have yielded distribution curves similar to figure 2–1. It seems that about 300 billion payments annually are for less than $10, and about 300 billion payments are for cash. These 300 billion are not the same transactions, but, in general, most transactions for less than $10 *are* in cash.

As long as inflation persists, the number of transactions crossing the $10 benchmark will increase. As the cost of operating payments networks declines, the cost of an on-line authorization will drop, making it economically feasible to replace cash for payments under $10. This combination of improved network economics and increased volume of purchases of $10 or more has been the accelerating trend of the last ten years.[11] During this time, as near as can be estimated, cash transactions as a percentage of all payments has not been reduced and the need for coins and small bills has increased.[12] Important factors that have contributed to the increased demand for cash are: inflation; increase in population; increased urbanization of the population; increased hoarding of currency; continued growth of the underground economy; and increased use of American currency outside the United States.[13]

The most likely scenario for the next decade and beyond is that the number of low-value transactions will continue to increase and that factors such as sales taxes and the proliferation of automated vending will increase the need for a wide range of low-value coins and bills, especially pennies and dollar bills.

Minting and distributing coins, and printing and circulating dollar bills of good quality are important to the management of currency for payments. As inflation has risen, the number of coins needed to complete a purchase has increased. Nickels and dimes and even quarters won't buy much any more, and so demand for dollar bills is high. The overworked dollar deteriorates under so much use, and the quality of dollar bills declines, causing problems for the banks who circulate them and the consumers who use them.

With inflation, the value of metals used in coins has sometimes exceeded their face value, requiring the Mint to replace the coins with cheaper alloys. Also, as noted above, inflation increases demand for higher value coins, and when the "coin" is a banknote, the need to replace paper with metal poses new problems for the Comptroller of the Currency.

Sales taxes, which are levied as a percent of a purchase, produce fractional values that have to be rounded to the nearest penny. Because of sales taxes and since many items are priced in cents, the need for pennies is high. At the same time pennies are hoarded, mostly because they are bulky to carry and don't have much purchasing power. Pennies are only an approximate solution and are expensive to manufacture and keep in circulation.

In a dynamic economy, the fixed values of coins is a static force that slows commercial activity. Because coins and dollar bills do not perfectly match the cost of goods and services sold, some businesses are forced to keep expensive inventories of small change and to forego some sales because of lack of change; other businesses manufacture substitute payments media to speed the payments process (and make money from pre-paid sales); consumers overpay sales taxes; pricing for some goods—such as in vending machines and mass transit—becomes approximate because exact change cannot be easily supplied; and untold millions of dollars are lost to fraud (short-changing, slugs, foreign coins) or forgetfulness.

A modern economy is judged to need six or seven values in a coin set.[14] The United States, according to theory, should have six coins ranging in value from two cents to one dollar. If, however, one of the "coins" could have a variable value, from a fraction of a cent to the total cost of a purchase, many of the inefficiencies stemming from the above diseconomies would disappear. As long as the inefficiencies thus eliminated were not replaced by new inefficiencies, and if any new diseconomies were less than the old diseconomies, then a Pareto Optimum would be achieved.

In the "ideal coin set" of the payments system of the future, there appears to be a role for a variable value coin.

A prepaid variable value coin for use in pay telephones was developed by Mars Electronics in the mid 1980s but shelved because the cost of the technology was too high for the proposed application.[15]

Using prepaid media to faciltate transactions is not a new concept. Metal tokens for transit and telephones, for example, are widely used around the world. Interest in prepaid cards, however, is growing rapidly. Technology, changing patterns of consumer behavior, and a shift in the underlying demand for coins for low-value transactions are among the contributing factors.

Prepaid Cards As a Payments Medium

Today's system of coin and currency is a combination of historical accident and 19th century technology that meets but does not fully satisfy the payment needs of an increasingly mobile, urban, and time-conscious society.

New technologies, especially computer-based technologies, provide payments alternatives that are better than coin and currency in many situations. This next section focuses on prepaid cards as the most likely substitute for cash for low-value payments.

A number of technologies are available for prepaid systems. These run from simple applications with metal tokens or paper punch cards to futuristic prototypes using laser technology or advanced computer techniques for "super smart cards." Of the technologies available on the marketplace today, those which can currently, feasibly, be used for a prepaid card to replace cash are enhanced magnetic stripe cards, integrated circuit cards, and contactless cards. All these technologies provide the capability of storing value in a memory carried on the card. This value can be withdrawn from the card in any unit of account, including fractions of cents.

None of the existing technologies being used to replace coins and currency for payments have the potential, at least not within the limits of current knowledge, to replace all cash. All of the alternatives under consideration require a transfer of value. In terms of today's technology, this means that a mechanical, electro-mechanical, or electronic terminal needs to be used to capture the value. No matter how small or inexpensive these terminals might be, it seems hard to envision an environment where one might transfer value to a pesky kid to induce him to go play somewhere else, to cite but one example.

Magnetic Stripe Cards

Magnetic stripe cards for prepaid applications are widely used around the world. In the United States, magnetic stripe technology is used for paper fare cards in the Washington, D.C. Metro, for vending machines in prisons and office complexes, and for school cafeterias and similar facilities. The University of Maryland will soon be introducing a "Collegecard" for applications ranging from dorm access to prepaid funds for purchases in cafeterias, bookstores, laundromats, and so forth. Coca-Cola, Inc., issues prepaid cards for its vending machines at corporate headquarters in Atlanta. Magnetic stripe cards with bar codes are being tested by Citibank and others to capture cardholder information for customer loyalty programs in stores.

Prepaid cards have assumed a significant role for consumer payments in Japan, and a magnetic stripe card is frequently used for this purpose. The telephone card is the most widely distributed—700 million have been issued since 1982, 300 million in 1988 alone.[16] In 1989, an estimated 100 million magnetic stripe cards, incorporating different technologies, will have been sold for prepaid applications.[17] Prepaid magnetic stripe cards are being issued by several consortiums for use in retail locations. In many instances, prepaid card readers will be hooked into the stores' point-of-sale systems and linked to the bank-operated networks. Companies participating in prepaid card programs include the Japanese subsidiaries of Coca-Cola, McDonald's, and Baskin-Robbins.

In Korea, Watermark technology is used with magnetic stripe cards for public telephones. A holographic card from Landis and Gyr is widely used in Europe for prepaid telephone cards, notably in the United Kingdom. A number of major companies in the U.K. and elsewhere in Western Europe use magnetic stripe cards for controlling meals in subsidized cafeterias. An advanced technology magnetic stripe card is being tested for access control in a sports stadium in Sweden. In Norway, magnetic stripe "token" cards are used for mass transit, taxis, and tolls.

Smart Cards

The term *smart card* is generally used to describe cards that contain computer chips for information storage and processing. Given what appears to be the unlimited potential of computers, it seems likely that this technology will be effectively adapted to a portable card, key, or other pocket-sized object. Rudimentary applications using computer chips in cards are already being tested around the world.

Of the smart cards in use, the ones with the greatest market presence are the simplest. The card used for French payphones is a memory chip which can store and decrement value. Although the French tend to include these cards in a smart card count, the cards are not in fact smart since they have no computing capabilities. The term is more appropriately used for integrated circuit cards, both EPROM and EEPROM; these are read/write cards which not only can store and decrement value but also can store and process other types of information, add and delete data, compute value, and perform other, similar functions. Also included in the broad definition of smart cards are the "contactless cards."

Integrated circuit cards work along the same principle as a floppy disk on a computer. The computer chip is embedded in a standard plastic card and is read when the card is placed in a reader with contact heads. Contactless cards hold a computer chip sealed inside a plastic card, which is consequently somewhat thicker than a standard card, with wires that run through the card, serving as antennae. As a result, the contactless card need only be laid on the surface of a terminal to be read; it does not have to be inserted in a slot or placed in a precise position. The chips for both integrated circuit and contactless technologies can be placed on a key or other support. The major manufacturers have produced and tested "smart keys."

Except for the French telephone cards, which rely on destructive decrementing, smart cards have not been used very much as a prepaid medium. The emphasis of the technology is on "transaction management" —that is, the ability to store and manipulate many types of information.

Among the applications of integrated circuit cards where preloaded value has been a feature are:

Club Med.   This group uses cards in several resorts to manage all services for vacationing guests; the most popular feature has been the use of the card to replace "bar beads."

Cinema.   A preloaded card can be purchased for access to certain movie theaters in Paris. The smart card manages discounted prices, and the readers track daily revenue according to type of ticket; this latter feature is important because theater personnel are compensated according to daily sales of full-price tickets.

Sports Complex. An experiment being conducted by Barclays Bank at the Dallington Country Club in England includes a prepaid petty cash function for the bar.

The contactless card is typically used in high-security situations. Midland Bank has issued the contactless card for students and faculty at Loughborough University in the United Kingdom. The card has preloaded value, credit, and user identity features. It has worked satisfactorily and is being extended to retail businesses away from the campus complex.

Replacing Cash with Prepaid Media

Thus far, we have established the reasonable—but not unassailable—premise that there are a lot of low value cash transactions that might be handled efficiently by a new payments medium. There seems to be consumer interest in using prepaid cards. Existing card technologies are being tested for prepaid applications and appear to be acceptable in at least some environments. The questions explored in this section will deal with specific instances of where prepaid cards are or might be preferable to cash.

Benefits associated with different payments media include acceptability, speed, accuracy, security, certainty, convenience, durability, flexibility, portability, and data capture.

For that sector of the consumer population that holds and uses coin and currency primarily for making payments, a prepaid card that can conveniently store and transfer value could be an improvement over metal coins and paper bills for small, recurring payments. Among the benefits are more accurate change (machine errors being less likely than human error), potentially faster transaction time (although this depends on the type of transaction and the type of technology), greater portability, and, for some, greater peace of mind in having the right change for the next day's transactions.

For retail businesses, it seems that cash payments of less than $10 are being made with 25 percent or less of coins and currency in circulation. People, nonretail businesses, and banks hold roughly 75 percent of coins and low-value banknotes in circulation.[18] We rely on our merchant base to turn over their cash supply quickly, to compensate for all the coins and bills held by individuals, businesses, and banks. The sectors with inventories of coins that must be managed efficiently are food services, vending machines, retailers, game machines, pay telephones, mass transit, and parking meters.[19] Businesses involved in these seven sectors bear the burden of making coins and currency an effective means of payment and are the ones most interested in applying technology to improve the use of coins and bills, or to replace them.

Food services, particularly fast-food franchises and cafeterias in schools, hospitals, and health care facilities, at the workplace, or in public locations such as museums and airports, experience problems with making change and with employee theft from cash registers. Speed of transactions is usually a concern. Restaurants may have promotions or discounts. Cafeterias may need to manage special menus, price subsidies, or customer eligibility.

Vending machines and games machines lose sales when potential customers don't have the right change; installing and maintaining bill changers create new costs. Robberies of machines and employee theft as well as vandalism are major concerns. Vending machines for drinks, food, and snacks are expanding the number of choices and extending their price range to higher value items. In addition to familiar items such as cigarettes, newspapers, and machines in laundromats, vending services today include dispensing stamps, movie tickets, freshly baked bread, items of clothing, and toys, to cite a few examples. Vending machines and games machines merge and emerge as lottery ticket terminals with keyboards that distribute tickets and select "instant winners."

Retail sector employees, from taxi drivers to designer clothing boutique *vendeuses*, are potential victims of armed robberies at their place of work. Their employers, in addition to the cost of providing physical security to their workers and customers, are faced with often costly "slippage" at the cash register. Problems in making change can cost retailers a lost sale or anger customers who have been short-changed.

Telephone booths and parking meters require constant maintenance to deter vandalism and to prevent coin boxes from choking. The phone company or the department of city streets may lose revenue if a potential customer doesn't have the right change. The loss may be far greater, however, for the consumer who didn't make that phone call or risked a parking ticket.

The prevalence of fare cards and tokens in most urban transit systems shows that, when it comes to moving masses of people, cash is considered a cumbersome means of payment. New York, London, Paris, and Tokyo are among the cities where transportation authorities are evaluating ways to improve their prepaid systems. In addition to maintaining or bettering entry–exit times for riders, mass transit executives are looking for ways to make the sales process faster, more cost-effective, and more secure. New prepaid technologies are also being tested to refine variable fares based on distance, time of day, and type of rider.

For these key commercial sectors, a prepaid card would have to match or better the main characteristics of transactions now performed. These are:

Substituted
- low value
- regular (in terms of time, frequency)
- consistent (in terms of what is expected/received)
- anonymous (human contact is not needed/desired).

Improved
- speed of transaction
- efficient data capture
- verification of authenticity.

Enhanced
- time and/or date validation
- variable pricing
- personalization (marketing data, coupons, etc.).

Economic benefits that can be captured and turned into profits by replacing cash with a prepaid means come from two major sources:

- reducing costs associated with coin and currency
- improving or adding benefits to the transactions performed with coin and currency.

An issuer, a bank issuing a prepaid card, for example, may be reducing internal costs or improving internal benefits. The issuer's primary objective, however, is to profit from the opportunity of offering businesses and their customers an alternative means of payment by capturing for the issuer's own benefit some of the reduced costs or improved benefits that would go to a payor or payee.

Revenue for a prepaid card issuer has two major components: interest earned on deposits and fees collected from transactions, whether on a per transaction basis or from a service fee. Other features that can generate revenue, depending on the technology used, could be cardholder insurance against loss, advertising on cards, and the sale of information zones to carry or capture information for third parties.

Costs are more diverse. In general, the costs are parallel to costs that already exist in the present environment of coins and currency. These include manufacture, distribution, physical collection, inventory, physical security, integrity, and netting and settlement. A prepaid medium reduces some costs and increases others; more important, it redistributes them. There is the cost of manufacture of the cards or whatever physical device is used to replace coins and currency for storing and transporting value. There is the cost of loading value into the cards. There is the cost of the acceptance devices. Value must be transferred from the devices to the appropriate recipient. Security needs must be met. Counterfeiting value must be prevented.

Some of the costs of coin and currency are currently borne by the government. Creating a substitute payments medium entails transferring these costs from the public sector to the private sector. Low-value payments presently occur largely outside the purview of banks. As issuers and managers of a payments medium for low-value payments, banks would assume a role comparable to that which they play now in the operation of electronic funds transfer networks. Some losses, such as those from counterfeit currency, which are not generally a cost to the bank in the present environment, would be a cost and potentially a large liability to any bank that took on the role of issuing a new payments medium. To compensate for new costs and greater risks, banks would have to have the opportunity to profit from fees generated by adding new characteristics to the payments medium. Creating an acceptable substitute is not sufficient; the new payments medium must include enough improvements and enhancements to provide the banks with opportunities for profit.

Most prepaid cards in use today are single function cards; to get any real improvement in the management of day-to-day, low-value transactions, the consumer must buy multiple cards. Or, the consumer might buy a multiservice card that would permit him to prepay for certain goods and services in budgeted amounts, through value loaded into discrete sectors of the card. Holding multiple cards or a card with multiple services with value prepaid for specific services might actually increase the amount of value that a consumer needs to hold as inventory for low-value payments. To avoid this, one of the requirements for a prepaid card as an economically rational replacement for coin and currency is that the value stored in it be accepted for more than one type of transaction.

A second requirement is that a prepaid card should not be any more costly in terms of idle funds than a cash withdrawal. Prepaid cards seem a marginal alternative to coin and currency unless the card can conveniently be emptied to exactly the last unit of value.

Since money stored in bank accounts is more productive to the economy than money held as currency in circulation, consumers should be able to deposit unneeded value from prepaid cards into bank accounts. A "fair" prepaid card should be easily redeemable for its remaining value, and an efficient prepaid card would redeem that money not as cash but as a bank account deposit.

If, however, a system is put in place that allows consumers to recapture the value held in cards, questions of validity become important. A bank might like reassurance that the value being redeemed in the card exactly matches the card's original value less legitimate transfers. A cardholder might like to know that only he (through a PIN—identification number— or other identification) could tap the monetary value not applied to transactions. Even better, a cardholder might want to add value to a card, keeping its capacity for paying for routine transactions within parameters that he determines.

A "fair" system for prepaid cards, one that lets consumers get the most productivity from the value which they carry with them, requires a clearing mechanism. This mechanism would replace what is essentially a laissez-faire government policy for turning out coins and currency. That is, governments issue coins and currency and take reasonable steps to see that these are not counterfeited and are backed by an implicit "promise to pay" on the part of the government; but these governments take few steps to see that these same coins and currency are used efficiently or that their implicit value is put to productive use.

Banks may be more efficient managers for low-value transactions, but the cost of the potential fraud from counterfeit value in a poorly conceived network is a major deterrent in the face of uncertain information about acceptability in the marketplace.

It is apparent that the circumstances under which a card is used for prepaid value or to manage transactions impact on its security. When payments are conducted off-line, as is the case for most prepaid magnetic stripe and smart card applications, one method of security is that the card issuer know the cardholder and be in a position to negotiate differences if either the card system fails or the cardholder abuses the privileges associated with the card. The potential for fraud increases the further away the cardholder is from the authority and control of the card issuer.

An off-line network for prepaid cards to supplement the existing on-line network must have other security measures besides the ability to identify and discipline cardholders. And yet, most off-line or prepaid systems in operation today rely almost exclusively on the ability of the card issuer to control the actions of the cardholder through the environment in which the card is used. This phenomenon has led to the development of the terms "closed environment" and "open environment." Examples of closed environments include the Club Med or the Dallington Country Club, noted above. A university is also an example of a closed environment because, even though access to the campus is open, the facilities for which cards are used are generally available only to pre-screened users. Prepaid cards for toll roads or for commuter passes operate in open environments, but the cards are for a single service and there are numerous opportunities to verify the identity of the holder and the validity of the card. Cards for movies, McDonald's, public telephones, vending machines in public areas, and other general uses operate in an open environment. It is unusual for a single card to accommodate multiple applications in an open environment.

When direct control of the environment or the cardholder presents unacceptable or infeasible solutions for transactions security, other measures must be taken. Identifying technologies and techniques that need to be put in place to ensure the secure distribution of multiservice, prepaid value cards in an open environment is the main obstacle to the introduction and deployment of these cards.

Consumer Preferences for Bank Deposits and Cash

Given the obstacles, are applications of computer technology for prepaid transactions of limited significance, or are they the beginning of a trend that will accelerate as participants become confident of their ability to manage revenue, costs, and risks? This section uses the context provided by basic economic theory to propose that there is a theoretical indifference among consumers as regards payments media and also to show that there is a form of "surplus value" which can be captured if the "monopoly" of government-issued coin and currency is open to competition from privately issued prepaid transactions media. If the following arguments are correct, then there could be an economic incentive to invest in technologies for prepaid media, perhaps even in preference to additional investment in electronic network technology.

The fact that, where other payments media exist, cash is used primarily for low-value payments suggests that consumers have a preference for storing value in bank accounts. Coins and banknotes do represent value: a promise to pay backed by the government that authorizes their issue. Their long tradition as a convenient and anonymous way to transport and transfer value has been enhanced by stable governments which assure their widespread acceptance at face value.

At one time, a metal coin was explicitly worth its face value, as measured by weight. As payments have become more complex, the role of coin and currency has changed. Today, they are infrequently a means of

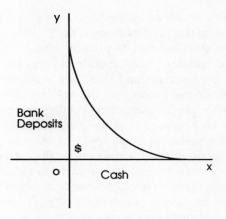

Figure 2-2. Consumer Preference Curve for Holding Value for Payments Transactions—Bank Deposits and Cash (Coin and Currency)

storing value and more often a means of facilitating transactions. Cash has been replaced by other payments media such as checks and wire transfers to resolve two of the problems of money transfer in this modern world: distance and value. The problems of volume (when value is not an issue) are still met primarily though coin and currency. Bank deposits have become the preferred means of holding value, as well as a channel for transactions, whether paper-based or electronic.

Coins and currency are held by consumers for convenience in making certain types of payments. In figure 2-2, using the classic economic analysis of a consumption curve based on two goods, on the x axis we have the intrinsic value of the privacy or convenience of holding cash for financial transactions and on the y axis we have the value of holding funds on deposit at a bank. This may be a positive value to the consumer in terms of interest paid, or the mitigation of a negative value by keeping a balance high enough to avoid service fees or interest paid to the bank, in the case of an overdraft, or it may be an intrinsic value of accountability, security, or other factors.

Given that any consumer, and consumers in the aggregate, are going to hold some or all of their assets for transactions, we are curious as to how much of this they might hold literally in cash—coin and currency—and how much in bank deposits.

At one end of the curve, we have a consumer who holds all his transactions value in cash; and unlike most consumers in economic theory, this one really exists! At the other end of the curve, we have the consumer who keeps all his money (value) in a bank. Although less frequently observed, this consumer also exists in the person of certain eccentric millionaires who themselves never carry cash.

The existence of payment instruments such as checks, debit and credit cards, and electronic transfers makes it possible for even our less affluent citizens to approach the no-cash end of the curve. Improvements in technology that facilitate cash-back on check and debit card transactions and the introduction of ATMs which accept cash deposits make it easier for a consumer to move up and down his payments media preference curve in response to changing needs.

We know that, on aggregate, the amount of cash held for transactions represents 80 percent to 85 percent of all the payments activity in the economy, but very little value. So, in aggregate, most of our citizens are high up on the y axis.

Much of the activity of retail banking is helping the consumer, as an individual and in the aggregate, to adjust his position on the payments media preference curve so that he never holds more cash than needed for transactions. Most American consumers are comfortable managing their finances to maximize bank deposits and minimize cash holdings, and have shown themselves willing to accept technology that changes the way they do this. Much of retail banking activity is created by consumers moving back and forth along their preference curves in a narrow range around their optimum. Successful banking technology, such as automated teller machines, helps consumers maximize the benefit of their choices.

If consumers seek to maximize the efficiency of their holdings of bank deposits by trading back and forth between cash and bank-facilitated payments media, then prepaid cards can be a more convenient way of holding value for small transactions. These prepaid payments media would replace cash but create bank deposits held by a third party and shift the distribution of value without reducing the amount held by the consumer.

The small but important role that travelers cheques play as a means of payment suggests that there are some circumstances in which a consumer will prefer prepaid payments media. The use of travelers cheques for transaction convenience is debatable, since the checks are comparatively a chore to procure and to cash. Other factors such as protection, portability, budgeting, and planning clearly enter into a consumer's decision to purchase travelers cheques. Logically, these same factors should apply to cash, and a consumer demand for a prepaid medium to replace cash can be hypothesized.

Prepaid cards can be an acceptable alternative to both cash and bank

64   MONEY AND PAYMENTS

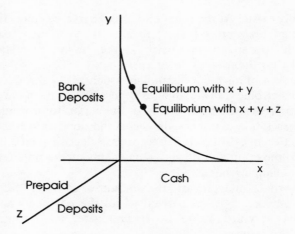

Figure 2–3. Consumer Preference Curve for Holding Value for Payments Transactions, Including Prepaid Media; Payments Media Decisions

deposits, but in an environment where bank deposits are already high, there appear to be greater opportunities for replacing cash. Indeed, it would appear that there are more opportunities for growth and improved productivity in creating new payments media, a new dimension, than in further improving on methods for accessing existing bank deposits.

Using a prepaid payments medium adds a third dimension to the payments media decision curve. On the z axis, shown in figure 2–3, are deposits of the consumer's cash which are held in a third-party account, presumably a bank account, but not the consumer's bank account and not necessarily at the same bank where the consumer holds his funds on deposit.

The z axis denotes value held in deposits for travelers cheques, money orders, prepaid cards, and certain types of scrip. Travelers cheques, for example, are bought for convenience and security. They are applicable to a wide sphere of payments transactions and are used to replace regular checks or cards for high-value transactions and to obtain coins and currency to be used in low-value transactions. Tokens and fare cards for mass transit have a narrow sphere of acceptability but are valued because of their convenience and the predictability of the payment.

Travelers cheques, oriented toward high-value transactions, tend to replace other payments media on the upside of the consumer's consumption curve. Prepaid cards, oriented toward low-value transactions, replace coin and currency on the downside of the consumption curve.

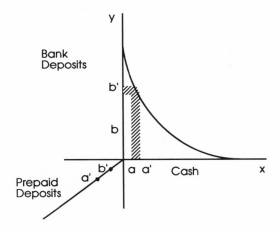

Figure 2–4. Consumer Preference Curves for Holding Value for Payments Transactions—Bank Deposits, Cash, and Prepaid Media; Payments Media Decisions

Figure 2–3 represents how value might be transferred from the consumer's bank deposits to cash holdings if the consumer has a viable prepaid medium as a payments alternative. A consumer could choose to transfer money from a bank account to purchase prepaid media, shifting downward on the preference curve. With prepaid media, the amount of "cash" could be augmented by cash equivalents. The consumer has slipped down the y axis and moved out along the x axis.

The shaded area in figure 2–4 suggests alternatives for shifting value when prepaid media are available. If the total value which the consumer holds for transactions is c, then, without prepaid cards, $a + b + b' = c$. If the consumer shifts bank deposits held for transactions convenience into prepaid cards, then the amount of cash and cash equivalents (prepaid cards) would increase and $a + a' + b = c$. If the consumer reduces holdings in currency by the amount used to purchase prepaid cards, then, once again, $a + b + b' = c$. Another possibility is that the consumer will pull value from other sources, increasing both his own bank deposits and deposits held with a third party to cover prepaid media; in this case, $a + a' + b + b' = c'$. The total value held for transactions would increase from c to c' and the curve itself would shift outward to find a new point of equilibrium.

All things being equal, a consumer should be willing to transfer some bank deposits held for transactions into prepaid media. When these bank deposits are used to buy prepaid media, money passes from the consumer's account (y axis) to a third party (z axis), and increases the consumer's "cash" represented on the x axis. When the switch is from coin and currency to prepaid media, value is deposited in bank accounts on the z axis, while "cash" remains stable at point a. Switching from coin and currency to cash equivalents such as a prepaid card creates new bank deposits.

The minimum impact of a prepaid card would be to shift bank deposits from one account to another. The maximum impact would be to increase liquidity with the addition of an attractive new means of payment. A logical assumption is that, once consumers accepted prepaid cards as a reliable alternative to coin and currency, the amount of government-issued cash in circulation would be reduced while bank deposits held in the private sector would be increased.

A measurable shift from currency in circulation to bank deposits would affect the monetary base, which might have implications for regulatory policy. On the aggregate these shifts might not be important. For individual banks, however, holding deposits and collateral to back prepaid cards instead of vault cash to meet customer demands could be significant.

If the consumer has made the decision to shift value into prepaid media, we can assume it is because he is satisfied with this distribution. The bank deposits on the y axis have been assigned an intrinsic value associated with increasing income or reducing costs and with certain types of payments convenience and security. The cash holdings on the x axis are associated with anonymity and convenience, especially for small payments.

Surplus value that the consumer can't use, because he is buying transaction convenience and has already maximized his/her choices, is transferred to third parties represented by the z axis. One way of describing this phenomenon is to state as a hypothesis that, once existing payments networks have maximized transaction efficiencies represented by the tradeoff between cash and bank deposits, new productivity from payments efficiency comes not from moving higher up the y axis but by expanding the opportunities with the addition of new dimensions. It is also possible that it is easier to move consumers with a preference for cash from the x axis to the z axis than it is to push them up the y axis with an array of payments media linked to bank deposits. This may explain the success of prepaid cards in Japan and of eurocheques (which have many of the features of a prepaid instrument) in West Germany.

The consumer, in showing his preference for holding money as bank deposits or as cash, can choose only among available options. Just as holding value for investment purposes is influenced by, among other things, rates of return and liquidity, holding value for transactions is influenced by factors such as acceptability and availability of payments alternatives.

A payment typically has three major participants: the payor, the payee, and the issuer of the payments medium. The choice of means of payment for any particular transaction is the result of a combination of factors:

- preference of the payor, based on his own evaluation of the costs and benefits associated with his choice;
- preference of the payee, who can and often does specify the form as well as the timing of a payment, based on his evaluation of the associated costs and benefits;
- availability of payments media. Within the limits of government regulation, a variety of media are supplied to the payments system; the offerors of these media (mostly but not exclusively banks) have also evaluated the costs and benefits associated with their choices.

The costs that each participant associates with a transaction can be explicit costs, or implicit costs, including an opportunity cost.

Observation suggests that consumers, as payors, go to a certain amount of trouble in order to have cash or other payments media on hand to make purchases in line with the constraints of the marketplace. At the same time, there appear to be tradeoffs between "transaction convenience" (always having the right change, for example) and "value convenience" (keeping a balance in a bank account at a certain level, for example). A consumer choosing a payments medium which maximizes his convenience for a particular transaction is consciously or unconsciously responding to decisions made by the payee and by the providers of payment services.

It is possible to construct consumer indifference curves regarding payments media and to identify a point that maximizes payor utility within the constraints of the marketplace.

If we put the need to store value on the y axis and the need to have value on hand for transactions on the x axis, we can hypothesize a series of consumer indifference curves (see figure 2–5). Along these curves, a consumer will be satisfied with any combination of payments media. With the constraints imposed by the real world, the consumer must find a utility indifference curve that maximizes his preference for storing value, given what the payee will accept, and by the availability of payments media—and their costs, if any.

If we draw the consumers' utility curves and the constraints of what is accepted as payment in different situations, we have a map that indicates

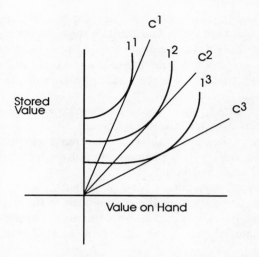

Figure 2–5. Consumer Indifference Curves: Allocating Value and Transactions
Convenience Given Marketplace Constraints for Accepting Payments Media

maximum utility for any given set of payor choices among payments media,
with payee constraints, in different payments environments.

Since we believe that consumers prefer to hold money for value, not
transactions convenience, that is, in bank deposits not as cash, a consumer
will prefer the highest utility curve I^1. His ability to achieve the maximum
utility is curbed, however, by the willingness of payees to accept direct
transfers of value, such as checks or direct debits, in lieu of cash.

The business of retail banking is in large part centered on providing the
payments media that give the payor and the payee maximum utility. Their
objective has been to lower the costs and increase the convenience
associated with accepting different payments media. We could hypothesize
that I^3 shows aggregate consumer utility for banks deposits and transactions media in the banking environment of the 1960s, represented by C^3. I^2
could be the current situation, with C^2 representing the aggregate of costs
and delivery constraints with today's electronic networks. I^1 could be
society's hypothetical objective for maximum utility at minimum delivery
cost. The question relevant to this analysis is the amount of investment
needed to get us to I^1. Diminishing returns to scale will eventually (may
already) prevail in using technology to help consumers get the maximum
utility from the value held in bank accounts. To date, the attention of
banks has been on improving the payment delivery systems that give the

consumer the best available access to his bank deposits. Not only do banks do this to provide services to customers in a competitive environment but also it is to banks' advantage to have value held as bank deposits instead of as coin and currency.

It may be that instead of investing to further improve the utility of bank deposits and transactions convenience for specific consumer market segments, banks would be better off investing to maximize aggregate bank deposits through the transactions convenience of prepaid cards.

For society as a whole, the greatest potential benefit of a prepaid card is not the marginal benefit in transaction facility, but the economic benefit of more productive funds.

Acknowledgments

Peter Hirsch, Battelle Institute, London, arranged for me to meet with Dr. Peter Harrop during a visit to London in February 1990. I was pleased to be able to use his excellent publication as a reference work because Dr. Harrop and I share many of the same views on the potential of technology to provide a better alternative to coin and currency.

Among the many others who provided me with ideas and information in the preparation of this chapter, special recognition is due Richard W. Epps and Richard H. Urban at CoreStates Financial, Philadelphia, and John Love, Faulkner & Gray, Chicago.

Glossary of Terms

Following are some of the terms that technology has recently introduced into the banking vocabulary and which are used in discussing prepaid cards and smart cards.

Contactless Card. A connection between smart card and interfacing device that does not use a contact surface. Signals are transmitted by high frequency.

Disposable Card. A medium designed for a predefined, short period or a specific amount. When the time lapses or all the value is used, the card is no longer valid and is discarded.

Destructive Decrementing. Method of decrementing value from a prepaid card by which the space carrying the value is removed from the card. In the case of a smart card, the memory space carrying value or information is permanently erased, or "burnt."

EPROM. Electronically programmable, read-only memory. A semiconductor memory that is erasable with ultra-violet light.

EEPROM. Electronically erasable, programmable, read-only memory. Nonvolatile memory carried in an integrated circuit card.

Hologram. A three-dimensional picture made by placing images so that the pattern is created by light reflection on the surfaces.

Integrated Circuit Card (ICC). The international standards designation for smart card, referring to the type of chip carried on the card.

Optical Character Recognition (OCR). Character fonts that are machine-readable by optical techniques; a standard for use in bar codes.

Personal Identification Number (PIN). Numeric or alphanumeric code used by a cardholder for verification of identity.

Watermark. A process originally developed for printing and used in security printing whereby very slight differences in paper width, caused by rolling or pressing the paper, create a pattern which can be seen when the paper is held to the light. The same concept applied to magnetic stripe technology creates a unique design on the stripe.

Zones. Areas of smart card storage designated for free access, limited access, or no access.

Sources

International Association for Microcircuit Cards. *Procedural Guidelines for the Integrated Circuit Card*. London: INTAMIC, 1989.

Svigals, Jerome. *Smart Cards*. New York: Macmillan, 1985.

Notes

1. The "electronic money" era was recognized in 1965 by the American Bankers Association, with the creation of the Checkless Society Committee under the direction of Dale L. Reistad. The group's goal was to identify electronic replacements for checks and cash. Dale Reistad is credited with coining the phrase "the checkless, cashless society."

2. Bank for International Settlements, in *Payment Systems in Eleven Developed Countries* (Bank Administration Institute, 1989), reports 84 million large-value wire transfers in the United States in 1987, for a total value of $281 trillion. It has become increasingly cost effective to use similar technology for payments in retail locations, providing authorizations and capturing data for interbank transfers for credit card and debit card transactions. Economies of scale and refinements in technology that drive down the cost of point-of-sale terminals and telecommunications links combine with increasing numbers of cardholders and card payments to lower the per-transaction cost.

3. Elinor Solomon addresses the influences of electronic transfers on money measurements in chapter 1.

4. Peter Harrop, in *The Future of Payment Media* (London: Financial Times Business Information, 1989), estimates 1,400 transactions per capita in the United States. David B. Humphrey and Allen N. Berger, in "Market Failure and Resource Use: Economic Incentives to Use Different Payment Instruments" (May 1988), estimate 0.4 percent of value of payments is in cash. See also note 6.

5. Bank for International Settlements (1989).

6. Bank for International Settlements (1989) gives a total of 59 billion noncash transactions in the United States in 1987. Sources of estimates for cash transactions are referred to in note 4; also the author revised estimates prepared by Paul B. Henderson, Jr., and published in "Modern Money," *Electronic Funds Transfer and Payments: The Public Policy Issues*, edited by Elinor Harris Solomon (Boston: Kluwer-Nijhoff, 1987).

7. Harrop (1989).

8. U.S. Department of the Treasury, "An Assessment of United States Currency and Coin Systems with Long Range Planning Recommendations," 1979.

9. Harrop (1989).

10. Harrop (1989).

11. Annual volumes of electronic funds transfers are reported in *Bank Network News* and *POS News*, published by Faulkner & Gray, Chicago, IL. Point-of-sale card transactions, for example, grew from 14.4 million in 1985 to 157.2 million in 1989.

12. U.S. Department of the Treasury, *Annual Reports*.

13. Dr. David D. Whitehead, Federal Reserve Bank of Atlanta, discussed with the author his findings on currency and the underground economy. By his estimate, 85 percent of U.S. currency may be held outside the United States.

14. Harrop (1989).

15. The "coin" used contactless technology and a simplified computer chip, preloaded with value, in a coin-sized plastic case. The coin fit into existing coin receptacles. When the value was exhausted, the coin was retained in the pay phone. As long as value remained in the coin it could be used to pay for phone calls of varying cost.

16. *Japan Weekly Monitor*, July 24, 1989.

17. Harrop (1989).

18. Harrop (1989).

19. Harrop (1989) gives the following distribution for coins held by commercial sectors in the United Kingdom: food services—37.8 percent; vending—32.3 percent; retail—19.5 percent; games—5.5 percent; telephone—2.7 percent; mass transit—0.7 percent; parking meters—0.3 percent.

II MONEY FLOWS: STABILITY AND FINANCIAL CYCLES

Part I examined the nature of electronic money and its microeconomic foundations. Part II considers the system dynamics, the business cycle today, and the macroeconomic policy control questions. The spotlight is on stability both in global dimensions (chapter 3) and in narrower money control and money flows perspective (chapter 4).

The communications revolution produces a universal awareness of global events.[1] An example was the tearing down of the Berlin Wall, as widely transmitted evidence of what a free market economy can do (Haberler, chapter 3). The ability to move money and information swiftly helped resolve the 1987 and 1989 stock market crises in expedited manner. However, the information technology perhaps can speed up that market response in disquieting manner in the downward direction, too.

Such questions of recent market volatility have been much discussed by economists (Humphrey, 1987; Tobin, 1987), the press, scholarly conferences (Reserve Bank of Kansas City, 1989) and influential policy makers (Greenspan, 1990, Brady Commission, 1988). The New York Federal Reserve Bank has examined the detailed operations of the different electronic nets and the information flows moving there (see references, chapter 1). Much attention has been paid to those innovative financial techniques as instrumental in the amplitude of the short-term swings.[2]

The situation gets very complex, however. The money base supports a variety of information with money-like characteristics moving on electronic nets prior to net settlement in bank-linked money. As shown earlier in Chapter 1, these flows generally moving at the speed of light (such as those in worldwide futures or options markets) are probably the most volatile of all.

Chapters 3 and 4 ask the consequences of this explosion of new, partially hidden, payments activity. Is it possible that something fundamental has been altered in the nature of the economic fluctuations—such as duration of cyclical swings, amplitude, or patterns at or around equilibrium? If so, what role, if any, is played by the mechanisms of electronic funds transfers? Even more broadly, do we still have a business cycle as conventionally known? To whom does one turn for answers to such fundamental questions?

Haberler's Economic Contributions

On the occasion of Dr. Gottfried Haberler's 90th birthday celebration at the American Enterprise Institute in June 1990, Professor Paul Samuelson observed a fact well known by all economists: Gottfried Haberler has been a "giant among giants," one of the "few most valuable economic scholars" of the epoch of the 20th century.

Dr. Haberler's classic *Prosperity and Depression* (1937) has been the definitive study of business cycles, both pre- and post-Keynes. This work also explicitly introduces dynamic processes, including time lag effects, into economic theory.[3] My current re-reading indicates it to be more relevant than ever to modern economic fluctuations and the processes of change. In addition, hundreds of Dr. Haberler's other writings (including the *Theory of International Trade*, 1936) have been theoretical milestones for guiding generations of subsequent policymakers and great scholars, among them Professor Samuelson.

Paul Samuelson (1939) created the famous multiplier/accelerator models of damped and explosive oscillations, with stability implications. The work in which he pioneered continued on. The Harvard University fiscal and monetary policy seminars of Profs. Haberler, Hansen, and Williams come to my vivid recollection; they provided a forum for debate of dynamic issues in an unforgettable atmosphere of intellectual enthusiasm. The ideas generated there in the late '40s and early '50s coincided with studies of Frisch, Harrod, Domar, Solow, and Baumol, among others.[4]

By the mid '60s disenchantment with the nonlinear dynamic models set in, due both to their mathematical intricacies and the later ascendency of the "new classical" (linear) models such as those of Lucas and Sargent and Wallace. However, the march of compelling scientific evidence in physics, astronomy, and weather has underscored their importance in obtaining realistic results. The search was on for finding a most interesting subset of nonlinear dynamics, "chaos," that holds out the promise for finding deterministic patterns out of seemingly random (stochastic) economic fluctuations.

At the same time, the computer technology and advances in mathematics have provided valuable new analytical techniques for recognizing nonlinearity if it exists (Brock, Brock and Sayers) as well as solving the complex differential equations by indirect numerical means (see references in chapter 4).[5]

The Business Cycle Dynamics: Chapter 3

We are deeply honored that Dr. Haberler, who made the fundamental contribution (1937) on business cycle dynamics, has consented to contribute a new work, "What Happened to the Business Cycle?," to this book.

Dr. Haberler analyzes present business trends, and finds no clear pattern typical of the past emerging. Indeed, Dr. Haberler questions whether such a thing as a "classic" business cycle even exists any more. In summer 1990 the U.S. economy was in the final stages of a protracted and most unusual eight year expansion. What circumstances may be perhaps responsible for this longevity in business upswing?

He seeks answers in a contrast between the present spirit of awareness and a much less enlightened past. The record of public policy during the years of the Great Depression of the 1930s was very poor. For one thing, the Federal Reserve let the basic money supply shrink by about 30 percent. For another it showed the bad judgement to raise interest rates in 1931 in the midst of the Depression.

Later on in the decade of the '30s, the Fed's timing was equally unfortunate. The eventual expansion was badly mismanaged by President Roosevelt's "New Deal." Against the advice of John Maynard Keynes, the Federal Reserve slammed on the monetary brake. The result was a short but very vicious depression (May 1937–June 1938). The Federal Reserve clearly had overreacted.

Dr. Haberler believes that policy performance is much improved now. The grievous mistakes of the Great Depression will not be repeated by any of the leading industrialized countries. Monetary policy in the 1980s, and hopefully in the 1990s, has been much better than in the 1960s and 1970s. In addition, flexible exchange rates have helped countries protect themselves from the real impact of a financial crash (1987) and control inflation and maintain expansion (the United States in 1983–1984 or West Germany in 1989–1990).

Even before the August 1990 Persian Gulf crisis, however, Dr. Haberler worried about the possible recurrence of another oil shock, like the ones that hit the United States in the 1970s. In order to lessen the inflationary shock of any trouble in the Middle East, he urged a sharp increase in the federal tax on gasoline. In addition to reducing U.S. dependence on foreign oil, a large tax on gasoline would over the years yield hundreds of billion of dollars in additional revenues to the U.S. Treasury and also have beneficial effects on the environment.

The Persian Gulf crisis now underscores these same points and it also sets the stage for a full-blown recession. Given the outbreak of war, we risk inflationary recession, a much more serious problem than a deflationary one because it severely constrains monetary policy options (see Dr. Haberler's postscript).

What, then, is the nature of today's business cycle? Dr. Haberler suggests that perhaps the German *Konjunkturschwankungen* is the better term. It easily translates into "business fluctuations" which

Milton Friedman has proposed as a substitute for "business cycles" because variety rather than uniformity is implied. Even if we disregard extraordinary situations as the present one, and compare business cycles in the 1960s and early 1970s with the late 1970s and 1980s, we find significant differences.

The Short-Term Money Control Model

In the next chapter, physicist Dr. Thomas Solomon and I look further at the characteristics of economic fluctuations. But the focus is different. The focus is the nature of stability in money flows systems.

As described in chapter 1, if electronic money becomes part of a money whole, the supply of effective money can become quite elastic. The distinctions between money—that which will buy financial assets as well as goods and services—and its rate of throughout-day use may easily blur.[6] What seems useful here is analysis of money flows in their totality (including the elusive electronic) as forces moving markets and altering stability conditions. Also most important will be the cyclical reactions of the other market participants, and (in this work) the "reaction function" of the central bank in particular.

"Money Stability and Control: The Perverse Effect of Feedback Loops," chapter 4, follows this approach in steps. Part I develops a basic nonlinear model that describes the time variation of the money supply and the Fed's attempts to control it (prices and income initially held constant). The role of time lags (next introduced) is very important in perverting policy goals, as highlighted earlier by Professor Milton Friedman.

What is interesting here is the "quantum leap" introduced by electronics into the already difficult money control process. The ability of EFT to move money faster (that is, to raise significantly the system's "saturation level") can make the situation worse: it increases the fluctuations of any unstable money and interest movements, in the presence of policy time lags. Consequently, the Fed must respond more cautiously to correct money deviations than in a pre-EFT era, in order to achieve exactly the same results.

In the next step (part II), we expand the money control model to include feedback effects from interest rate changes to money changes, and vice versa. The broader concept of money flows including velocity as well as money is incorporated into the model here. The (continuous) money turnover rate is studied for the possible effects of higher electronic speeds. The money velocity (turnover) and flow demand functions are related to the conventional money demand function.

With higher money flows speeds, the policy delay times become more relevant than ever, as potentially destabilizing elements. A "heating up" of the critical money flows parameter can shift the system more quickly into instability. The argument is strengthened that the Fed may have to cut down its money corrective attempt, in order not to destabilize the system. Indeed, the "feedback" relationships between money and interest rate changes may amplify all the effects, including even random noise.

Given the dynamics in an EFT regime, it comes as no surprise that the Federal Reserve has leaned quite heavily upon Fed funds rate control—one with little significant time lag in implementation. The present mix of "information based" targets has the added advantage of decoupling and defusing any money and interest rate chain reaction, in the event of instability. With market-oriented targets, the unhappy spectacle of money and interest rate volatility feeding back upon one another becomes a less likely prospect.

Notes

1. As information and payments flows approach the speed of light, we approach (but do not achieve) a holistic globe. The familiar analogy is the hologram, where every feature of the image is encoded at every point across the whole photographic plate. In such a situation (defined by the so-called nonlocal character of quantum states) it is not possible to consider each particle as existing separately, in the absence of the other. For a good nontechnical explanation see Davies (1984, pp. 219–220).

2. For example, the "circuit breakers" just authorized by the Securities and Exchange Commission in July 1990 were imposed by the New York Stock Exchange on August 7, 1990, to help contain the one-day sharp 93 point drop in the Dow Jones Industrial Average. As selling pressures mounted in the wake of grim news from the Mideast, the Exchange announced restrictions on index arbitrage, a form of program trading in which investors shuffle money between stock-index futures and broad baskets of stocks, depending on which is cheaper. Also in the first half-hour of trading, another set of circuit breakers took hold at

the Chicago Mercantile Exchange. The Standard & Poor's 500-stock index futures sank suffiently below their Friday close to trigger a trading limit for the futures at the MERC (*Wall Street Journal*, August 7, 1990, pp. C1 and C17).

Global aspects of the volatility made possible by world trading in futures and options, along with an interesting discussion of the mechanisms, are treated by the Federal Reserve Bank of Chicago (May/June 1990). Becketti and Sellon (1989) also analyze the differential sector effects, including those on short- versus long-term rates of different types.

Unlike modern macroeconomists, Irving Fisher includes the early 20th century equivalent of such financial transactions in his V_T along with purchases of all the intermediate components which go into production of, say, flour or a piece of machinery (see chapter 1). Fisher apparently was something of a technology enthusiast, too. There is much discussion of payments revolutions—and the resulting altered payments habits of individuals and business firms—in his *Purchasing Power of Money* (1911).

3. See Haberler's *Prosperity and Depression*, 3rd ed. (1946, pp. 8–11, 83ff, 249–254, 302ff.).

4. Samuelson (1990); Baumol and Benhabib (1989); Haberler in Koo (1985), part V; *Prosperity and Depression* (1946 expanded ed.), part III.

5. A modern personification of the Holy Grail, for economists, is that unique subset of nonlinear dynamics called, in something of a misnomer, "chaos." Chaos is defined as a nonlinear dynamic system with sensitivity to initial conditions; a random event such as a butterfly flapping its wings in Hong Kong can affect the state of weather in New York.

However, chaotic systems contain within them ordered fluctuations which otherwise appear to be random (stochastic) in nature. (For a careful interpretation for economists, see Baumol and Benhabib, 1989.) The cyclical model of true chaos in a "hard" science such as physics is deterministic. But even in "noisy" chaotic systems—such as any in economics would surely turn out to be—much valuable information could be obtained by the embryonic techniques of chaos researchers. The new information could lead, eventually, to a better identification or prediction of cyclical turning points and the boundaries ("strange attractor") toward which the business cycle tends to return.

Is it just possible that some of what we economists call random or "white noise" may be part of the endogenous dynamic model? Gleick (1987) tells the amusing story (pp. 83–85) about economics professor Hendrik Houthakker's encounter with Dr. Benoit Mandelbrot at Harvard's Littauer Center in the Harvard yard. Mandelbrot, the mathematical father of fractals (quite similar to "strange attractors" in chaos), made a querulous joke when he saw Professor Houthakker's blackboard: "How should my diagram have materialized ahead of my lecture?" Professor Houthakker didn't know what Mandelbrot was talking about. The diagram on his blackboard represented eight years of cotton prices.

6. It is not generally clear whether particular payments fluctuations are due to a rise in transactions V, or in the sundry money permutations (electronic and conventional M) with which the V_T is paired. This lack of precision, even confusion, brings to mind the Heisenberg "uncertainty principle." This principle of quantum mechanics states that you can know either the position of a particle or its momentum, but not both at the same time. (Uncertainty of momentum) × (uncertainty of position of a particle) = a constant ($\neq 0$).

As electronics steps up the transfer of money toward the speed of light, while attenuating the links between electronic money and the money base, it becomes difficult also to distinguish between money in motion (flow) and money at rest (particle). Focusing on money flows (ϕ, or $M\gamma$, as discussed more fully in chapter 4) gets around this particular problem somewhat, while obviously not resolving it.

References

Baumol, W.J., and J. Benhabib. 1989. "Chaos: Significance, Mechanism, and Economic Applications." *Journal of Economic Perspectives* 3 (Winter).

Becketti, Sean, and G.H. Sellon, Jr. 1989. "Has Financial Market Volatility Increased?" *Economic Review*, Federal Reserve Bank of Kansas City (June).

Brady Commission [U.S. Presidential Task Force on Market Mechanisms]. 1988. *Report of the Presidential Task Force*. Washington, D.C., January.

Brock, W.A., and Chera L. Sayers. 1988. "Is the Business Cycle Characterized by Deterministic Chaos?" *Journal of Monetary Economics* 22.

Davies, Paul. 1984. *Superforce*. New York: Simon and Schuster.

Federal Reserve Bank of Kansas City. 1989. *Financial Market Volatility*. Symposium, Jackson Hole, WY, August 17–19, 1988.

Federal Reserve Bank of Chicago. 1990. "Globalization." *Economic Perspectives* (May/June).

Friedman, Milton. 1960. *A Program for Monetary Stability*. New York: Fordham University Press.

Gleick, James. 1987. *Chaos: Making a New Science*. New York: Viking Penguin, Inc.

Greenspan, Alan. 1990. Testimony before the Financial Institutions Supervision Subcommittee, Committee on Banking, Finance and Urban Affairs. U.S. House of Representatives. Chicago, IL, May 14.

Haberler, Gottfried. 1937. *Prosperity and Depression: A Theoretical Analysis of Cyclical Movements*. Geneva, Switzerland: League of Nations.

Humphrey, David. B. 1987. "Payments System Risk, Market Failure and Public Policy." In Elinor H. Solomon, ed., *Electronic Funds Transfers and Payments*. Boston: Kluwer Academic Publishers.

Koo, Anthony Y.C., ed. 1985. *Selected Essays of Gottfried Haberler*. Cambridge, MA: The MIT Press.

Samuelson, Paul. 1939. "Interactions Between the Multiplier Analysis and the Principle of Acceleration." *Review of Economic Statistics* 21, 75–78.

Samuelson, Paul. 1990. "Gottfried Haberler as Economic Sage and Trade Theory Innovator." *Wirtschafts Politische Blatter: Gottfried von Haberler zum 90*. Geburtstag (1990 .37).

Tobin, James. 1987. "Monetary Rules and Control in Brave New World." In Elinor H. Solomon, ed., *Electronic Funds Transfers and Payments*. Boston: Kluwer Academic Publishers.

3 WHAT HAPPENED TO THE BUSINESS CYCLE?

Gottfried Haberler

As this is being written in August 1990, the U.S. economy is still in the cyclical expansion that started seven and a half years ago (in November 1982), the longest cyclical expansion on record. What are the reasons for the exceptional longevity of this expansion? One reason surely is that there has been no supply shock, nothing compared to the oil crisis in the West that followed the embargo on oil exports from the Middle East triggered by the Israeli-Arab War of 1973.

True, there have been some alarming stock exchange crashes, one around the world in 1987, and one in Japan in 1989–1990, which were widely expected to bring on a recession. That this did not happen suggests that national and international monetary management in the seven leading industrial countries has greatly improved. What I have in mind here is that in the 1980s—and we hope in the 1990s—monetary policy has been much better than in the 1960s and 1970s.

The Great Depression of the 1930s and the Business Cycle

But before discussing the business cycle problem as it presents itself today, I will briefly analyze the nature and causes of the Great Depression of the

Solomon, E.H., (ed.), *Electronic Money Flows.*
© 1991 Kluwer Academic Publishers. ISBN 0–7923–9134–9. All rights reserved.

1930s. Today it is inconceivable that any of the leading industrialized countries would make the horrendous policy mistakes responsible for the Great Depression of the 1930s.

The Great Depression was a world-shaking event, which brought Hitler to power and thus can be said to have led to World War II. Moreover, for years it caused a profound change in the intellectual climate in which economic policy was made. It shook confidence in free markets and free enterprise; it bolstered the prestige of Soviet Russia, whose economy seemed to be immune to the disaster that had engulfed the West. Many became convinced of the superiority of central planning. Marxists could say, "We told you so. This is the end of capitalism!" Some radical followers of Keynes—"Marxo-Keynesians," as Schumpeter called them—took the same positions. Keynes's own view is not so clear. There are passages in *The General Theory* that lend themselves to that interpretation. But in 1937, one year after *The General Theory* was published, Keynes, to the great astonishment and dismay of some of his followers, said it was time to curb inflation even if it meant a little more unemployment.

Actually, the main policy mistakes that produced the disaster and the country that made them can be identified beyond any reasonable doubt. To put it bluntly, they were due to the policies of the United States who was universally accepted after World War I as the dominant military, economic, and political power of the world. Unfortunately, it did not make good use of its power. To be sure, other countries, too, made policy mistakes and had their own depressions, in some cases more severe than in the United States—Germany, for example. At this point, however, I will confine myself to saying that other countries' mistakes had very little effect on U.S. policy. The U.S. depression was homemade.

The most serious mistake was made by the Federal Reserve; it must carry a large part of responsibility for the disaster. It let the basic money supply shrink by about 30 percent, both through acts of commission (for example, by raising interest rates in 1931 in the midst of the depression, when the British pound was cut loose from gold and declined in foreign exchange markets) and through acts of omission (by failing to prevent the collapse of thousands of banks). One need not be a monetarist to understand that such a sharp deflation would have catastrophic consequences.

Another great mistake was that in 1931, in the midst of the depression, the Hoover administration proposed that taxes be raised; Congress accepted the proposal, and taxes were raised in 1932. It should be mentioned, however, that a step was taken to reduce the adverse effect of the tax rise by establishing the Reconstruction Finance Corporation to make loans to distressed banks. This tax policy was entirely in the spirit of the time, however, and in no way changes the fact that Hoover was a great president. On top of it all, Congress enacted in 1930 the skyscraper Smoot-Hawley tariff, which greatly accelerated the spread of the U.S. depression around the globe.

The ensuing expansion lasted four years, April 1933 to May 1937. Unfortunately, it was badly mismanaged by President Roosevelt's New Deal. Against the advice of John Maynard Keynes, who recommended that economic policy should first concentrate on recovery from the depression and prevention of any relapse, the Roosevelt administration initiated a large number of social reforms, all of them costly and some downright damaging. The power of labor unions, for example, was sharply increased, and agriculture was heavily subsidized. Wages rose faster than productivity, and prices rose sharply, although the rate of unemployment still was high. Thus the Federal Reserve felt it was forced to step hard on the monetary brake. The result was a short but vicious depression, from May 1937 to June 1938. In 13 months the gross national product (GNP) declined by about 12 percent. Industrial production fell by 32 percent, and unemployment shot up from 11 percent to 20 percent.

This clearly was an enormous overreaction. It reminds me of what my old teacher Ludwig von Mises said: Trying to cure an overdose of inflation by an overdose of deflation is like trying to put a man who has been run down by an automobile back on his feet by letting the car run over him in the opposite direction.

The record was dismal indeed, but I hasten to point out that after World War II the United States did a most effective job rebuilding the shattered world economy. America's most important contribution to world prosperity was that unlike in the 1930s when the U.S. depression spread across the globe; in the post-World War II period the U.S. economy was kept on an even keel, several recessions (none of them coming anywhere near a depression) not withstanding.

In several international conferences under the aegis of the General Agreement on Tariffs and Trade (GATT) the tariff walls of the major countries, including the U.S. Smoot-Hawley tariff, were greatly reduced. In addition, the United States made important initiatives to revitalize the world economy through the speedy economic rehabilitation of the defeated nations, Germany and Japan. Aggressive moves of Stalin's USSR probably speeded up U.S. efforts. Be that as it may, the U.S. reaction was the right one. The spectacular rise of the German economy from the ashes of Hitler's Third Reich and the equally impressive rise of the Japanese economy changed the world outlook demonstrating what a free market and free enterprise—that is, capitalism—could do. The U.S. actions can thus

84 MONEY FLOWS

be regarded as bringing about the demise of communism, which became apparent in 1989 when the wall between East and West Berlin came down. As East Berliners went shopping in droves in West Berlin, the whole world could see on television the difference in the standard of living between the West and a communist country—one that in its pre-Communist period had enjoyed the same standard of living as the West's.

But the subject of this chapter is what happened to the business cycle. I do not believe that the Great Depression can be regarded as a "normal" downphase of the traditional business cycle. As proof of this, consider several reasons why business cycle upswings have been followed by downswings.

In many cases the upswings of business cycles have been marred by inflationary excesses. It stands to reason that high inflation cannot be eliminated without some sort of recession; this clearly was not the reason for the Great Depression. On the contrary, 1920 to 1929 was regarded as a period of exceptional price stability—so much so that many experts optimistically thought the business cycle had been overcome.

Then late in 1929 came the boom and the crash on the New York Stock Exchange. They surely could have been regarded as sufficient reason to expect a recession and to take the appropriate action to deal with the liquidity crises. But the recession was converted into a Great Depression by the horrendous policy mistakes mentioned earlier. Without the sharp contraction of the money supply and the failures of the banking system, the 1929 recession could not have degenerated into the Great Depression.

The Business Cycle in the Present Situation

I repeat, I find it inconceivable that any leading industrialized country or any member of the Group of Seven or the Group of Ten would make the horrendous policy mistakes that were responsible for the Great Depression. We can, therefore, rule out any economic contraction nearly severe as the Great Depression, except in the case of war, revolution, or some other catastrophic event.

There is, however, one possibility that cannot be ruled out, and it is all the more important because the United States could guard against it by measures that would also be most beneficial on other grounds. What I have in mind is an oil shock, like the ones that hit the United States in the 1970s, caused by wars in the Middle East. The next time, nuclear weapons could be involved.

What the United States should have done years ago and should do now is to increase sharply the federal tax on gasoline. U.S. dependence on imported oil has markedly increased in recent years, and gasoline prices are lower in the United States than in any other industrialized country. In addition to reducing U.S. dependence on foreign oil, which is clearly in our national interest, a large tax on gasoline would over the years yield hundreds of billions of dollars in additional revenues to the U.S. Treasury.

Such a tax would also have beneficial effects on the environment. The exhaust of motor vehicles, trucks, and automobiles, which accounts for much of the air pollution, would be sharply reduced. Fewer cars would carry only one person because drivers would form car pools or use public transportation. Many other ways would be found to combine trips and save gasoline. The use and production of oversized gas-guzzling limousines, which choke traffic, pollute the air, and crush the highways, would be curbed.

In Los Angeles and some other areas where rush hour traffic has become a nightmare, authorities have tried to solve some of the problems by creating regulations and building large bureaucracies to enforce them. Putting a high tax on gasoline and letting market forces do the rest would be much cheaper and more efficient and would not require any additional bureaucracies.

On the question of what happened to the business cycle, I am concerned only with the industrialized countries in the West, the Group of Seven, and some countries that follow them, such as Switzerland and Austria in Europe, Taiwan in Asia, and some others. These countries have experienced such a long period of cyclical expansion that some say the business cycle has perhaps been overcome. The *Economist* on June 9, 1990, carried an article, "Topping the Business Cycle," expressing the hope that a worldwide recession may be avoided. "Perhaps the biggest reason for this hope," the *Economist* argues, "is that the big economies are currently less synchronised than for many years. In the 1970s, countries' business cycles were closely aligned: they boomed and went bust in step." The *Economist* does not explain how this lack of sychronization would be possible under the system of fixed exchanges that it has recently espoused ("Time to Tether Currencies," *The Economist*, London, June 9, 1990).

It is not hard to find cases where flexible exchange rates have helped countries to adjust their accounts. Three cases have been suggested by Allan Meltzer:

1. The 1987 stock market crash. Prior to the crash there was an effort to fix exchange rates. After the crash the exchange rates were

allowed to fluctuate, reducing some of the effects of a crash on a real economy.

2. The United States in 1983–1984. A large expansion in the appreciation of the currency and increased imports helped control inflation and maintain expansion.

3. West Germany in 1989–1990. After the wall came down, the appreciation of the real exchange rate helped prevent inflation rising.

In 1990 the expansion in the United States celebrates its 8th birthday, the longest cyclical expansion on record. It has survived several stock exchange crashes, ups and downs of the dollar in the foreign exchange market, and other disturbances.

In the United States voices can be heard arguing that the business cycle "has gone out of business," as the *Washington Post* put it. This means that there will be no recession or only a very mild one. Two reasons usually given for this optimism are, first, that monetary policy has become much more skillful and, second, that the services industries have increased rapidly.

That the Western industrialized countries' monetary management on the national and international levels has become much better than in the 1980s and 1990s is surely true. It is also true that output and employment are much more stable in services industries than in goods-producing industries and that the sharp rise in services industries is therefore a stabilizing factor.

Be that as it may, the fear of a recession has sharply increased in the past few months for two reasons. First, the growth of the U.S. economy has slowed and, second, even before the outbreak of the war in the Persian Gulf, the probability of a new oil shock had been anticipated.

Thus the stage seems to be set for a recession. Given the large rise of the price of oil caused by the war in the Persian Gulf, the recession is likely to be inflationary, not deflationary. An inflationary recession is a much more serious problem than a deflationary one. The sharp rise in oil prices raises the costs of all oil-using industries and poses a dilemma for monetary policy. If the Federal Reserve wants to stop inflation, it has to raise interest rates and reduce the supply of money. These actions, of course, make the recession worse. In other words, they increase unemployment. If the Federal Reserve wants to alleviate the recession, that is to say, reduce unemployment, it has to lower interest rates and increase the money supply. These steps, of course, would intensify the inflation.

The best policy surely is to keep the price level stable and not try to push unemployment down by inflation. That policy never works. The reason is that people find out what is going on and take steps to protect themselves by asking for higher prices and wages. In other words, inflation accelerates quickly.

Market forces, if given a chance, will bring about the necessary adjustments. That does not mean, however, that nothing can or should be done to speed up the process of adjustment. On the contrary, in every country there are numerous restrictions imposed by governments, labor unions and other groups that protect the status quo. These restrictions should be removed in order to ensure greater mobility of labor and wage adjustments. Protectionist pressures to restrict imports should be resisted.

In many countries labor unions have become a powerful force whose impact on the economy on the whole has been negative. They push up wages and so create unemployment. And they make any wage reduction almost impossible, which slows down the adjustment process. In some important cases unions in particular industries have managed to keep their wages substantially higher than wages of workers with the same qualifications in other industries.

A well-known case is that of the U.S. automobile industry. The United Auto Workers (UAW) over many years has managed to keep their wages 50–60 percent higher than wages in manufacturing industries in general. That obviously is a most unsatisfactory situation. It reduces general labor productivity.

In the international sphere it has led to grotesque consequences. When the export of Japanese automobiles to the United States assumed large proportions, the U.S. automobile industry and union demanded protection. The U.S. government responded by proposing to the large Japanese automobile firms that they "voluntarily" restrict the export of Japanese cars to the United States. The Japanese exporters accepted this proposal with alacrity, because this produced what was in effect a U.S.-sponsored foreign export cartel for the monopolistic exploitation of the American people. That the automobile exporter can act like a monopolist is due to the fact that there are only a few large firms involved and that, in addition, the Japanese government takes a hand in the distribution of the quotas among the few exporters.

To clarify the meaning of the term *exploitation*, suppose imports are restricted by a tariff; in that case the difference between the costs of the Japanese producers and the price an American buyer has to pay is collected by the U.S. Treasury. In the system of "voluntary" export restrictions, the difference goes to the foreign exporters. So much on this topic in the present chapter.

Deflationary recessions do not pose a dilemma for monetary policy. If in a recession prices decline, clearly monetary expansion is needed.

What has all this to do with what is called the "classic" business cycle? Is there such a thing as a classic business cycle? Perhaps the German word *Konjunkturschwankungen* is a better term. It easily translates into "business fluctuations," a term Milton Friedman has proposed as a substitute for "business cycles" because it suggests variety rather than uniformity. Even if we disregard extraordinary situations, like the present one, that are complicated by war and revolution, and compare business cycles of the 1960s and early 1970s with those of the late 1970s and 1980s, we find significant differences.

Postscript

Since this paper was finished in August 1990, a major issue has been the looming recession. The war in the Persian Gulf, by driving up the oil price, has intensified this issue. The coming recession will be an inflationary one, a case of stagflation. An inflationary recession poses a dilemma for the central bank. If it keeps money tight to reduce inflation, it exacerbates unemployment. If it pursues an expansionary policy to reduce unemployment, it increases inflation.

The chairman of the Federal Reserve Board, Alan Greenspan, seems to be well prepared for this situation. Reportedly he said, "I have learned to mumble with great incoherence." This remark reflects his understanding that the central bank is subject to conflicting pressures from those who want to curb inflation and those who want to reduce unemployment. The current rate of inflation is unacceptable because it would accelerate when people became convinced it would not be eliminated.

The aim of monetary policy should be long-term price stability. The present unacceptable rate of inflation should be phased out; market forces will find jobs for the unemployed. Of course, well-designed structural changes in the labor market and elsewhere would be highly beneficial.

Finally, a word about deflationary recessions in which output and employment drop and prices fall. Unlike an inflationary recession, a deflationary one does not pose a dilemma for the monetary authorities. If prices fall, surely an expansionary policy is indicated.

Unfortunately, this postscript is limited. I confine myself to saying that none of the postwar recessions was deflationary, but the depression of the 1930s was definitely deflationary.

Let me end with the last two lines of the world-famous book, *Tractatus Logico-Philosophicus*, by Ludwig Wittgenstein: "Whereof one cannot speak, thereof one must be silent."

4 MONEY STABILITY AND CONTROL: THE PERVERSE EFFECTS OF FEEDBACK LOOPS

Thomas H. Solomon[1] and Elinor H. Solomon

From 1979 to 1982, the Federal Reserve implemented a policy in which an attempt was made to control the money supply with minimal regard to the interest rates. This policy was well grounded in established monetarist theories that predicted that careful control of the money supply would lead to stable interest rates and prices (M. Friedman, 1956). The result, however, generally was viewed as unsatisfactory. Interest rate fluctuations were more volatile and erratic than earlier. Even more surprising, though, was the instability of the money supply itself, which fluctuated at unprecedented levels. The failure of this policy, which will be referred to as the "monetarist experiment," presents an intriguing real-world "laboratory" where new theories of economics can be studied.

Traditional equilibrium theories offer no satisfactory explanation, either for the "monetarist" failure of 1979–1982 nor—perhaps even more puzzling—of the Fed's apparent better luck with policy control in the years following its formally announced abandonment of monetarism in 1984 (Wallich, 1984). New approaches are required to resolve these nagging questions (B. Friedman, 1988). Poole (1988) recommends new analysis of money demand elasticities and the market's response to unexpected money. Rational expectations theories emphasize the role of expectations and money supply surprises (Cornell, 1983; Roley, 1982; Urich, 1982).

Solomon, E.H., (ed.), *Electronic Money Flows.*

Money market models using reaction functions, borrowed from engineering control systems, examine interactions between the Fed and public behavior (O'Brien, 1984; Radecki, 1984). Barnett has searched for the presence of chaos and strange attractors in money aggregates (1987, 1988). Other experts highlight financial markets volatility and its causes (Kansas City Federal Reserve Bank, 1988, 1989). Earlier work has suggested that electronic funds transfer (EFT) speed is instrumental with respect both to the observed money volatility and the money control failures (Simpson, 1984; Simpson and Parkinson, 1984; Solomon, 1984).

Theories of dynamical systems have been applied successfully in the physical sciences for over two decades, but have only recently received attention in economics. Important examples have been the work of Grandmont (1987), Brock (1987, 1988), Brock and Sayers (1988), and Baumol and Benhabib (1989). All owe a major intellectual debt to the dynamic business cycle theories of Haberler (1937) and Samuelson (1939), who identified the internal or endogenous mechanisms that could be responsible for economic fluctuations.

In this chapter, we analyze the monetarist experiment with a new dynamic approach in which the *rate of change* of the money supply and interest rates are controlled by feedback from current and previous levels. We believe that this test case can illuminate some of the advantages of dynamic models, which may be particularly important in the current information age when the extraordinarily high speed of funds transfer (see chapter 1) can make equilibrium approaches obsolete. We also hope to illustrate some of the (sometimes unpredictable) effects of EFT and rapid communications upon money flows, volatility, and system stability.

The work can be divided into two sections. The first develops the basic nonlinear model, concentrating only on the money supply and the Fed's attempts to control it. It is shown in this section that a time delay in the implementation of the policy can lead to an instability of the money supply, undercutting the monetarist experiment at its roots. The implications of EFT on the fluctuations of an unstable money supply are also presented here. In the second section, we expand the model to include feedback effects from interest rates. The concept of money flows is incorporated into this model. It is proposed that increases in money flows due to EFT can amplify the feedback and further destabilize the system.

Background: The Unanswered Puzzles, 1978–1982

Many in the economics community view the monetarist experiment as largely counterproductive, adding to the Fed's problems in money growth

control rather than improving control mechanisms (Tobin, 1987; B. Friedman, 1984; Roley, 1982; Cornell, 1983). The following observed results are
examples of that disappointment.

1. Short-term interest rate movements were more volatile and more
    erratic than usual between 1979 and 1982. This was not entirely
    surprising since economic wisdom suggests that policymakers can-
    not set money growth (a quantity) without letting interest rates (a
    price) move freely with the market. The only question was how
    wide the swings would be. Unfortunately, rate volatility exceeded
    expectations by far. The wide business cycle swing during this
    period, from inflation and high employment to the most severe
    depression since the 1930s, contributed to these unusual interest
    rate fluctuations. How much less they might have been in the
    absence of money growth targeting is anybody's guess.
2. The most surprising result of the new policy was the failure of
    money growth, the very thing targeted, to respond properly. In-
    deed, short-run money growth control was farther away from its
    target rather than closer to it. While M1 growth was pushed down in
    the long run, the Fed's efforts to control money aggregates coin-
    cided with more M1 volatility in the short-term. The near-money
    aggregates, M2 and M3, behaved even more badly. M2 growth,
    which incorporated many new kinds of money market accounts
    created in 1982 post-deregulation, continued upward even in the
    long-term while M3 moved erratically in both the short- and long-
    term (B. Friedman, 1988).
3. Markets were characterized by greater volatility and rapid asset
    turnover, especially over later phases of the monetarist period. This
    phenomenon appeared related to the dawning of the new electronic
    money age. Whether the money control attempts added to the
    already existing fact of market volatility has attracted much specula-
    tion.
4. There was a peculiar asymmetry in money growth response, relative
    to official Fed monetary aggregate targets. Specifically, money
    growth was much more frequently above than below target between
    1979 and 1982. Why?
5. Paradoxically, money growth became much less erratic post-1982,
    when the Fed's major focus on monetary aggregates—and, in
    particular, M1 transactions money—was officially abandoned. To
    an increasing degree, the Fed funds targets have been upgraded at
    the same time that money growth targets have been downgraded. It
    is interesting that the Fed has had more success stabilizing money

growth, at least in the short-term, when it has not tried so hard to
do so.

This chapter examines these paradoxes and the possible effects of
electronic funds transfers (EFT) as a new factor specifically to be considered. We model the monetarist experiment with a series of differential
equations, following the approach discussed in chapter 1 in which money
supply and interest rates are viewed as continuous (rather than discrete)
variables. The first section introduces the model, examining the Federal
Reserve control of money supply. In the second section, interest rates and
money flows are incorporated into the model. Prices and income initially
are held constant.

Basic Models—Money Supply Targeting

Description of Model

The monetarist experiment can be described as a negative-feedback (control) system with the Federal Reserve as the controlling mechanism. The
Federal Reserve compares the value of the money supply M to the target
value M*, and takes actions to push M to M*. In its simplest (and ideal)
form, a negative-feedback system of this nature is described by the
equation

$$\frac{dM(t)}{dt} = -f_m \left(M(t) - M^* \right), \tag{1}$$

with $f_m > 0$. This is a simple, linear, differential equation whose solutions
can be determined analytically. $M(t)$ approaches the target M^* (which is a
stable solution for all values of $f_m > 0$) exponentially as a function of time.
The parameter f_m (the slope of the Federal Reserve response function) is a
measure of the "tightness" of the control. The larger the value of f_m, the
quicker M approaches M^*. In any practical situation, external noise
produces fluctuations in the value of the targeted variable (here M). If
the fluctuations are large, a large value of f_m will be required to keep M
near M^*.

The system represented by equation (1) will always provide complete
control of an otherwise fluctuating variable M, if f_m is large enough. This
equation, however, is a gross simplification of a realistic model of a
negative-feedback system. In any real control system, there is a time delay
τ between the measurement of the controlled variable and the action taken

to change it. In the case of Federal Reserve control of the money supply, there is a delay of at least two weeks. Money supply during one week is measured, then announced on Thursday of the following week. The Fed takes actions to correct deviations (buying and selling government securities), according to the discretion of the Open Market Committee, perhaps the following Monday or later. These actions produce changes that take several or more days (or weeks) to ripple through the economy, before resulting in the full expected change in the money supply, based on the new reserves and the applicable reserve requirements. Federal Reserve actions to correct money imbalances must depend for their effectiveness on the combined responses of banks, borrowers, and the public, hence the considerable lags.

The presence of time delays in negative-feedback systems can have serious impacts on the ability of the system to mantain control. Equation (1) can be modified to take a time delay into account:

$$\frac{dM(t)}{dt} = -f_m \left(M(t - \tau) - M^* \right). \tag{2}$$

This is the simplest example of a delay differential equation with negative feedback (Glass and Mackey, 1988).

In general, delay differential equations (which are nonlinear equations) cannot be solved analytically; numerical simulations must be used instead. Equation (2), however, has been studied extensively for various control systems and analytical solutions can be found (Hayes, 1950). The solutions are of the form

$$M(t) = M^* + (M_o - M^*)e^{\lambda t}, \tag{3}$$

(figure 4–1) where M_o is a constant determined by the initial conditions and $\lambda = \mu + i\omega$ is a complex constant determined by the values of f_m and τ. The solutions are stable (converging) or unstable (diverging) oscillations, depending on the value of μ. In the limit of $\tau \to 0$, as is the case in equation (1), $\omega = 0$ (there are no oscillations) and $\mu < 0$ for all $f_m > 0$ (the steady state $M = M^*$ is always stable against perturbations). If there is a nonzero time delay, however, there will be a critical value of f_m, above which the steady-state solution will not be stable. Specifically, M^* will be unstable ($\mu > 0$) if $f_m > \pi/2\tau$ (Glass and Mackey, 1988). The larger the delay τ, the smaller the value of f_m required to keep the system stable.

The implications of the above analysis to Fed control of the money supply are significant. If fluctuations in M due to external variables are large, the Fed will be tempted to tighten its control, increasing f_m. In the

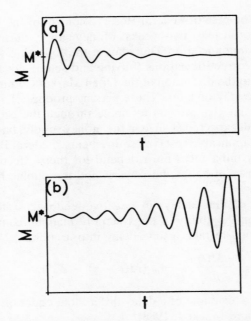

Figure 4–1.   Solutions to Standard Delay Differential Equation (Equation 2)
Notes: (a) $f_m < \pi/2\tau$, $\mu < 0$. The solution $M(t) = M^*$ is stable. (b) $f_m > \pi/2\tau$, $\mu > 0$. The solution $M(t) = M^*$ is unstable.

presence of a time delay, though, increasing f_m could cause the system to become unstable, resulting in fluctuations in M that are far greater than in the uncontrolled case. The Fed must exercise greater caution with a large delay time.

The results presented thus far concern only the steady state solution $M = M^*$ and its local stability. The simple model of equation (2) should be considered as an approximation whose validity becomes questionable at large deviations of M from M^*. When the oscillations become sufficiently large, additional nonlinear terms that have not been included in the model will become significant, limiting the growth or drop in M and, perhaps, allowing for the possibility of disordered (and maybe chaotic[2]) fluctuations.

Various factors can limit the growth or drop of M in situations where the steady state is unstable. Effects of large changes in M on the interest rates (r) and feedback of the resulting changes in r on M will be considered in the next section. Practical considerations also become important if fluctuations become too large. A lower limit is necessary, since the public must

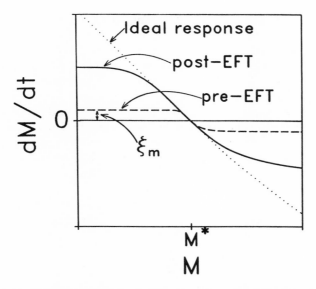

Figure 4–2.   Saturation of the Federal Reserve Response Function by Technological Clogs
Note: The ideal response function (dotted line) is only possible if the market can
exchange money at infinite rates. In the EFT era (solid curve), the response
function is saturated, but at a high level ξ_m (the height of the plateau above zero).
In the pre-EFT era (dashed line), ξ_m is small, and saturation effects can be
dominant.

hold a certain amount of money for daily expenses. Similarly, the government will create only a finite amount of money, so an upper limit must also
exist. (The fear that endless money creation will produce an upward spiral
of price inflation produces an effective upper constraint.) These practical
limits can be incorporated into the model by imposing firm upper and
lower cutoffs in M, but this naive approach produces artificial results with
sharp kinks in graphs of $M(t)$. Implementation of softer, more realistic
practical limits is nontrivial and could form the basis of future studies.

Technological considerations can also limit the growth or drop of an
unstable M. The model of equation (2) assumes that the economy is
capable of transferring money at an infinite rate. This is clearly not the
case. Limitations of the funds transfer mechanism will cause the response
function of the control system to saturate at large values of $|dM/dt|$ (figure
4–2). The level of the saturation will depend on the technology available.
Before the communications and electronics revolution, transferring money

required a laborious procedure involving the transfer of paper money between the Fed and investors, resulting in a low saturation point in the response function (dashed curve in figure 4–2). With the advent of EFT, money can flow at much higher rates ($|dM/dt|$ can grow much larger than before). Investors and "Fed watchers" have their personal computers plugged directly into both the financial data base and the brokers' lines. Execution of portfolio preferences, based upon new information and revised expectations about the tradeoffs between return and risk, is both fast and easy. The financial system is therefore able to transfer money at much higher rates, resulting in a much higher level of saturation in the response function. The unconstrained ("ideal") case of equation (2) is represented by a dotted line in figure 4–2.

Saturation effects can be incorporated into the control model by replacing the linear response function of equation (2) with a sigmoid function (see figure 4–2):

$$\frac{dM(t)}{dt} = \xi_m \frac{\theta^n - X^n\,(t - \tau)}{\theta^n + X^n\,(t - \tau)}, \tag{4}$$

where $\xi_m = |dM/dt|_{max}$ is the saturation level, $\theta = -\xi_m n/2f_m$ and $X(t - \tau) = (M(t - \tau) - M^* - \theta)$. For M near M^*, this function reduces to the linear response function of equation (2) with slope $-f_m$. The parameter n determines the transition between this regime and the flat regime for $|M - M^*| \gg 0$. If n is small, the transition is gradual, whereas if n is large, the transition is sharp.

With the saturation of equation (4), unstable solutions will no longer grow indefinitely but will instead level off at a finite value (figure 4–3). The magnitude of the oscillations can be quite small in magnitude, and may even be small enough such that, in the presence of external noise, the steady-state solution $M = M^*$ will appear to be stable (figure 4–3C). Effectively, a small saturation level is analogous to a decrease in the Fed's response f_m.

This analysis implies that inefficient money transfer mechanisms (pre-EFT) can damp fluctuations in what would, without saturation, be an unstable control system. Advances in communications technology enable the rapid exchange of money and securities, increasing ξ_m and making the money supply more susceptible to catastrophic fluctuations. As a result, any attempts to control money supply in the EFT era will be difficult, unless steps are made to decrease the delay time of the control system significantly. This is analogous to the effect on the stability of the stock market of the increased rate of exchange caused by program trading, widely recognized as an important contributor to the speed of the collapses

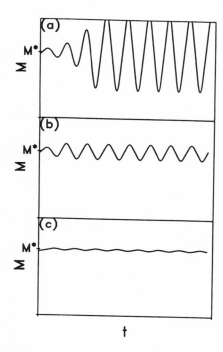

Figure 4–3. Effects of Saturation on an Otherwise Unstable Control System
Note: For all three figures, $2f_m\tau/\pi = 1.43$, well above the threshold for instability of the solution $M(t) = M^*$. (a) $\xi_m = 0.05\ M^*$/day (EFT levels?). Fluctuations in $M(t)$ grow to 50 percent of M^*. (b) $\xi_m = 0.01\ M^*$/day. Fluctuations in $M(t)$ are smaller but still not negligible. (c) $\xi_m = 0.001$ (pre-EFT levels?). Fluctuations in $M(t)$ are damped by the saturation.

(and later revivals) of October 19, 1987, and, more recently, October 13, 1989.

Discussion

It is clear from our simplified model that time delays can alter, dramatically, the stability of money supply targeting and may have been largely responsible for the failure of the monetarist experiment. It should be noted that the effects of time delays in economic systems have been addressed in previous studies, including the classic work of Milton Friedman (1960) who pointed out the disruptive effects of "inside" and "outside" lags between Fed policy and implementation in money systems. The instability caused by time delays may not have been important in the past because of the low saturation level ξ_m that was common before the advent of EFT, which would act to smooth out fluctuations in $M(t)$, as in figure 4–3C. In the current information age, though, EFT increases ξ_m sufficiently such that the saturation will no longer damp the instability.

From a policy perspective, it would appear that rigid money control has negative payoffs. A stable money growth path can be achieved most effectively if the slope of the Fed response function is small. It is possible, in fact, that no attempted control of the money supply $(f_m = 0)$ is better than control with a moderate response. (This may partially explain the success of the approach of the later post-monetarist years.) The result is a disturbing paradox of sorts. If the Fed tries too hard to achieve its promised monetary growth targets, given the presence of a significant lag between measurement of M and the action taken to change it, it moves farther away rather than closer to targets. Massive open market sales to achieve full money growth correction promptly can be self-defeating, and can result in greater amplitude and volatility of money aggregates. Intuitively, the Fed recognized this fact through its accommodation to the "feel of the market" as the years wore on.

It is possible that the Fed was being asked to do the technically impossible, in its attempted money control regime, especially in an era when technology and deregulation were opening up many new money forms and money-shifting possibilities. The Fed recognized its dilemma early, about 1980. The Federal Open Market Committee (FOMC) proceeded to back away from the money growth targets by discretely "renormalizing" the target base. Another technique was to stretch out the time periods for achieving money growth goals. The Fed would then be reneging on its money growth promises somewhat, but out of technical necessity rather than any base motive such as a deliberate desire to "cheat." The inclusion of the Fed funds constraint was an additional deviation from a policy of strict monetarism. Even within a rather broad five- or four-point band, the Fed was imposing a binding upper limit upon interest rates, with inevitable bending of the money goals. There is thus considerable justification for allegations that monetarism was never given a full test (Rausche, 1983). But perhaps such a test was not possible without inviting instability as the Fed correctly surmised.

Interest Rates and Money Flows

Our models so far have considered only the variations in money supply, neglecting possible interactions with other variables. Specifically, we have not included the effects on M of interest rates, inflation, income changes, and exogenous shocks due to unforeseen events such as international conflicts or exchange rate disturbances. We will not attempt in this chapter to build a comprehensive, realistic model that includes all of these variables. The interest rate r, however, is a particularly important piece of the puzzle, since variations in r are intimately connected to variations in M. For these reasons, it is not appropriate to hold r fixed in the model.

Money Flow Concepts

In the current EFT era, the coupling between interest rates and the money supply cannot be captured by the conventional M, which is a measure of the end-of-day balances. The rapid turnover of money with EFT amplifies the feedback effects on the interest rates of changes in conventional money aggregates. To examine the coupling between M and interest rates r in this era, it is necessary to incorporate the concept of money flows into the model. The expansion of the concept of money and the rapid money flows caused by EFT are discussed in detail in chapter 1. In this section, we give a concrete definition of "money flow" and show how EFT, by increasing money flow, can destabilize the monetary system.

The basic idea can be summarized as follows: the money flow ϕ is defined by the relation $\phi = M\gamma$, where γ is the continuous turnover frequency of all money M throughout the day. Increases in transactions rates caused by EFT are represented by increases in γ. We assert that the money flow can be thought of as an "effective" money supply, since it measures the total transactions power of the money supply. If the turnover frequency γ is, say, three times per day, there is more effective money (or money flow) than if $\gamma =$ one time per day, since, on the average, each dollar is involved in three times more transactions. In other words, the same total money M can finance more transactions if γ is large.

The concept of money flows will be incorporated into the model in the coupling term between money supply changes and interest rate changes. A certain change in the conventional money supply dM/dt has a larger effect on the interest rates if γ is large. Thus, γ is, effectively, an amplification term.

Description of Expanded Model

In the expanded model, interest rates are a second independent variable $r(t)$. The effects of r on the money supply are taken into account by adding an additional term to equation (2):

$$\frac{dM(t)}{dt} = -f_m \left(M(t - \tau) - M^*\right) + l_m \left[r_e - r(t)\right]. \qquad (5)$$

The additional term accounts for the public's response to changes in r. If the current value of r differs significantly from the average public expectation value r_e of future interest rates, assets will be converted between cash holdings and long-term investments, changing M. For example, if the interest rates are higher than expected, the public will shift from liquid assets to long-term investments, lowering M. There is no significant time delay in this term, since public responses to shifting interest rates are very fast. The parameter l_m represents the magnitude of the public's reaction.

A few comments should be made about equation (5). We are looking primarily at the effects of interest rates on the stability of money control systems. For this reason, we write the response functions in their simplest, linear form. (It should be noted that the equation is nonlinear, though, because of the time delay in the control term.) We have dropped the technological saturation of the control term equation (4). A fully dynamic model would include this saturation, as well as a saturation of the public's reaction function (the second term). Furthermore, the second term would be dependent on M, since people can only invest a finite amount of money.

The parameter r_e is particularly interesting, since it concerns public perceptions of the state of the economy. As a first approximation, we have chosen to hold r_e fixed. However, a more realistic model might have r_e as a variable, since expectations of future interest rates can depend sensitively on M and r. Fed watchers might base r_e on the current value of M and on the expectation that the Fed will act to move M toward its target.

It is necessary to add a second equation to describe the variations in r:

$$\frac{dr(t)}{dt} = l_r[r_e - r(t)] - c_1 \gamma \frac{dM(t)}{dt}. \qquad (6)$$

The first term is the counterpart of the second term of equation (5). The actions taken by the public in response to deviations of r from the expected value r_e will affect the interest rates as well as the money supply. This is a stabilizing term. If the r is higher than expected, the tendency of the public to make long-term investments will drive r down toward r_e. Conversely, if r is lower than expected, the public will tend to liquidate long-term investments, driving r up.

The second (and coupling) term of equation (6) incorporates the concept of money flows described earlier. This term is derived from conventional theories of money demand and supply. We start with a variation of the money demand function (figure 4–4):

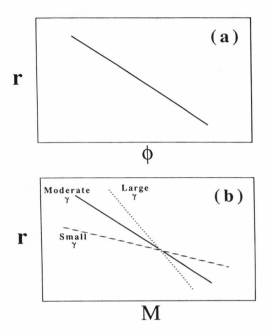

Figure 4-4. (a) "Flow Demand Function." (b) Conventional Money Demand
Function
Note: The flow demand function (a) is invariant with respect to changes in γ. The
slope of the conventional money demand function increases with γ.

$$r = r_o - c_1\phi \qquad\qquad (7)$$

$$= r_o - c_1\gamma M, \qquad\qquad (8)$$

where r_o and c_1 are constants and γ is the money turnover frequency
defined earlier. The function is written in a fairly conventional sense as
both linear and downward sloping to the right, although in this case r is the
dependent variable rather than M. We have deviated from the conventional approach in one crucial aspect, though. Instead of the money supply M
in equation (7), we use the money flow ϕ (effective money supply) as the
independent variable. It should be noted that this approach reduces to the
conventional approach if we assume the technology base to be constant, in
which case γ can be absorbed into the proportionality constant c_1 in
equation (8). The "flow demand function" equation (7) is invariant with
respect to changes in the technological base (figure 4-4A). This is not true

with the conventional money demand function equation (8), whose slope changes with γ (figure 4–4B).

To determine the *change* in r caused by a change in M, we take the time derivative of equation (8), resulting in the second term of equation (6). This term represents motion along the traditional money demand curve or its reciprocal here, the money velocity curve. Money and interest rates are negatively related through this term, just as they are in any given money demand function (if M increases, r will decrease). The turnover frequency γ amplifies the feedback between dM/dt and dr/dt. In the EFT era (with large γ), small changes in M will cause the same change in r as larger changes in M in the pre-EFT era, since each money "bit" turns over more times, on the average.

Results and Discussion

We have been unable to determine an analytic expression for the condition of stability of the expanded model equations (5) and (6). We therefore turn to a numerical approach, integrating equations (5) and (6) to simulate the time evolution of M and r in the vicinity of the equilibrium solution ($M(t) = M^*$, $r(t) = r_e$). We note first that if $l_m = 0$, equation (5) reduces to equation (2) and the solution $M(t) = M^*$ is stable if $f_m < \pi/2\tau$. We are interested in the effects of the addition of interest rate coupling on this stability.

Figure 4–5 shows the results of simulations with $2f_m\tau/\pi = 0.32$. In the absence of interest rate coupling, the solution $M(t) = M^*$ is stable with this product of f_m and τ. Simulations are shown with three values of γ, holding c_1, l_r, and l_m constant. It can be seen that if γ is sufficiently large (figure 4–5C), the system will become unstable.

These results can be interpreted by examining equations (5) and (6). The coupling between the two equations is determined by the magnitude of the coefficients l_r and $c_1\gamma$. We assume the parameters c_1, l_r, and l_m to be constant, independent of technological base. The money supply turnover frequency γ is, therefore, the parameter of greatest interest in these discussions. If γ is small (figure 4–5A), the effects of changing M on r are small, and the stabilizing (first) term for equation (6) dominates. In this situation, r is fairly steady, as are, presumably, asset prices in the market. Arbitrage, market speculation, and other market forces (the sum of whose effects are contained in the parameter l_r) pull the market back onto an ordered path should any instability threaten.

If γ increases, due to advances in communications technology, the

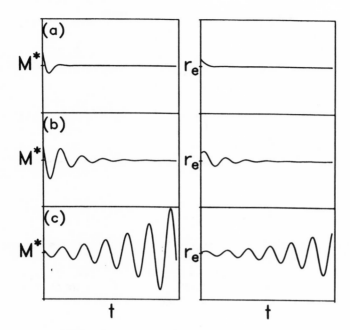

Figure 4–5. Amplification of Feedback Between Interest Rates r and Money Supply M by Different Money Turnover Rates γ
Note: The three graphs on the left represent variations in M as a function of time t. The graphs on the right represent variations in $r(t)$ with the same parameters. For all three simulations, $2f_m\tau/\pi = 0.32$, well below the threshold for instability of the solution $M(t) = M^*$ in the absence of interest rate coupling. $l_m = 0.099$ M^*/day per percentage point change in interest rate. $l_r = 0.1$/day. (a) $c_1\gamma = 2.0$ percent/M^*; (b) $c_1\gamma = 7.0$ percent/M^*; (c) $c_1\gamma = 10.0$ percent/M^*. See text for discussion.

second term of equation (6) becomes significant (figure 4–5B). Fluctuations in M cause fluctuations in r. If γ is large enough (figure 4–5C), the stabilizing term of equation (6) is not able to control the fluctuations. The fluctuations in r feed back on the money supply through the second term of equation (5) and enhance the fluctuations in M, which, in turn, feed back on r again through the second term of equation (6). The process continues indefinitely, resulting in the complete instability of both M and r.

These results imply that control of the money supply (as attempted during the monetarist experiment) is particularly difficult if feedback from interest rates is considered. Increases in rate of money turnover γ require careful (and compensating) policy adjustments. The problem of control of

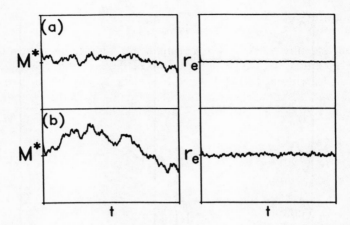

Figure 4–6. Amplification of Random Noise in $M(t)$ by Feedback Between Interest Rates r and Money Supply M
Note: Noise level is 0.07 M^*/day; l_m = 0.05 M^*/day per percentage point change in r; l_r = 0.1/day. (a) $c_1\gamma$ = 2 percent/M^*; (b) $c_1\gamma$ = 10 percent/M^*. Noise-induced fluctuations in M and r are higher if γ is large, as in (b).

the money supply caused by time delays is exacerbated by a large γ, and requires the Fed to lower the slope f_m of its response function even further below the condition $f_m < \pi/2\tau$ to keep the market stable.

It should be noted that the effects of γ on market fluctuations are not limited to a model with Fed control of the money supply. Increasing γ will amplify noise-induced fluctuations in M also. We demonstrate this with simulations (figure 4–6) in which the first term of equation (5) (the control term) is replaced by a random noise term. We believe that technological increases in money turnover rates will amplify any fluctuations in M and r, regardless of the source of these fluctuations.

Finally, we have tried implementing a very crude Fed funds constraint into the model. Specifically, we turn off the Fed money control term (first term of equation (5)) whenever interest rates go above (or below) a certain level. In this situation, we find that we can reproduce some of the asymmetry observed in actual money movement relative to the money growth targets, since interest rates tended more frequently to hit the top rather than the bottom of the Fed funds band. By cutting off control at the upper limit of the Fed funds band, greater monetary expansion was allowed.

Policy Inferences

Our models of the monetarist experiment are admittedly somewhat simplistic. The equations aim to grasp some of the essential features of the control policy without getting tangled in specific details. Nevertheless, it is probable that some of the conclusions drawn from these models are independent of the specific details. These conclusions have implications for Federal Reserve policy that we discuss below.

The "Mix" of Targets

Interest rate targeting may be more effective than money targeting, from the perspective of control dynamics, predominantly because the delay times associated with interest rate control are very short (almost instantaneous). The recent success of Fed control policies (post-1984) is an example. Chairman Greenspan continues to utilize monetarist theory, in relation to the broader long-term monetary aggregates, while targeting with great short-term precision the crucial Fed funds rate, without time lags. We see now also an eclectic mix of a variety of intermediate targets, market-oriented as in the years following Chairman Martin's Treasury-Federal Reserve "accord" of 1952.

A policy of mixed targeting can sever the feedback loop between M and r discussed in the second section. Fluctuations in M will have limited effects on r, since r will be controlled actively by the Fed (with success, due to the small delay). With r stable, there will be no feedback on M.

The "Feel" of the Market in Central Banking Parlance

It can be argued that an "information-based policy" in which the Fed looks at market results to determine its strategy is more stable than a policy of rigid adherence to a specific target. Effectively, by broadening its policy and easing up on its targets of money supply, the Fed reduces the slope of its response function f_m, increasing the stability of the system.

Chairman Greespan's present cool and cautious approach, like then-Chairman Martin's "leaning with the wind" stance following the 1951 accord, seems to be working. Both approaches have been eclectic, slow, information-based, and market-oriented, rather than rigid and unyielding.

Conclusions

Each of the monetary theories currently in favor contributes to what we believe to be a possible story behind success or failure of any one policy, including monetarist policy. Dynamical approaches almost certainly have important contributions to make to this story. Electronic funds transfer, with its heightened money flows, mandates (in our view) a careful examination of the monetary dynamics, made more complex and more important by the potential of the new money technology.

We have made an attempt to apply nonlinear dynamics to the real-world monetary puzzles of the late 1970s and the 1980s and, in particular, to the role of EFT in making that monetary world more complex. The ability of these models to explain some of the puzzling features of the monetarist experiment and of more recent policies indicates the possible suitability of this approach. We stress the preliminary nature of these models. Much more work needs to be done to examine all the relevant aspects of Federal Reserve control policy. In addition to improvements to the response functions described earlier, other modifications may prove interesting. Addition of fluctuating inflation rates to the model, as well as variable interest rate expectations r_e, may produce a model with bounded (and possibly chaotic) fluctuations that can be compared to those of the monetarist experiment. In addition, the role of "Fed watchers" who buy and sell assets based on their predictions of future Fed activities (based on Fed policy) has not been addressed in the current chapter. The activities of these traders may provide additional instability to the system.

Finally, any good understanding of market fluctuations in the EFT era requires Federal Reserve data on ongoing money flows throughout the day, with parallel measurements of daily money turnover rates (or flow velocity). Knowledge of the behavior of extremely short-term fluctuations in M and r is essential for a complete understanding of the effects of rapid communications on money and interest rates.

Acknowledgments

We are pleased to acknowledge useful discussions with M. Mackey, Thomas Simpson, Jeffrey Marquardt, and Anthony Yezer, and the fine technical assistance of Derric Ward. Some of the numerical work was done with equipment provided by the University Research Initiative program under Contract No. DARPA/ONR N00014-85-K-0759 to Princeton University.

Notes

1. During the writing of this chapter, Thomas Solomon was with the Departments of Physics of the University of Pennsylvania, Philadelphia, PA 19104 and Haverford College, Haverford, PA, 19041.

2. A chaotic system is defined as one that is "sensitive to initial conditions" (Gleick, 1987) in the sense that any uncertainty in the initial state of the system grows with time, preventing long-term predictability.

References

Barnett, William, and Ping Chen. 1987. "The Aggregation-Theoretic Monetary Aggregates Are Chaotic and Have Strange Attractors." In W.A. Barnett, Ernst Berndt, and Hal White, eds., *Dynamic Econometric Modeling.* Cambridge, England: Cambridge University Press.

Baumol, William J., and Jess Benhabib. 1989. "Chaos: Significance, Mechanism, and Economic Applications." *The Journal of Economic Perspectives* 3 (Winter).

Becketti, Sean, and Gordon H. Sellon, Jr. 1989. "Has Financial Market Volatility Increased?" *Economic Review*, Federal Reserve Bank of Kansas City (June).

Brock, W.A. 1987. "Distinguishing Random and Deterministic Systems: Abridged Version." In J.M. Grandmont, ed., *Nonlinear Economic Dynamics.* Orlando, FL: Academic Press, Inc.

Brock, W.A. 1988. "Introduction to Chaos and Other Aspects of Nonlinearity." In W.A. Brock and A.B. Malliaris, eds., *Differential Equations, Stability, and Chaos in Dynamic Economics.* New York: North Holland.

Brock, W.A., and Chera L. Sayers. 1988. "Is the Business Cycle Characterized by Deterministic Chaos?" *Journal of Monetary Economics* 22, 71–89.

Cornell, Bradford. 1983. "The Money Supply Announcements and Interest Rates." *The American Economic Review* (September).

Federal Reserve Bank of Kansas City. 1988. *Financial Market Volatility.* A Symposium, Jackson Hole, WY, August 17–19.

Friedman, Benjamin M. 1988. "Lessons on Monetary Policy from the 1980s." *Journal of Economic Perspectives* 2 (Summer).

Friedman, B., and M. Friedman. 1984. "Lessons from the 1979–82 Monetary Policy Experiment." *The American Economic Review* (May).

Friedman, Milton. 1956. "The Quantity Theory of Money, A Restatement." In M. Friedman, ed., *Studies in the Quantity Theory of Money.* Chicago: University of Chicago Press.

Friedman, Milton. 1960. *A Program for Monetary Stability.* New York: Fordham University Press.

Glass, L., and M.C. Mackey. 1988. *From Clocks to Chaos.* Princeton, NJ: Princeton University Press.

Gleick, James. 1987. *Chaos: Making a New Science.* New York: Viking Penguin Inc.

Grandmont, J.M. 1985. "On Endogenous Competitive Business Cycles." *Econometrica* 53, 995–1045.

Haberler, Gottfried. 1937. *Prosperity and Depression: A Theoretical Analysis of Cyclical Movements.* Geneva, Switzerland: League of Nations.

Hayes, N.D. 1950. "Roots of the Transcendental Equation Associated with a Certain Difference-Differential Equation." *Journal of the London Mathematical Society.* 25, 226–232.

Koo, Anthony Y.C., ed. 1985. *Selected Essays of Gottfried Haberler.* Part III, "Inflation and Business Cycles," and Part V, "Money, Real Balance Effect, and Other Essays." Cambridge, MA: The MIT Press.

O'Brien, James M. 1984. "The Information Value of the FOMC Policy Directive under the New Operating Procedures." *Journal of Money, Credit, and Banking* (May).

Poole, William. 1988. "Monetary Policy Lessons on Recent Inflation and Disinflation." *Journal of Economic Perspectives* 2 (Summer).

Radecki, L.J. 1984. "Targeting in a Dynamic Model." *Quarterly Review*, Federal Reserve Bank of New York (Summer).

Rausche, R. 1984. "Comments on Henry Wallich's Presentation." *Journal of the Midwest Finance Association*, Chicago (April 5).

Roley, V.V. 1982. "Weekly Money Supply Announcements and the Volatility of Short-Term Interest Rates." *Economic Review*, Federal Reserve Bank of Kansas City (April).

Samuelson, P.A. 1939. "Interactions Between the Multiplier Analysis and the Principle of Acceleration." *Review of Economic Statistics.* 21, 75–78.

Simpson, Thomas D. 1984. "Changes in the Financial System: Implications for Monetary Policy." *Brookings Papers on Economic Activity* 1, 249–272. (Brookings Institution: Washington, D.C.)

Simpson, Thomas D., and Paul F. O'Brien. 1985. "Implications of Electronic Funds Transfer for Monetary Policy." *Staff Studies*, Board of Governors of the Federal Reserve System, Washington, D.C.

Solomon, Elinor Harris. 1984. "Monetary vs. Interest Rate Targets Revisited: The Role of Market Expectations." Presentation for the Annual Meeting of the American Economic Association. Dallas, TX, December.

Tobin, James. 1987. "Monetary Rules and Control in Brave New World." In E. Solomon, ed., *Electronic Funds Transfers and Payments.* Boston: Kluwer Academic Publishers.

Urich, T.J., and P. Wachtel. 1984. "The Structure of Expectations on the Weekly Money Supply Announcement." *Journal of Monetary Economics* 13 (March).

Wallich, H.C. 1984. "Recent Techniques of Monetary Policy." *Economic Review*, Federal Reserve Bank of Kansas City (May).

Walsh, Carl G. 1984. "Interest Rate Volatility and Monetary Policy." *Journal of Money, Credit, and Banking* 16 (May).

Wicksell, K. 1936. *Interest and Prices: A Study of the Causes Regulating the Value of Money.* London: MacMillan & Co.

III THE SEAMLESS GLOBAL MESH

Part II examined the underlying nature of business and financial fluctuations, and the recent correction of mistakes past made. Part III continues on in discussion of the international mechanisms, and the reforms yet to come. Dr. Thomas Simpson (Federal Reserve Board) and Dr. Yoshiharu Oritani (Bank of Japan) analyze the process whereby money and capital flow around the earth in an almost "seamless" 24-hour web. Oritani focuses on payments networks, Simpson on the broader capital markets mesh around the clock.

Both make concrete suggestions on how best to promote efficiency and safeguard system integrity. Oritani suggests the forging of tighter links between central banks directly, in guarantee of payments finality. Simpson emphasizes the private market route, including eventual simultaneous settlement and multilateral payments netting across instruments. This approach will reduce gross payments flows and market "churning" as well as lessen risks.

Road blocks exist to implementation in both cases, however: some political, some legal, and some based upon the unwillingness of holders of present subsidies to part with them—a theme running throughout the book.

Dr. Oritani, Manager of the Institute for Monetary and Economic Studies of the Bank of Japan, has payments knowledge unique around the world in his key post at the BOJ. He has conducted extensive research on payments and macroeconomic questions with his staff. Oritani also has a technology background to match his formal economics training, which makes his analysis particularly valuable and a vital element in the whole story presented here.

Dr. Oritani stresses the ongoing globalization of the payments network, as more communications satellites are launched and many trans-Pacific optical fiber cables are put in place. One form of new global network consists of a financial institution's in-house electronic connections with overseas branches. A second type utilizes a commercially operated global telecommunications network: for example, Euroclear or SWIFT.

In both cases the possibilities for explosive growth are great. So also is the likelihood of rising competition between payments networks. Currently most of the world's financial transactions are concentrated in the three major financial centers—New York, London, and Tokyo. But that status quo may not continue. This is because financial globalization will reduce the need for separate regional financial centers.

Which country's international financial center in the end will win out may depend on whether its payment network can survive the competition. The decisive factor favoring survival will not necessarily be how large a country's cumulative surplus of balance of payments may be. Rather, it will be the underlying support or "infrastructure" within each country—the payment network, the country's political stability, legal framework, and accounting systems.

Dr. Oritani emphasizes the fact that systemic risk, too, presents new global dimensions. Such risk arises originally in one country, but now there is the danger of its careening in a chain reaction toward the other side of the world.

Dr. Oritani carefully analyzes the role of the central bank here. He notes the unique and critical nature of services provided by the payments system. The present "club" goods approach, whereby member banks develop rules under central bank sponsorship, must be reinforced. Oritani argues powerfully for continued central bank independence from government pressures, in order to contain risk and promote effective competition.

In order further to prevent risk "spillover," central banks must work together to establish a fail-safe and efficient payment network. The ideal payment network of the future, Oritani believes, should have each country's central bank as the core (see Oritani's figure 5–3). A global network of central banks may minimize systemic risk for several reasons. First, a central banking network could facilitate a cross-border funds transfer, with finality of settlement. An international link could facilitate a quick extension of credit whenever central banks might want to play the role of lender of last resort. Such cooperation would be important also as a first step toward creation of a global central bank that issues unified money.

Chapter 6 is authored by the nation's leading expert in analysis of financial markets innovation, Dr. Thomas Simpson, Associate Director of Research and Statistics, Federal Reserve Board of Governors. We are proud to be able to present it here. Dr. Simpson's compelling chapter broadens the payments analysis to a global capital markets focus. Simpson highlights, as does Oritani, the present high degree of interdependence among national financial markets. He discusses the specific efforts among regulators and financial exchanges to enhance soundness and stability. Simpson stresses the ongoing tradeoffs between efficiency gains and system strength, in a kind of mirror image to similar difficult policy choices that beset regulators within the present retail electronic scene (discussed in chapter 8).

The technology presents many new opportunities for world-wide trading. The expanding availability of risk-shifting foreign exchange instruments—currency futures, forwards, swaps, and options—helps investors seek higher returns while providing an opportunity to hedge against adverse developments at home. Issuers, too, see distinct opportunities to lower their cost of capital by placing securities with foreign investors.

Dr. Simpson portrays vividly the resulting 24-hour seamless web of securities trading, the passing of the baton from Tokyo to London to New York by a different team at each of the globally positioned securities firms, with the shift in daylight zones around the earth.

How do the mechanisms work and how ought they to work, in terms of desirable change? In order to answer this question, Simpson analyzes the desirable attributes of a market system, including auction, dealer-based, and open-outcry. He analyzes the changes wrought by electronics and provides specific illustrations of seamless trading within state-of-the-art markets, such as that for U.S. securities and foreign exchange.

Dr. Simpson shows the important advantages of electronic trading systems including the better "paper trail" and detection of abuses. Set forth also are their drawbacks, such as lessened liquidity or the tendency to escape regulation through deflection of trades to other markets.

One major difficulty, of course, is the risk that between the time that a transaction has been arranged and the time of actual settlement, the counterparty to the transaction will fail to deliver on its end of the bargain. That particular problem ("counterparty risk") can be reduced by shortening settlement times. In the limit, transactions could be settled at the time they were made ("instantaneous" settlement). But this would require a highly developed electronic system that included book-entry holdings of the security in a depository. Any proposal such as this has been highly unpopular to investors who have a strong preference for physical possession of the asset.

The existence of time zone differences introduces "intraday risks," too. For example, in a yen-dollar transaction, the buyer of yen receives access to the yen balances during the business day in Tokyo a half-day before the dollar balances must be delivered to the seller of yen during the business day in New York. A similar time lapse problem can arise when securities are bought in one financial center in one hemisphere but settled in another hemisphere.

In both of Simpson's examples, the intraday risks would be eliminated if payments systems were open around the clock. Payment could then be made at time of delivery. The payments system of the Federal Reserve would be open to make dollar payments during the Tokyo and London business days. Or, the Bank of Japan and the Bank of England could offer dollar accounts that could be used in settling foreign transactions in their business hours while the Federal Reserve is closed.

Simpson believes the recommendations of a private group called the Group of Thirty to be of particular merit as a model for the future trading and exchange systems. The Group hopes to strengthen systems, partly through standardization and simultaneous trading and settlement. However, it will be some time before the proposed recommendations can be implemented. Meanwhile, other measures can be taken to reduce risks and enhance efficiency.

Particularly interesting among them is the multilateral clearing house route, with private members putting up the collateral. Simpson analyzes the use of clearing houses in stock exchanges, futures, and options, and demonstrates the logic for extension of the netting possibilities. A large international bank will make a vast number of yen-dollar transactions on a given day, both yen sales and purchases. Similarly, a large brokerage firm will, on any given day, place many buy and sell orders for shares in IBM. The *net* buy or sell position will be small relative to the *gross* size of transactions.

Netting arrangements take advantage of this principle and reduce the size of payments flows that need to be made. The total value of liquid assets needed for clearing and settlement is lowered. In addition, the existence of the clearing house guarantee on transactions, if credible, can enhance customer confidence in the system. Balanced against these advantages are the costs of risk control, in particular curbing the moral hazard incentives that accompany the mutualization of risk.

5 GLOBALIZATION OF PAYMENT NETWORK AND RISKS

Yoshiharu Oritani

The recent development of information telecommunications technology has created global networks for instantaneous transmission of information. The technology in turn has made possible immediate financial transactions and payment settlement around the world. At the same time, however, it has intensified competition among international financial centers and heightened risks. In order to respond to these issues, close cooperation among central banks of the major industrial countries and the development and installation of a highly cost-efficient and fail-safe network for settlement of payments are indispensable.

Development of the Globalized Payment Network

Factors Contributing to Development

The basic factor contributing to the ongoing globalization of the payment network is the high-tech progress being made in information telecommunications technology. This technology has recorded quantum growth

Solomon, E.H., (ed.), *Electronic Money Flows*.
© 1991 Kluwer Academic Publishers. ISBN 0–7923–9134–9. All rights reserved.

with such advances as launching of communications satellites and installation of the optical fiber cables in the trans-Pacific submarine cable (completed in 1989).

The accelerated deregulation of the value-added network (VAN) has also served to promote the rapid increase in the establishment of global communications networks. Since financial transactions and payment settlements are basically performed by means of telecommunication, the impact of electronic telecommunications on payment procedures is greater, the wider the area is that is covered by technology.

Consequently, globalization of the telecommunications network has served to promote globalization of the payment network through two separate routes. One is indirectly through development of a global network required for collecting information on financial markets and contract matchings by means of the telecommunications network. This in turn has increased the volume of global financial transactions and, as a result, demand for global settlement of financial transactions has grown. The second route is directly through the establishment of the global network for instantaneous payment made feasible by advances in the telecommunications technology. With increasing convenience and cost efficiency of the payment system, the volume of global transactions has increased and spurred the development of the network.

The extensive development of the global payment network has become inevitable because globalization of the payment network has been promoted by the continuing advancements of the telecommunications technology.

Developing Forms of Global Payment Networks

When the networks of payment systems become globalized, they fall into the following two general forms.[1]

The first is depicted in figure 5–1. Here, a country's dedicated payment network becomes globalized by being linked with the international in-house network of a financial institution. This type is based on a financial institution's in-house on-line network connecting its overseas branches, and is made feasible by the development of technology for interconnecting networks.

The other form is depicted in figure 5–2. In this second case a global network is not based on any in-house network. It is, rather, a global payments network, utilizing the services of a commercially operated global telecommunications network.

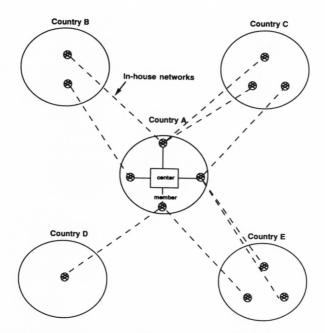

Figure 5-1. Global Network Based on In-House Networks

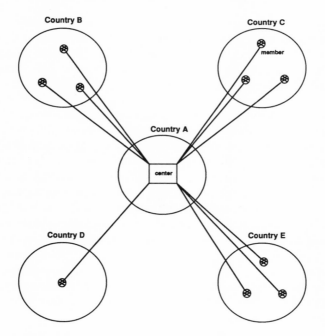

Figure 5-2. Global Network Directly Linked with Members

In one such type the center for settling payments is an entity independent from the one operating the network. The network could be a public utility that offers global telecommunication services (such as Euroclear, based on utilizing the GE Mark III as a host computer). Another network of this type is SWIFT, the global network without a center for settling payments, whose main purpose is to transmit payment information among financial institutions. The second form of network system for global settlement of payments has its centers in the United States and Europe. Presently there is no center for global payments with an operational base in Japan.

Globalization of Risk

Concomitantly with globalization of the payment system network, the risks inherent in the system have been globalized. The major risks include the following: (1) loss of status by a country either as a center of a payment network or as an international financial center, or (2) the globalization of a payment network's so-called systemic risk.

Risks of Retreat from International Competition

International Competition Among Payment Networks. As each nation's payment network is becoming globalized, competition among the networks is intensifying. Under these circumstances, network users in each country will find it easier—more than in the past—to use the services of foreign networks, in addition to their domestic one. The user will prefer to employ the network offering the best cost efficiency and reliability; and consequently the inferior network could lose out in the international competition.

Some argue that "users will prefer to use the service of the payment network of the creditor's country, just as they prefer the creditor country's currency." This argument is based on the premise that does not clearly differentiate between a currency's function for storing value and its function as a means of exchange. For instance, when Japan's surplus in its balance of payments grows cumulatively and an upward valuation of the yen can be anticipated, the trend for choosing the yen as a store of value will increase. Nonetheless, if the cost efficiency and reliability of Japan's network is inferior to those of other countries' networks, the yen will be little used as a means of payment.

Competition Among International Financial Centers. Currently most of the world's financial transactions are concentrated in the three major financial centers—New York, London, and Tokyo. With the expanding globalization of the payment network, competition among these financial centers could intensify. This is because globalization of the payment network, together with that of the information network on financial transactions, will have the effect of reducing the significance of financial transactions conducted separately in regional financial centers. It could also reduce the necessity for the existence of financial centers in many countries of the world.

Which country's international financial center will win out in the competition will depend on whether its payment network can survive the competition. In this instance, the decisive factor favoring survival will not necessarily be how large a country's cumulative surplus of balance of payments is but rather how adequate is its infrastructural support for international financial transactions—such as the payment network, as well as the country's political stability, legal framework, and accounting systems.

Globalization of Systemic Risk

The globalized payment network entails various risks, which could instantaneously spread worldwide through the network. Major issues are not only the relative risk affecting the actual users of the network but also the so-called systemic risk which affects third parties in a chain reaction because they happen to subscribe to the service to the network.

Participants in the payment network—banks and others—are directly exposed in general to two types of risks: credit risks and liquidity risks. Credit risk occurs when the payment network accepts remittances of funds that the remitter does not possess. Credit risk is inevitable, especially when the payment system finally settles the net credit and debit position of participating banks after a lapse of time following completion of the transactions. Liquidity risk occurs when the account of a participant in the transactions turns to deficit in the short term—and when the participant's plan for remaining liquid fails and it cannot raise the needed funds to remain liquid at short notice.

Both types of risks entail systemic risk. Systemic risk occurs when the relative risk involving only the two parties in a transaction "spills over" so as to affect multiple participants (banks, etc.) in a chain reaction. This occurs when a bank participating in a network becomes insolvent and its creditor banks become insolvent as a result. Or, the chain reaction effect of liquidity risk may occur without necessarily any of the participants falling into the worst case of insolvency; it may occur as a result of a simple mistake, such as a numerical error occurring in a remittance transaction.

These systemic risks may arise originally in the payment network confined to a single country; however, as the network expands globally, there is the danger that the trouble originating from one participant on one side of the globe may produce a chain reaction among participants on the other side of the world.

How To Cope with Globalization of Risks

The basic requirement for forestalling retreat from international competition is the establishment of a payment network that is both cost-efficient and fail-safe. To ensure this, the network must be designed to cope with any systemic risks. The following sections describe the three ways by which this can be accomplished.

Establishment of an Efficient Payment Network

It is essential to establish a fail-safe and efficient payment network in order to forestall any declines in international competition. The actual designing and development of an efficient system should start with the conversion of a system based on paperwork to that based on electronics. The new system must include payment systems transferring funds and securities.

Various kinds of obstacles confront the creation of an electronics payment system, of which the major ones are: (1) the technical cost of developing the system, and (2) inconvenient regulations and tax treatments. The technical cost of establishing an electronic system has been reduced by the recent cost reductions achieved in computer hardware and the development of software (for instance, Computer Aided Software Engineering). On the other hand, the second type of obstacle cannot necessarily be eliminated by the development of technology. In order to forestall the risk of retreat from international competition, any obstacles in a nation's regulations and tax structure that hinder conversion of the paperwork type to the electronics kind should be reformed beforehand.

Assuring Fail-Safe Operation of the Payment Network

In order to cope with these risks of credit and liquidity, it is imperative that parties directly involved in transactions take the necessary precautions. In the case where relative risks could develop into a chain reaction-like systemic risk, this can be prevented by cutting off the direct interdependence among the banks.

The central bank of a nation is in the position effectively to implement this requirement because settlement by transfer of funds among the participants' deposits held in the central bank would constitute "finality" to the transaction. Finality is defined by President Corrigan of the Federal Reserve Bank of New York (Corrigan, 1990) as follows: "Finality means that at the very instant an institution receives an advice of payment of confirmation of delivery through a system for a particular transaction, the money in question is 'good money,' even if at the next instant the sending institution goes bust."

The central bank is authorized to create "good" money in the form of bank notes and deposits held at the central bank. Therefore, when both the remitting bank and the bank receiving the remittance are participants in the payment network overseen by the central bank, the insolvency of the remitting bank will be prevented from affecting the bank receiving the remittance.

If any bank other than the central bank is responsible for operating the payment network, however, it may be impossible to prevent the insolvency of the transmitting bank from affecting other banks. In such a network where a payment netting scheme is employed, when a bank's debit position cannot be settled, the position of all banks participating in the system will be recalculated—after eliminating the amount of funds that cannot be settled; this is referred to as "unwinding." In most such instances, the remittance of funds from the insolvent bank is regarded as being void. In this case, in addition to the liquidity risk, caused by the fact that the anticipated funds had not been remitted at the anticipated time, a credit risk may arise from the insolvency. The latter could chain-react to cause insolvency among the participating banks.

Hence, in order to enhance the fail-safe functions of the payment network of each country and cope with globalization of system risks, participating banks should opt for joining the payment network with each country's central bank as the core. This will ensure finality to settlement of accounts.

Maintenance and Reinforcement of the "Club" Rules

The services provided by the payment system are not, by nature, strictly private goods, nor are they strictly public goods. According to Buchanan's definition (Buchanan, 1965), they could best be described as "club goods." This is because the services provided by the payment system—such as the transmittal and receiving of remittances—jointly benefit all members in the network. In other words, the services fulfill the necessary and sufficient condition of club goods "collectively consumed" by all participants. This aspect of the club goods differentiates them from private goods. On the other hand, membership in the payment system can be limited because of the application of "exclusion of nonmembers from club goods." In this sense, club goods differ from public goods.

Consequently, the payment system cannot be permitted to operate without rules and regulations. The payment system works in a manner unlike the market for clearly private goods, whose transactions are based on the principle of laissez-faire. Nonetheless, since the payment system's services are not purely public goods, it should not be operated under the government's rules and regulations, either. For this reason, the payment system traditionally has been operated as an interbank club sponsored by the central bank—an entity intermediate between the government and the private sector—under rules and regulations subscribed to by the member banks.

This tradition has been respected by all governments of industrially advanced countries, where no government holds supervisory power over the payment operations of the central bank. The reason for this is as follows. In addition to the club goods characteristics of the payment network operated by the central bank, the bank's monetary policy comprises measures designed to ensure liquidity for the member banks and cope with the aforementioned liquidity risk. Consequently, should the government hold supervisory power over the central bank's payment operations, there could exist the danger of the government's intervening in the central bank's monetary policy. This threat would imperil its independence from the government.

Be that as it may, any payment network based on rules and regulations that contravene the above requirements of nonintervention from the

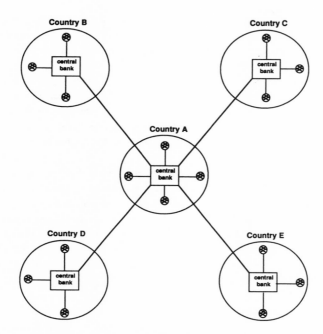

Figure 5–3.   Global Network Linking Central Banks

government will lose credibility and, consequently, it will be exposed to the risk of its international competitiveness declining. Hence, it becomes imperative that the rules on club goods be maintained and reinforced.

Cooperation of Central Banks

As for desirability of the international competition among payment networks mentioned earlier, the discussion of the desirability is deeply related to the discussion on international competition among national currencies. This is because the payment network of the central bank can be regarded as a flow aspect of money. On the desirability of competitive money supply, there is no consensus among monetary economists. While economists such as Friedman (1959) supports the monopolistic supply of money, other economists such as Hayek (1976) argues for a competitively determined supply of money. The separation of opinions on the supply of money reflects the differences of approaches to the European Monetary Union. While the Delors Report supports the unification of money in the European Community (EC), the United Kingdom argues the competing currency approach.

Since the scheme of the competitive supply of money has not yet proved to work in the history, the scheme can not be acceptable in the global market. Then, it is natural to pursue the unification of money in the globally integrated market. As the first step to the global central bank that issues unified money, the cooperation among central banks is very important.[2]

One of the examples of such cooperation is to link payment networks of the national central banks. This linked payment network would be the third type of global network, and is depicted in figure 5–3. A global network of central banks would contribute to minimize systemic risk resulting from the globalization of the payment networks. This is because the network can facilitate a cross-border funds transfer with finality and a quick extension of credit to a troubled bank when a central bank, or central banks, want to play the role of lender of last resort.

Notes

1. Frankel and Marquardt (1987) described the postwar structure for making international large-value payments and analyzed changes affecting the global payment system structure.
2. The international competition of national currencies and national payment networks has some possibility to increase the risk of worldwide depression or inflation. Because the competitive supply of money scheme is argued to have the risk of inflation, and because the lack of the lender of last resort in the competitive currencies scheme could increase the risk of bank failures and subsequent depression, the central bank has an important role to play here. The central bank can issue money without a limit and stand neutral, not as a competitor. This fact makes it possible for the central bank to play the role of the lender of last resort. (This point is clearly stated by Goodhart, 1988.)

References

Buchanan, James M. 1965. "An Economic Theory of Clubs." *Economica* (February).
Corrigan, E. Gerald. 1990. "Perspectives on Payment System Risk Reduction." In David B. Humphrey, ed., *The U.S. Payment System: Efficiency, Risk and the Role of the Federal Reserve.* Boston: Kluwer Academic Publishers.
Frankel, Allen B, and Jeffrey C. Marquardt, 1987. "International Payments and

EFT Links." In Elinor Harris Solomon, ed., *Electronic Funds Transfers and Payments: The Public Policy Issues*. Boston: Kluwer Academic Publishers.

Friedman, Milton. 1959. *A Program for Monetary Stability*. New York: Fordham University Press.

Goodhart, Charles A.E. 1988. *The Evolution of Central Banks*. Cambridge: The MIT Press.

Hayek, F.A. 1976. *Denationalisation of Money*. The Institute of Economic Affairs.

6 TRENDS IN GLOBAL SECURITIES MARKETS

Thomas D. Simpson[1]

Development of the financial system globally has been very rapid and related to the revolution in the field of electronics. This has especially been the case for securities markets which have benefitted from vast advances in information processing, both hardware and software systems, and tele-communications. This technology is particularly well suited for securities markets. Investors require timely information on prices and underlying factors influencing prices and the ability to complete transactions quickly. Also, in recognition of the risks associated with such transactions—in particular, the prospect of failure of the transaction for a variety of reasons—accurate information on the parties transacting and terms of the transaction are required as well as systems that provide for timely transfer of ownership and payment. Modern electronic technology enables this information to be gathered and disseminated quickly, and highly complex transactions to be processed promptly and accurately.

Another important factor contributing to the globalization of financial

The views expressed in this chapter are those of the author and do not necessarily reflect the views of the Board of Governors or other members of its staff.

Solomon, E.H., (ed.), *Electronic Money Flows.*
© 1991 Kluwer Academic Publishers. ISBN 0–7923–9134–9. All rights reserved.

markets is the increasing international diversification of investment portfolios. With increasing awareness of investment opportunities abroad and
a growing dependence on developments in other economies, investors
around the world have been seeking potentially higher returns or hedges
against adverse developments at home. The expanding availability of
risk-shifting foreign exchange instruments—currency futures, forwards,
swaps, and options—has facilitated this process by enabling investors to
cover the foreign exchange exposure arising from investing in a foreign
security. Moreover, the existence of internationally diversified portfolios
by investors around the world, operating in different hemispheres and time
zones, has been increasing the demand for being able to transact in a
security outside the normal operating hours of the home market. Issuers,
too, see distinct opportunities to lower their cost of capital by placing
securities with foreign investors and thereby broadening and diversifying
their investor base. As a result, the marketplace for an expanding number
of securities, both bonds and stocks, has become global in scope.

Accompanying this development has been a growing concentration of
the management of financial assets in the hands of professional institutional managers and the trading of portfolios of securities. The rising concentration of assets reflects a choice by individuals, either directly or through
employment arrangements, to delegate responsibility for asset management to pension funds, life insurance companies, and mutual funds. In
the equities area, efforts to reduce risk and limit the effects of large
transactions on the prices of individual securities have led to the use of
well-diversified portfolios of stocks. Moreover, empirical studies have
demonstrated that returns from a diversified portfolio of stocks representing the market generally cannot be enhanced by efforts to select carefully
individual stocks, implying a preference for baskets of stocks representing
the market. Complementing this trend has been the introduction of futures
and options on such stock indexes.

An Illustration

A good example of a state-of-the-art global securities market is that for
U.S. Treasury securities. In this market, there is nearly "seamless"
around-the-clock trading in these securities. The market opens each day in
the Far East (Tokyo) while it is evening (of the previous day) on the East
Coast of the United States. A number of securities dealers—most with
trading operations also in London and New York—stand ready to buy or
sell the more popular issues at posted bid or offered prices. When trades

are completed, prices are transmitted around the globe within moments over on-line financial news services. Facilitating the market in Treasury securities during this time period is a special evening session for trading futures contracts in Treasury bonds on the Chicago Board of Trade; the availability of the futures market complements the cash market by enabling dealers and investors to adjust their overall positions and exposures to price movements. Dealers are more willing to make markets if they are able to hedge their positions as they add to or reduce their holdings of the security in the course of making a market. Thus, market liquidity and depth are enhanced by the availability of such risk-shifting instruments. Also complementing the market for Treasury securities during this time period is the availability of the foreign exchange market. Buyers and sellers in Japan can hedge the foreign exchange risk associated with dollar-denominated securities in the highly developed foreign exchange market. Some of the dealers in Treasury securities also serve as dealers in foreign exchange.

As trading in U.S. Treasury securities is winding down in Tokyo, it is opening up in London, and a different team at each of these securities firms takes over. Futures contracts on Treasury bonds on LIFFE (London International Financial Futures Exchange) complement trading in the cash market in this time zone. From London the baton is passed to New York (and the Chicago Board of Trade futures pits) which continues to be the mainstay of the market.

The Treasury securities being traded around the clock are held in book entry (electronically) on the books of the Federal Reserve System. Owner-ship is transferred and payment is made the next business day in the United States. (A trade made, for example, on Tuesday in Tokyo—Monday night in New York—would settle on Wednesday in New York, about a day and a half later.) An important feature of transactions in Treasury securities is the use of federal funds—balances on the books of Federal Reserve Banks—as the payment medium. These balances are transferred from the account of the buyer's bank (or the clearing bank used by the buyer's dealer) to the account of the seller's bank. These transactions are made over the Federal Reserve's wire transfer network—Fedwire—and they are final; they cannot be reversed in the event either party fails to deliver.[2]

A question to be asked at this point is, Where is the global financial system headed? In the process, are investors likely to be offered better terms and lower costs? Will the market system of the future be a safer one? What is the likely role of electronic technology? In this regard, it seems obvious that less cumbersome and costly market systems will displace more costly ones. Also, more sound market systems will tend to displace less sound ones, especially if the move to a stronger system does not entail much higher costs. Thus, those innovations that boost efficiency without adding to risk will displace others. Similarly, those that enhance soundness without sacrificing efficiency will displace others. At some point, efficiency gains might only be available at the cost of soundness or vice versa. At this point, a choice will have to be made between efficiency and strength of the system. This is a particularly interesting question because a disruption in one market can spill over to other markets and to the economy, and thus compromises in the area of soundness on the part of one market can have significant effects on others. In other words, there are important externalities in securities markets implying that risks in one market have consequences for others.

Attributes of a Market System

Investors seek a variety of attributes in a market system for securities. Several such attributes stand out. Information on recent prices, and perhaps recent transaction volume, as well as the current price at which the security can be bought or sold is valued highly. A timely means of submitting orders and a clear, fair, and efficient procedure for matching orders also are important. These attributes are sometimes called *market transparency*. Next, the investor values prompt confirmation of the trade and not being exposed to the risk of a failed trade in the event that trades cannot be reconciled. Finally, a sound clearing and settlement system is regarded as being very important. Sellers want to be sure that they will receive payment when they deliver securities, and buyers want to be sure that they will receive the securities they bought when they part with their funds.

It might also be useful to contrast the principal types of market-making systems for securities as well as their related derivatives. The two principal types are the specialist and dealer market-making systems. Under the specialist system, sometimes labeled an "auction" market system, all buy and sell orders in a particular security are directed to a central location, the specialist. The specialist then attempts to match buy and sell orders following certain exchange rules. The specialist has an obligation to maintain an "orderly" market in the security and attempt to avoid sharp movements in price, and for this purpose maintains a relatively small inventory of the security to meet excess demand or has cash or a line of credit to acquire an excess supply. In some cases, the order book of the specialist is public information, and in others it is not. The specialist system is used by the major stock exchanges in the United States and Japan.

In dealer-based, over-the-counter markets, there are competing market makers who post bid and offer prices at which they are willing to buy or sell the security. These prices typically are binding, at least up to a certain quantity. In some cases, the market system will have in place procedures for directing orders to the dealer with the best price. In any event, the dealer will need to maintain an inventory of the security to meet demand if his offer price is hit, and, of course, ready access to cash if his bid price is hit. Dealer-based systems are used in the U.S. Treasury securities market, the foreign exchange market, and various equity markets around the world (for example, the International Stock Exchange in London and a segment of the U.S. market regulated by the National Association of Securities Dealers, or NASD).

In addition, there is the open-outcry system, traditionally used for the trading of futures contracts. Under the open-outcry system, customer orders are brought to a central trading floor ("pit") where a number of floor traders ("locals") compete through their bids and offers. Initially, the orders are filled by these locals who take temporary positions in the contract. Later, position imbalances of individual floor traders may be redistributed to other floor traders through trades among themselves or by posting sufficiently attractive bids or offers to bring in buyers or sellers from off the floor.

Automation is greatly affecting all of these market systems. Electronic systems for delivering orders to the specialist have been in use for some time, and now orders for entire portfolios of individual stocks can be submitted by machine in seconds. In the dealer-based markets, elaborate electronic systems have been developed to receive dealer bid and offer prices, along with corresponding amounts that would be bought or sold, and for matching incoming orders with the best available price. Electronic technology also is being used increasingly in open-outcry systems for recording trades and for doing trade comparisons.

Moreover, the major U.S. futures exchanges have been developing electronic trading systems—similar to those available in dealer markets—for use in trading futures contracts outside of regular exchange hours. Some foreign futures exchanges have expressed an interest in these electronic systems for trading their instruments outside of exchange hours. These systems are able to accommodate the trading of securities and other financial instruments, besides futures contracts, during times when their markets are closed and could conceivably replace existing trading systems.

Meanwhile, some major securities exchanges have indicated that they are developing electronic trading systems to be used in after-hours trading in securities listed on their exchanges.

Clearly, electronic trading systems have many advantages. They can provide market participants with nearly instantaneous reports on the price and volume of the most recent trade, and current bid and offer prices. In addition, trade comparisons can occur instantaneously on these systems. They hold the potential also for facilitating prompter clearing and settlement of transactions, working in tandem with electronic payment systems for moving cash, and thereby reducing this source of risk to the system. Dealers and clearing organizations also can reduce their risk exposure by imposing real-time risk control procedures on customers and members. For regulators, too, there are some important advantages of electronic trading systems. Such systems can provide more accurate and more readily available information on the trading activity of individual market makers and brokers, a better "paper trail," and thereby make it easier to detect trading abuses and other violations of securities laws. This, in turn, could enhance investor confidence in the marketplace.

Electronic systems also have been seen to have some drawbacks. One potential drawback associated with dealer-based market systems is lessened liquidity. It has been argued that dealers are likely to be unwilling to commit themselves to buy or sell large amounts of a security at their posted bid and offer prices for fear of being exposed to traders who have acquired, in a prompter fashion, information bearing on the fundamental values of those securities and could more quickly take advantage of this information gap in an electronic market. To limit their exposure to such developments, it is argued, dealers will reduce the size of an order that they are willing to commit themselves to fill at their bid or offer prices, implying that larger orders may have more price effects in this type of market. This implies that there will continue to be a need for some mechanism for arranging large block trades, such as the "upstairs" trading on the New York Stock Exchange where large, typically institutional trades are worked.

Another potential drawback is the possibility for electronic trading systems to develop outside the scope of regulation or to be based in a center having weak regulation. The availability of modern telecommunications facilitates trading on such systems from virtually any part of the world at any time of the day. The reason for concern about such a system is that a market failure could—because of important externalities—have significant effects on other markets if volume were deflected to these other markets or if a large loss by one or more participant were to affect the ability of such participants to discharge their obligations in other markets.

Risk in Securities Markets

A major source of risk in the global financial marketplace is the risk that
between the time that a transaction has been arranged and the time
settlement of that transaction occurs, the counterparty to the transaction
will fail to deliver on its end of the bargain. This is especially important as
transactions activity becomes more complex and interdependent and as
new players enter the markets, making it more difficult to rely on previous
informal relationships and understandings for ensuring contract compliance. Increasingly, portfolios are being managed by large institutional
managers who use a variety of financial instruments in their attempts to
meet their objectives, including financial futures and options, and in the
process they engage in an ever more complex chain of transactions. For
example, a manager wishing to raise the share of a portfolio in equities and
lower the share in money market instruments may first buy stock index
futures—in effect, to lock in current equity prices. Later, that manager will
acquire the equities in the index and simultaneously liquidate the futures
position. Similarly, a rise in money market rates, say, in the United
Kingdom, may encourage the manager to convert a portion of the portfolio's money market assets into U.K. instruments and to hedge the foreign
exchange risk using a foreign exchange futures contract, a swap, or an
option. The point to be made here is that a failure of the counterparty to
any of these transactions to discharge its obligation could jeopardize the
ability of our portfolio manager to meet his obligation and lead to
disruptions across a number of markets. This type of outcome would be
more likely the larger are the positions of that counterparty. Thus, such
counterparty risk can have significant systemic consequences,˙ going
beyond domestic markets.

Also, differences in clearing and settlement times across the various
financial instruments can pose strains on investors that result in strains on
the system. For example, if an investor chose to substitute Japanese for
British shares in his portfolio, he would not receive cash for the British
shares for at least two weeks but would need to pay for the Japanese shares
in three days. This places pressure on his liquidity, and he incurs the risk of
an adverse movement in the value of the British pound relative to the
Japanese yen—a risk that can be hedged, but at a cost.

These settlement risks can be reduced by shortening and synchronizing
settlement times. In the limit, transactions could be settled at the time they
were made. In other words, settlement would be instantaneous. This
would require a highly developed electronic system that included book-
entry holdings of the security in a depository (in contrast to physical

possession of the security by the owner or the owner's agent). This system would first verify that the seller has the securities about to be sold and that the buyer has good funds to pay for them. Once the price were determined, the securities would be transferred to the account of the buyer and the cash to the account of the seller. Settlement risk would be removed and the only risk to be concerned about would be operational risk should there be a breakdown in the system. Moreover, such a system has the potential for significantly lowering the overall costs of making securities transactions.

For various reasons, such a system is not practical at the present time for most securities markets. First is the existence of physical certificates for many securities instead of book-entry holdings. In the U.S. stock market, for example, a substantial portion of shares is held by the investor or the investor's agent in the form of certificates, requiring that the seller surrender the shares to his broker after the sale. This process takes time. In contrast, U.S. Treasury securities are held in electronic book-entry form on the books of the Federal Reserve and can be transferred quickly to the account of the buyer. Thus, an important step in shortening settlement times and systemic risk is the substitution of book-entry systems for physical certificates, a measure that has been highly unpopular to a segment of investors who has a strong preference for physical possession. Such a procedure for holding securities in electronic book-entry form also would reduce risk by facilitating simultaneous delivery versus payment (to be discussed more fully in the next section).

In some securities markets, payment conventions call for something other than same-day funds in return for securities. For example, in the U.S. equity market, settlement occurs typically after five business days, and payment is made in next-day funds; that is, the funds pass to the seller's account and can be used the day after settlement. To ensure that the buyer can meet his obligation, brokers usually ask for payment of good funds on the date of settlement, resulting in a day's float for the broker and some income that would be lost if payment were made in same-day funds as settlement times were shortened.

Another difficulty in the area of international securities markets is the existence of time zone differences and the inability to achieve simultaneous settlement because one system is closed. This is especially a problem in the foreign exchange market in which the payment system for one of the currencies to be exchanged is closed while the other is open. For example, in a yen-dollar transaction, the buyer of yen receives access to the yen balances during the business day in Tokyo a half-day before the dollar balances must be delivered to the seller of yen during the business day in New York. The seller is thus exposed to a settlement risk—should the buyer of the yen default on his obligation to deliver dollars in New York that day—because the U.S. payment system and the Japanese payment system do not operate during the same hours.

A smaller problem can arise when securities are bought in one financial center in one hemisphere and settled in another hemisphere. For example, when Treasury securities are purchased in Tokyo and settled in dollar balances in New York, an extra half-day transpires compared with when those same securities are purchased in New York. The extra time adds to the risk that one or the other counterparty will default, prompted in part by the larger scope for a large change in the price of the security. Even if a dollar payment system is utilized in Tokyo and the seller receives a dollar balance on the books of a banking office in Tokyo, final payment will not be made on that transaction until later in the day when New York is open and the buyer's deposit balance is debited. In this case, there is additional intraday counterparty risk that must be borne by someone.

In both examples, these intraday risks would be eliminated if payment systems were open around the clock. Payment could then be made at the time of delivery. Keeping payment systems open around the clock could mean that the payment department of each major central bank is kept open around the clock. For example, the payments system of the Federal Reserve would be open to make dollar payments during the Tokyo and London business days. Alternatively, key central banks in each time zone could offer accounts denominated in certain foreign currencies that could be used for making payments when the central banks that issue those currencies are closed. For example, the Bank of Japan and the Bank of England could offer dollar accounts that could be used in settling foreign exchange and securities transactions during their respective business days while the Federal Reserve is closed.

Group of Thirty Report

In recognition of the risks in the various securities markets around the globe, a private group called the Group of Thirty prepared a list of recommendations in 1989 that are serving as a model for many securities markets. They were offered as a means for strengthening national securities markets and the international system, partly through standardization. They might be viewed as an initial move toward a completely automated securities trading system. The key recommendations of the Group of Thirty (1989) report are:

- Trade comparisons between brokers should be completed no later than the next business day (T+1).
- Each country should have a central securities depository (CSD), designed to encourage maximum participation by the industry. This would enable securities to be held in book-entry form. Securities could be issued exclusively in book-entry form ("dematerialized") or held in certificate form at the CSD for the account of the owner ("immobilized").
- Each country should look into the feasibility of establishing a netting system for trades to reduce risk and promote efficiency. (A discussion of netting and clearing house arrangements will appear in a later section.)
- Delivery versus payment (DVP) practices should be used for settling all securities transactions. In a delivery versus payment system, the exchange of the security for cash is simultaneous, and the risk that the security could be paid for but not received, or vice versa, is eliminated.
- Payments should be made in same-day funds (that is, the seller would receive funds over which he had full control on the same day that payment was made, in contrast to next-day funds).
- A "rolling settlement" system should be adopted by all securities markets with an objective of settling all securities transactions by three days after the trade date (T+3). In a rolling settlement system, trades settle each business day at a specified interval after the trade. (This is to be contrasted with a system in which trades accumulate for a period of time, say, a week, and then are all settled at the same time.)

Clearly, these recommendations go a considerable way in reducing systemic risk in the securities markets and address a number of the problems identified earlier in this chapter. In particular, the shortening and standardization of settlement times, the use of book-entry systems, and the practice of delivery versus payment in same-day funds would reduce systemic risks. Moreover, adoption of these various recommendations would set the stage for further improvements in the settlement system, including still shorter settlement times.

Other Improvements to Clearing and Settlement Systems

Recognizing that it will be some time before a completely automated, virtually simultaneous trading and settlement system is in place, there are other measures that can and are likely to be taken to reduce risks and enhance efficiency, consistent with the recommendations of the Group of Thirty report. In particular, netting arrangements are being developed and extended to a wider array of financial instruments.

Banks and brokers during the course of a day make numerous transactions in a given currency or security on behalf of their customers. In the case of foreign exchange contracts, a large international bank will make a vast number of yen-dollar transactions on a given day, both yen sales and purchases. Similarly, a large brokerage firm will, on any given day, place many buy and sell orders for shares in IBM. In both instances, on a typical day, buy and sell orders will be of crudely similar orders of magnitude. Thus, the *net* buy or sell position will be small relative to the *gross* size of transactions. Netting arrangements take advantage of this principle and reduce the size of payments that need to be made. In the process, they reduce liquidity pressures on the system and lower risk.

Basically, there are two types of netting arrangements that are available. The first is bilateral netting. In this case, each bank or broker nets transactions with each other bank or broker and makes a final settlement in the amount of the net position vis-a-vis that entity. For example, Bank A may have an obligation to Bank B to buy $1 billion of yen and sell $1.2 billion of yen. Under a bilateral netting arrangement, it would be required to deliver $0.2 billion of yen and would receive $0.2 billion in U.S. dollars from Bank B on that day. Outlays in this example have been reduced from $1.2 billion to $0.2 billion, a reduction of more than 80 percent. This reduces the size of payments and liquidity pressures substantially. It also reduces risk. If Bank A defaults on its obligation to Bank B, Bank B would be exposed to potential losses on the $0.2 billion net payment of yen from Bank B and not the $1.2 billion gross payment. The potential for such losses has systemic consequences, and measures that reduce such losses reduce systemic risk.

A multilateral netting system goes well beyond a bilateral one. In a multilateral scheme, netting is done across all member positions vis-a-vis all other members and a single payment of cash or delivery of securities or foreign currency is made by each participant on its net position with all other participants. For example, suppose on a particular day that Bank A has a net dollar-yen position with Bank B—one in which it owes Bank B $8 billion of yen (in return for an equivalent amount of dollars). Suppose also that its net position with Bank C is one in which it receives $2 billion of yen. Bank B in turn owes Bank C $4 billion of yen. In this case: Bank A could make a net payment of $6 billion yen (in return for a like amount of dollars); Bank B would receive a payment of $4 billion yen; and Bank C would receive $2 billion yen. The advantages of multilateral netting rise rapidly with the number of participants.

In addition, multilateral netting systems can be used for more than one instrument. For example, netting could be done for dollar-Deutschemark (DM) transactions and yen-DM transactions. In this case, some further netting across instruments could be achieved to reduce payments even further. In the previous example, if Bank A were to be a recipient of $3 billion worth of yen reflecting its net yen-DM position, it would pay in $3 billion of yen—the $6 billion it owed on yen-dollar transactions less the $3 billion it receives on yen-DM transactions—instead of $6 billion.

Multilateral clearing systems typically take the form of a clearing house arrangement. In this case, brokers or banks become clearing members, and all transactions are netted across clearing members. The clearing member then makes a payment to the clearing house of its net position vis-a-vis all other members and across all instruments cleared by that clearing house. Of significance is the role of the clearing house as the counterparty to every transaction cleared through the clearing house. Because of this, each customer transacting through the clearing house can be confident that default on the part of the other party will not result in a reversal of the transaction. If the other party were to fail to deliver, say, the security purchased, the clearing house would purchase that security using its own resources and transfer it to the buyer at the time the buyer puts up his cash. Conversely, if the buyer of the security fails to put up cash, the clearing house would give the seller cash from its resources at the time the seller delivered the security and then sell the security to replenish its cash.

In practice, to limit risk to the clearing house and better control risks in the clearing and settlement system, there are certain rules about allocating losses. The initial loss resulting from a customer default is to be absorbed by the clearing house member (bank or broker). This provides an incentive to the member to have internal procedures in place that reduce the scope for a customer default (position limits, collateral on deposits, and so forth). In the event that the member cannot deliver, losses are picked up by the clearing house. To be able to guarantee all transactions, the clearing house must have adequate financial resources, including ample holdings of liquid assets. These resources come from the clearing house's members. When a loss occurs at the clearing house level because a member defaults, other members are obligated to replenish that loss. Formulas for replacing such funds call for members to pay a share of the loss based on their transactions with the defaulting member or their overall transactions with the clearing house. In other words, risk bearing in the clearing house involves a mutualization of risk on the part of the clearing members.

This mutualization of risk results in a strong vested interest on the part of each member in the financial condition of the other members. The failure of any one member can lead to significant losses being borne by the other members which could impair their ability to function. As a consequence, clearing houses typically set minimum financial standards for membership, set minimum standards for member dealings with customers, require frequent reports by members on their financial condition, and require notification of any adverse change in financial condition.

In summary, multilateral netting through a clearing house offers substantial clearing and settlement efficiencies, including a large reduction in the amount of liquid assets that are needed for clearing and settlement. In addition, the existence of the clearing house guarantees on transactions, if they are credible, can enhance customer confidence in the system and reduce systemic risk. Balanced against these advantages are the costs of risk control, in particular curbing moral hazard incentives that accompany the mutualization of risk.

Clearing house arrangements are typical for exchange-traded derivative instruments, futures and options. In the case of futures, the underlying commodity or asset—for example, wheat, gold, or securities—may be delivered for cash at the time the contract expires, or cash settlement may be required; in the case of cash settlement, a payment is made or received depending on whether the value of the underlying item has increased or decreased in value. To better ensure contract compliance, futures clearing houses specify that an initial payment—margin—must be made by both parties to the contract, and additional payments may be required daily (or even intradaily) depending on whether the change in the value of the contract moves against the customer. Variation in margin payments daily has been a key element of risk control for these clearing houses and can give rise to large sums of funds being moved daily on outstanding futures contracts.[3]

Stock exchanges also typically use a clearing house to clear or settle transactions.[4] Corporate bonds frequently are cleared and settled by a clearing house, and clearing house arrangements have been developed for U.S. Treasury securities. At the present time, foreign currency transactions are settled among banks on a bilateral basis, but, in recognition of the advantages of a clearing arrangement, efforts have been under way to explore the use of a clearing house arrangement to reduce credit and liquidity risks and achieve efficiencies.

The globalization of financial markets and the trading of securities in more than one financial center are leading to growing demands for linkages among national securities clearing houses. In cases where the security is held by a central depository in the home country, procedures are needed to transfer ownership of that security at that central depository when the transaction is made in another financial center. In addition, as we have noted, customers have a strong interest in a standardization of transactions procedures across markets—of which the Group of Thirty report is a symptom—and avoiding the added liquidity needs when such procedures are not standardized. Undoubtedly, much more will be done in the area of clearing house linkages. Risk control considerations will be an important aspect of these linkages. Also, there are some important differences in legal systems applicable to the various financial centers, and arrangements must be made for dealing with these situations if investors are to be confident that transactions will be completed under a variety of circumstances.

Conclusions

The global financial system is evolving rapidly, and electronic trading systems and payment systems are playing an important role in this process, owing to their lowering of transactions costs and the strong requirements of accuracy and speed. Speed is valued because portfolio managers want to make transactions quickly in response to new information and to cover any unwanted risk exposure. Speed also is desired to reduce counterparty risk exposure, a consideration that looms larger in the modern depersonalized world of global financial markets. Standardization of transactions procedures across financial instruments and national borders is important in a world in which transactions activity is so complex—involving futures, options, and swaps as well as securities and currencies and a large chain of purchases and sales across various markets. At the same time, these conditions are giving rise to greater demands for around-the-clock settlement capability in each currency for purposes of reducing settlement risks.

By expanding the array of financial assets held in investor portfolios—both domestic and foreign—and by reducing transactions costs, the linkages among national financial markets are becoming tighter, implying that developments in one market are having larger and prompter effects in other markets. There also is greater dependence through clearing and settlement systems, owing to growing linkages among clearing houses and the tendency for the large multilateral banking and securities firms to be involved in the various major financial markets. As a consequence, a problem in one financial center can potentially be transmitted to others quickly. The recognition of this interdependence with implications for global systemic risk has led to efforts to better coordinate policies among exchanges and regulators to enhance soundness and stability, while at the same time encouraging innovation and efficiency.

Notes

1. During the writing of this chapter, Thomas Simpson was a member of the staff of the Board of Governors of the Federal Reserve System.

2. Should the buyer fail to make payment to his bank, the bank (or dealer used) would gain possession of the securities, and these could be liquidated to cover the payment. In the event that the value of these securities diminished, the bank (or dealer) would incur the loss. Should the bank be unable to cover this loss, the loss would be borne by the Federal Reserve which has granted final payment to the seller's bank. Similarly, a failure of the seller to deliver would expose the seller's bank (or dealer) and potentially the Fed to a loss. For its part, the Fed has sought to reduce its exposure resulting from settlement finality to minimal proportions by limiting the size of each bank's exposure on Fedwire and the posting of collateral by banks to cover such exposure. The Fed also proposes to charge for intraday credit extended by the Fed.

3. Many of these features of futures clearing houses also apply to options clearing houses.

4. In the United States, the National Securities Clearing Corporation (NSCC) clears stock transactions while the Depository Trust Corporation (DTC) settles these transactions.

Reference

Group of Thirty, 1989. *Clearance and Settlement Systems in the World's Securities Markets*. New York and London, March.

IV MONEY AND SOCIETY: TECHNOLOGY AND THE WORLD AHEAD

Money and society become the focal point of the final part IV. In chapter 7, *Information Services, Demographics, and Some of the Dynamics of Change*, Kenneth Robinson—now Senior Legal Adviser to the Chairman of the Federal Communications Commission and a national telecommunications expert and commenter on new technology issues—looks at the demographic, regulatory, and social factors. Mr. Robinson brings to this chapter his knowledge, insights, and experience in a wide area of technology and telecommunications policy.

Robinson considers the fusion of telecommunications and finance. He examines the forces likely to propel both forward rather rapidly. Robinson analyzes the transformations wrought by the electronic information technologies on the financial services sector. He examines also the regulatory challenges, the undesired by-products. Moreover, such difficulties likely will be compounded throughout the 1990s, as a full-fledged "electronic banking" regime emerges—particularly in the United States, and also, to somewhat lesser degree, in Japan and Western Europe as well.

Robinson explains the reasons why electronic banking may rather suddenly engulf us. On the supply side, the 1980s saw a surge in U.S. corporate spending on communications and communications equipment. Now many applications of this capital outlay are visible to the retail consumer, such as "bar code" scanning and computerized stock management systems.

On the demand side, are the changes associated with an increasingly computer-literate population. Women who move into the general workforce appreciate the value of time-saving measures. They are ready for "teleshopping" of a type widely accepted in France. It is a great convenience that the order placed by home terminal in the morning produces groceries delivered on the doorstep in time for the working woman's evening meal.

These trends will likely continue. Much of the necessary retail electronic infrastructure is already in place. Moreover, the demographic factors are compelling. Today, some 30 percent of the workforce uses a computer all or much of the time. Computer literacy training has percolated even down to the preschool level. The number of U.S. households with a computer of some sort is projected to comprise more than half of all American households by the mid-1990s. Many "user friendly" interactive computer-communications services now directly target the home computer market, for example, the Sears-IBM "Prodigy" joint venture.

Some major legal impediments stand in the way of growth but will not block it altogether. The demographics are just too powerful. However, the regulatory barriers will constrain investments and induce vendor caution. Robinson cites, as an example, the present prohibitions on "information service" marketing, placed on the newly separated Bell companies under the 1982 AT&T antitrust consent decree.

The initial restrictions on Bell operations were relaxed in 1987. However, they remain an obstacle still to the optimum deployment of the switching and other facilities needed to support full-fledged teleshopping and other useful retail networks. Compounding the problem has been some reluctance on the part of Bell and other telephone companies to undertake the necessary long-term capital commitment.

In chapter 8, "The Tradeoffs: Banks, Consumers, and the Law," I look further at Robinson's regulatory, legal, and practical difficulties. The chapter discusses the specifics of cooperation, conflict, and resolution-solving at the retail EFT level today. The interaction among payments partners is examined. So also are the special problems lurking when nonbank partners are added—sometimes under legal duress—to the more homogeneous banking "mix," and joint ventures increasingly are utilized as the chosen entity for new payments operations. The cost and price incentives of the partners become difficult to unravel, and often become the source of conflict.

The role of market forces and the law in shaping these arrangements is discussed. We perceive a generally diminished central bank and antitrust division interest in conflict resolution, while the role of private litigators and the state attorneys general is enhanced. The economic issues under these circumstances tend to become polarized under heat of trial or arbitration.

Not yet on the horizon is any definitive guide to resolution of such problems between participants in the electronic payments area. The relevant body of payments information and analysis could, perhaps, be prepared in advance, but it is impossible, at least at present, to project all the major possibilities. An intellectual "brainstorming" effort such as that of the earlier NCEFT Commission (1977–1978), drawn from many sectors of society, could be useful. And one can always hope that the Congress will provide more definitive guidance. However framed, a greater public presence seems desirable now, as in the days leading to the formation of the Federal Reserve when similar kinds of payments difficulties and conflicts existed.

In the final chapter, 9, Professor Martin and Dr. Weingarten broaden the spectrum with analysis of the computer pathways within society. "The Less-Check/Less-Cash Society: Banking in the Information Age" presents the societal, privacy, and security issues and the attempts that Congress has made to protect the user. The technology is carefully explained by two of the leading experts in the field—with illustrations of the potential for damaging impact as well as great benefit in one of mankind's most profound revolutions.

From yet another point of view, that of concerned scientist and congressional technology director, Martin and Weingarten examine that technology and its infrastructure: the integrated circuitry and electronic building blocks, and the engineering specifics that have made the payments nets and flows possible.

In a payments media consisting of a stream of numbers encoded as discrete pulses (bits), computers can control the flow of information as it moves from point to point in the network. An intelligence capability opens up a wide variety of new services and changes the way in which old ones can be delivered. But while offering a tantalizing smorgasbord of new possibilities for the payments system, the technology also carries with it a set of vital new issues and problems. Some of these issues are mainly technological, such as security and vulnerability of systems to "viruses," "worms," and the like. Martin and Weingarten discuss technical safeguards for computer systems, which range from secure encryption to criminal laws written with updated language appropriate to the new era.

Of equal or greater importance, they believe, the right to privacy has been severely strained with the increased use of computer data bases for record-keeping. Before the advent of the computer, people used to collect a lot of information about others in the course of doing business, but usually it took too long or was too costly to compile or evaluate much of it. Electronics has changed all that. The computer has mass-produced transactional information and has also made its rapid and cheap access very easy.

Such information funnels incessantly into a maze of data bases, and documents the daily lives of almost every person in the United States—the time, location, and amount of phone calls, bank deposits and withdrawals, purchases, and driving records. Hovering over each individual is a web composed of this kind of very personal financial and other information.

The web is formed during his (or her) lifetime by means of increments to all the interconnected data bases. Much private information contained on one net within the web (say, bank balances or subscription lists) can pass to owners of other nets, through sale or tacit permission or, in many cases, unknown means. The individual does not know much about who holds this information about his lifestyle and tastes. Unfortunately, computerized records detailing the finances of private citizens have the potential for great abuse in the wrong hands. Legislative solutions have been proposed and enacted, but the technology involved is such a moving target that the law can barely keep pace with the new problems that can arise.

Finally, Martin and Weingarten believe, as do earlier authors, that technology now expands the theater of commerce and politics to global dimensions and increases the necessity for political and economic cooperation among nations. If the "coin of the realm" for nations is replaced with a single international electronic currency in the coming decade (as considered possible by Oritani), the lines of national sovereignty will be blurred.

7 INFORMATION SERVICES, DEMOGRAPHICS, AND SOME OF THE DYNAMICS OF CHANGE

Kenneth Robinson[1]

In 1909, American Telephone & Telegraph Co. (AT&T) bought a controlling interest in Western Union Telegraph Co., and began a program of shining up dingy telegraph offices, hiring more operators, and marketing new services. Telephone subscribers could order telegrams by phone, and a new class of inexpensive "night letters" was introduced. Company sales managers thus were able quickly and efficiently to communicate electronically with sales forces in the field. And, one immediate consequence of this seemingly modest telecommunications industry advance was to accelerate the advent of the mass consumption economy that the United States has today (Strasser, 1989, p. 23).

Information Technologies and Financial Services

The economic and societal consequences of that modest turn-of-the-century development in communications are small compared to the transforming effect that electronic information technologies have had, and will have, on the financial services sector. For at least a generation, U.S.-based commercial banks and securities trading companies have ranked among the principal customers of the regulated telecommunications and unregulated computer and data processing service industries, both at home and abroad, accounting for about 8 percent of this "Information Economy's" $400 billion in annual American revenues (see, generally, Fernandez, 1988, pp. 443 et seq.).

The views expressed here are the writer's alone.

Solomon, E.H., (ed.), *Electronic Money Flows*.
© 1991 Kluwer Academic Publishers. ISBN 0–7923–9134–9. All rights reserved.

So high a ranking reflects the fact that virtually the entire "wholesale" part of the financial services field—interbank payments and institutional trading, most notably—today depends on computers linked via communications facilities. With the possible exception of the federal government, no other single sector of our economy is so reliant on information technologies.

For bank customers, this transformation has meant efficiencies—presumably reflected in the interest rates and services charges they pay—and, in many instances, a broader range of choices. Telecommunications technology has made possible needed economic development and creation of jobs in locales far away from traditional money centers, such as South Dakota, where Citicorp has established a major processing facility. As noted in reports including the Brady Commission study following the October 1987 U.S. stock market collapse, this electronic automation has heightened trading volumes and velocity, and also affected central bank and other regulatory controls.[2] Any such commercial and regulatory challenges likely will be compounded throughout the 1990s, moreover, as the computerizing of the "retail" parts of the financial services field progresses, and a full-fledged "electronic banking" regime emerges—particularly in the United States and also, to a somewhat lesser extent, in Japan and Western Europe.

Contributing Factors

Several factors have driven, and should continue to drive, the advance of this phenomenon. On the supply side, there are the many fundamental changes that business, particularly U.S.-based corporations, has made in the way retail trade in particular is conducted. On the demand side, too, are all the changes associated with an increasingly computer-literate population—and the influx of women into the general workforce, and the consequent premium value that time-saving measures have commanded as a result.[3]

Major U.S. retailers in the 1980s appear to have adopted corporate strategies that seek to sustain (and, if possible, enhance) profit growth chiefly through recurring operating expense reductions. Previously, most U.S. firms assumed that a perennially buoyant U.S. economy and rapid population growth almost automatically would yield yearly profit growth. In the 1980s, however, projections were made that the balance of the century would see relatively slow U.S. gross national product (GNP) growth—ranging from 2 to 2.5 percent annually—and that consumer spending would also lag, in part due to the commercial dynamics associated with an older population (which tends to possess many products already), a lower household formation rate (due to very low birth rates in the 1960s and subsequent years), as well as an accumulation of consumer debt (and accompanying loss of consumer confidence and proclivity to buy generally).

At the same time, most major U.S. corporations appear to have assumed that electronic automation—greater use of computers, usually linked via communications—was perhaps the most promising means of accomplishing cost reductions. Focusing on internal cost-containment measures, moreover, as an intrinsically defensive commercial posture, apparently was compatible with the corporate philosophy of the times. Confronted with rising international competition and the uncertainties associated with an intensified marketplace for corporate control, most major U.S.-based companies chose to concentrate on maintaining their existing markets and improving aggressively to secure greater sales and new market share.

Consequently, the 1980s saw a surge in U.S. corporate spending on communications and communications equipment (which rose from about 6 percent to nearly 26 percent of total business equipment outlays). For the consumer, the most visible results were the advent of electronics-intensive gasoline retail outlets, for example, and the near-universal adoption of bar code scanning and computerized stock management systems in the grocery, convenience, and, increasingly, general merchandise retail outlets— enterprises that typically account for nearly half the total U.S. economy. Less visibly, systems that trade under the name "electronic data interchange" or "quick response" were adopted by many managements. They facilitated especially labor savings, including cost reductions due to the deliberate "de-skilling" of positions, coupled with significant inventory management economies as well.

This broadscale electronic automation also contributed efficiency gains in credit card operations. While customer acceptance of credit (or debit) card payment options lagged notably in some major sectors—a majority of American grocery store customers, for instance, continue to pay using paper checks—it expanded in others. The most recent U.S. Commerce Department estimates, for example, indicate that an almost astounding 15 percent of fast-food transactions in 1989 involved credit card payment. All indications, moreover, are that this trend will continue.

Continuation of the Trend

It will continue, first, because much of the necessary retail electronic infrastructure is already in place, as are the commercial imperatives favoring its more intensive exploitation. Second, there are an array of demographic factors alluded to before. Today, some 30 percent of the general workforce uses a computer system some or, in certain occupations, all of the time. Computer literacy training has also percolated down to the preschool level. In addition, the number of U.S. households with a computer of some kind stands at about 20 percent, and is growing by slightly more than 25 percent annually—which indicates that, by the mid-1990s, more than half (and possibly as high as 60 percent) of all American households will have a computer. While less than one-third of home computers today are connected to telecommunications facilities, moreover, that almost certainly will change.

Very user-friendly, interactive computer-communications services directly targeting the home computer market—such as the Sears-IBM Prodigy joint venture—have experienced healthy growth rates, particularly in higher-income, better-educated markets where the service has been marketed. Purchasing decisions entail an individual assessment of the potential benefits and the personal investment—both financial and in time—needed to capture those benefits. Five years ago, when computer literacy levels were lower, fewer consumers were willing to make the personal investment needed to use a home computer, or to access an on-line data base. That is less true today; among other things, that personal investment to attain some degree of technological facility has often been made as a condition of general employment. Couple that circumstance with the ease of purchase and use characteristic of mass market items distributed by telephone companies, and the prospects for growth in the "information services" field are good today and should become better.

Teleshopping Impediments

Existing, home-oriented, electronic information services already offer subscribers a variety of long-distance teleshopping options; and, indeed, some are supported in part through advertising sales. Some networks also offer bank customers the ability to retrieve account information, authorize some bill payments, and obtain a limited amount of financial services information as well.[4]

The current offerings, both in the United States as well as Canada, however, are clearly targeted at small, niche markets, not all subscribers, much less the public at large. How successful these services will prove in the short run in commanding widespread, ubiquitous support from either suppliers or consumers is uncertain.[5]

The argument is frequently advanced that a broad-based, electronic teleshopping system is unlikely to arise without some kind of external stimulus. The example of France Telecom's Teletel ("Minitel") network is as often put forward. There, the monopoly French telecommunications administration undertook an aggressive information network development program about a decade ago, designed around a low-cost home terminal that was supplied without direct charge. (The costs were recovered in line usage charges of about one French franc per minute, plus additional charges levied by the information service providers.) The French Minitel service, which this year secured its 5 millionth subscriber—comparable to some 24 million customers in the United States—entailed a long-term commitment on the part of France Telecom. And, while administrative limitations were placed on its services—chiefly to avoid direct competition with French newspapers—France Telecom had more flexibility to experiment with the service and its offerings than telephone companies in the United States have enjoyed previously.

In the United States, prohibitions on information service provision were placed on the Bell companies (which account for about 70 percent of U.S. local phone service) under the terms of the 1982 AT&T antitrust consent decree which caused the breakup of the former Bell system. While the initial restrictions were relaxed in 1987, many believe they were (and, in some regards, remain) an obstacle to the deployment of the switching and other facilities needed to support a full-fledged teleshopping (or similar) network. Compounding the problem has been some demonstrable reluctance on the part of Bell and other telephone companies to undertake the kind of long-term capital commitment toward development of new services that such a network entails. In addition, most residential and business telephone use in the United States currently is sold on a flat-rate basis, not the usage-sensitive basis commonplace in Europe.

France Telecom inaugurated its "Minitel" service in significant part to stimulate usage of existing telephone plant, and thus to increase its revenues. By comparison, increased local plant usage in much of the United States will not necessarily produce higher revenues under prevailing state-prescribed tariffs. That, coupled with the industry's traditional risk-adversity, make help explain why the United States today lags behind in deploying such networks.

Over time, pressures from their business customers to offer such services, in order to maximize return on those customers' information technology investment, as well as pressures from an increasingly computer literate and time-sensitive residential subscriber base, should result in the deployment of U.S. networks comparable to Minitel. Certainly the economics of some applications are compelling; not only are the processing and mailing costs associated with the current paper-based bill payments regimen steadily rising, for example, but much of the equipment that major "transaction" mailers installed in the late 1970s is now ending its useful life. Given the prevailing regulatory and judicial environment, however, that demise is not likely to happen soon.

Conclusion

Distinctive characteristics of the telecommunications and information services sectors generally include the extraordinary rate of growth (as a percentage of U.S. GNP, this field approximately doubled in the last 15 years, one of the few such examples) and the fact that developments of large-scale impact seem regularly to occur with minimal, if any, significant high-level policymaker, and often general public, awareness. In the last decade alone, at least four major applications materialized and yet managed to escape most people's awareness: cable television (which now passes 85 percent of U.S. homes and constitutes the principal video service delivery system in the country); personal computers (of which there are an estimated 60 million units); cellular radiotelephones (now used by some 5 million subscribers); and, of course, the now-ubiquitous facsimile machine.

Information services that rely on a blend of communications and computational capabilities, to date, have been used chiefly by larger businesses and the research establishment, although they have also attracted considerable attention on the part of the computer subculture both in the United States and abroad. Expanding the reach of these services hinges, in the short run, on resolving a variety of commercial and regulatory challenges. But in the longer term, demographic and economic factors almost certainly will mean their far broader dispersion and use.

Notes

1. During the writing of this chapter, Kenneth Robinson was the Senior Legal Adviser to the Chairman, Federal Communications Commission, Washington, D.C.

2. Chaired by Mr. Nicholas Brady, later named Secretary of the Treasury, *The Report of the Presidential Task Force on Market Mechanisms* is discussed in the 1988 and 1989 annual

reports of the Council of Economic Advisers, the most readily available research material. See *1988 Economic Report of the President* (1989, pp. 39–45) and *1989 Economic Report of the President* 1990, pp. 271–74.

3. It is not inaccurately said that the average married woman working outside the home—nearly 60 percent of all adult American women, at present—has two jobs: managing the household and working at another job. A result has been a surge in demand for time-saving services and products. Charts showing the percentage of retail sales accomplished through the mails or by telephone, as well as the use of electronic bank teller machines, for example, show a distinct correlation with the movement of women into the general work-force. Other indicators include the proliferation of microwave cooking appliances and convenience food products.

4. According to an October 1989 survey by the Yankee Group, telephone banking information systems (use of a touchtone phone to access customer account information) are now used by about 8.8 percent of U.S. households. About 2.2 percent use a telephone banking transaction system (i.e., use of a touchtone phone to transfer funds and pay bills). Only about 100,000 households, however, currently use a personal computer-videotext banking service.

5. Bell Canada, after a small-scale, two-year experiment with a variant upon the France Telecom Minitel service called "Alex," recently indicated plans for a major expansion of the service, with the goal of deploying some 500,000 terminals by 1994—about 14 percent of its subscribers.

References

Council of Economic Advisers. 1989, 1990. *1988, 1989 Economic Report of the President*. Washington, D.C.: CEA.

Fernandez, John P. 1988. "Electronic Banking and Financial Services." In *NTIA TELECOM 2000: Charting the Course for a New Century*. Washington, D.C.: Telecommunications and Information Administration, U.S. Department of Commerce.

Strasser, Susan. 1989. *Satisfaction Guaranteed: The Making of The American Mass Market*. New York: Pantheon Books.

8 CONFLICTS: BANKS, CONSUMERS, AND THE LAW

Elinor Harris Solomon

Some difficult yet major payments system problems have recently surfaced in private litigation and legal arbitration. The federal regulatory bodies have kept their distance, as has the Antitrust Division and the legislative branch of government. Except for the expert witnesses, academics have been uninvolved, while consumers are generally unaware both of the conflicts and their direct future impact.

Why should people care about how some extremely technical payments system disputes are settled? The reason is that they relate directly to the way that bank-like services can, and will, be transferred from payor to payee. They impact on retail pricing for consumers and, equally important, on the manner and kinds of money services available to the public. Furthermore, unless and until the private parties can amicably agree on basic responsibilities, the electronic payments modes may not be fully utilized. Because of risk of costly litigation, adoption of the new payments technology through joint ventures may be slowed. The expected consumer benefits of all the scale economies may fail to be realized fully.

Solomon, E.H., (ed.), *Electronic Money Flows.*
© 1991 Kluwer Academic Publishers. ISBN 0–7923–9134–9. All rights reserved.

Payments Concepts and Modes

A payments system includes the whole socioeconomic "ball of wax" for transferring money, the customs, laws, institutions, and participants, be they bank or nonbank. The gold standard provided the classical structure for transferring gold and other forms of gold-backed money from about the time of Adam Smith (1776). Much later, credit standards became the payments norm after the downfall of the gold standard in 1931. Then, as now, money consisted largely of deposits, paper (central bank notes), or coin. The money or its proxy, the paper orders to pay, were physically shipped around on the usual transport forms, with airplanes gaining ground because they provided greater collection speeds. As we approach the 21st century, people can transfer money through electronic funds transfer (EFT) and access money through the plastic card with either encoded magnetic stripe or computer chip. In the information age the electronic system transfers money through many diverse computer and telecommunications links.[1] While electronic payments modes transfer only a small amount by *number*, they are overwhelmingly predominant now in *dollar value* (see figure 8–1).[2]

Electronic impulses then furnish the directions to transfer money from one account, the buyer's, to another account, the seller's. These electronic impulses travel by "wire" or though the air, perhaps "downlinked" to the ground from geosynchronous ("geosync") orbit 22,000 miles above the earth. They can be "zapped" in milleseconds from the buyer's to seller's bank. It is no longer necessary painstakingly to load and unload paper orders to pay, on and off planes or trucks. The time lags and physical frictions are mimimized. Money can be constantly in motion, available for the purchase of goods and service throughout the day as money turnover becomes swift, almost instantaneous. Money transfers may be compared to a continuous fluid flow, potentially able to move around the world many times during the day. The change in relevant money flows concepts as money speeds approach the speed of light, are treated throughout this book by Martin, Moore, Robinson, and Solomon.

In this chapter we shift the focus toward a more earthly perspective, to the marketplace origins of the new payments forms. We look at the manner in which the exotic new money and money-transfer forms are being shaped by technology and the market, with the courts lurking in the background in the event of irreconcilable strife. We have seen that the concept of money constantly in motion presents some monetary policy puzzles and implications; the concept of money being transferred under untested technical conditions, by a lot of diverse and often strident payments parters, presents some legal and societal difficulties.

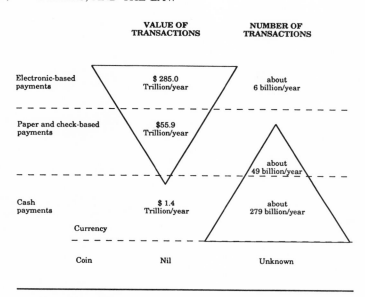

Figure 8–1.   The United States Payments Structure
Source: Paul Henderson (1987); Appendix Table 1A-1, 1987 data, Humphrey and Berger (1990).

Paper-based Systems

In the olden days, any system malfunctions seemed able to be handled in fairly precise ways, for a couple of reasons. First, the Federal Reserve retained a dominant role in the payments system, with little or no challenge. Second, payments rules were finely honed over time and clearly understood. Banks could clear through local clearing houses, correspondent banks, or the Fed Banks, depending upon business preferences, the area served, and the necessary clearing speed.

The old delivery mode (see figure 8–2) involved pretty much a one-on-one bank/customer relationship. That basic fact simplified decision-making. Bank 1 provided loans and services to the customer. The customer provided the basic "core" deposits and interest fees in return. The relationship was two-sided and often personal, as shown to the left in the figure. Clearing houses existed to handle local net clearing and settlement. Deposits were "cleared," or netted out, between other banks locally, say bank 2 and bank 3, through the clearing houses in correspondent balances, gold, or later, Fed funds.

Over longer distances the correspondent banking network did the job

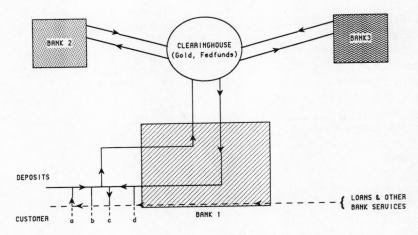

Figure 8–2. The Paper-Based Delivery Modes
—deposits flow; — — cash, loan, and services flow.

quite effectively. The small banker, who bartered his deposits for clearing and other services, was in a strong bargaining position. His "respondent" bank deposits were sought after by the big city banks, who tried to accommodate him through loans as well as payments services. The Fed Banks were always there as "clearer of last resort" if the private system did not work well for the individual bank. Central banks emerged and stepped in to settle corrosive questions in a forum of open discussion.

The Historical Sweep

A very long time passed in which all the arrangements could evolve in orderly fashion. The origins of the paper clearing system go back to the Renaissance and earlier. As checks (written orders to pay) evolved from goldsmith notes, it became inconvenient for people receiving checks to go to different banks to get their money. The goldsmiths (now called bankers) decided to meet at local clearing houses to clear bundles of checks. Each bundle contained checks of the other banks and included a list of the amounts due one bank from each other bank. The clearing house members then settled the net differences among themselves. Much later, in 1853, a more formal clearing house was established in New York in response to payments "chaos." Bank porters no longer had to crisscross each other's tracks to settle accounts, and net balances at the clearing house were settled in gold. Other regional clearing houses followed, in response to advantages of net settlement and major efficiencies.

All was not smooth sailing, however. One big problem prior to 1913 was the lack of prior certainty about check clearing cost and net settlement amount following collection. Checks were often collected at varying discounts below par, or face value. These discounts below par were called "remittance charges" or "nonpar" payments. The discounts, a percentage of the amount of the check returned for collection, were typically charged by country banks on their own checks mailed for payment from out of town.

Nonpar clearing fees cost either the city bank or its customer an amount that became known only at the time of final collection of the customer's check some days later. Charges were often applied haphazardly and at quite arbitrary rates. Critics argued that these fluctuating charges made the wrong party bear the cost—the check depositor (merchant or seller) rather than the check writer (buyer). It was frequently not clear to the merchant seller whether his bank would absorb the nonpar clearing cost for him. Even worse was the circuitous routing of checks, an outcome of the varying clearing charges. Often the roundabout process was the result of the merchant's bank efforts to avoid nonpar charges by finding a correspondent that had an agreement to collect checks at par from the check writer's bank. In a number of reported instances, checks meandered for hundreds of miles and several weeks to a final destination relatively near the sending bank (Gorton, 1984, pp. 3–11; Duprey and Nelson, 1986, pp. 18–29).[3]

The government in the 1913 Federal Reserve Act was finally called into play because private sector participants with conflicting interests could not resolve problems. Among its many other provisions, that Act required Federal Reserve Banks to receive from members, at par value, all checks drawn on other members. Eventually, most nonpar clearing was eliminated and payments routing paths shortened. But the old nonpar clearing issues have resurfaced at present within the context of the much debated interchange fee. Other electronic pricing issues are eerily reminiscent of the old. They generate a sense of *déjà vu.*

The Payments Partners and Their Point of View

Although the electronic innovations are not usually a money form, akin to gold or even deposits, they all make possible the *transfer* of money in quite ingenious ways. They have one other very important characteristic: they are capable of being offered by a variety of nonbank as well as bank suppliers. They thus broaden vastly the payments system horizons and its range of participants, diverse in focus and strategy.

Economies of scale lie in the relatively low cost of additional units of cross-selling grafted on to payments transfer nets, once the necessary hardware and software are in place. But systems are expensive to set up initially; member-owners can also incur much risk. Society has, accordingly, devised new institutions and legal forms to permit the systems to get off the ground and running. The joint venture is one of them.

Electronic systems may be established by single firms such as American Express in a "proprietary system" format. More typically, electronic systems take the form of a "joint venture" or legal arrangement between independent firms to cooperate on a specific operation. Joint venture members are a complex breed who have to learn to get along. They include the financial institutions that issue cards either for themselves (the primary members) or others (agent members). They also include the depository institutions (DI's) that handle the merchant side of the business. Also accorded membership are the DI's who put out ("deploy") the terminals. The joint ventures now being formed to offer home banking (Prodigy, for example) comprise merchant (Sears Roebuck), computer systems manufacturer (IBM), and other bank, merchant, and telecommunications links.[4]

The necessary cooperation can take other forms, such as outright merger or acquisition, but the joint venture has the advantage of being quick and easy to achieve. A joint venture is also easier to dissolve than a merger, once consummated. Any adverse effects on competition are better kept down, since the area of agreement is limited, while the need for the joint venture may be more compelling. Quite obviously, no one will want to assume joint responsibilities with rivals without the economic incentives to make it worthwhile.[5] But incentives do exist; payments partners, even where plastic rather than paper may be a medium for accessing deposits, bring joint and often subtle strengths to the bargaining table. Let's look at figure 8–3, which portrays cash flows through the automated teller machine (ATM) system, owned by many people jointly. We assume that the ATM is located at the merchant's store, say, a supermarket. The customer has bought groceries. He needs cash.

The consumer has handy an ATM card from the bank (or DI) where he maintains his deposit account, card-issuing bank C. The ATM card, and the system configuration of hardware and software, provide an alternative to the live teller for the purpose of obtaining cash. It is very convenient to be able to do this at the supermarket. In step 1, the cardholder uses his ATM card at the ATM terminal owned by bank or DI_a, and placed in merchant M's supermarket. The cardholder sends a set of instructions to

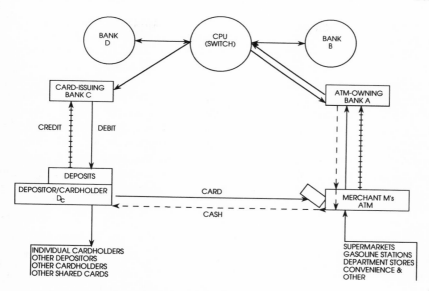

Figure 8−3. The Electronic ATM Flows
—message flow; — — cash flow; +++ deposits flow, depositor/cardholder D_c to bank C – merchant M to Bank A.

his bank for the necessary cash, by punching the proper commands into the supermarket's ATM.

In step 2, the electronic message flows from the ATM at M's supermarket, through to M's bank (DI_a), which in this example assumed the costs of installing the ATM in the store. The message continues to travel swiftly on to the central switch, or CPU, for transfer to card issuer (DI_c), through a processor that logs the transaction and deducts the cardholder's deposit account. The system CPU, at the same time, sends a message back in the reverse direction which instructs the ATM in the supermarket, in step 3, to produce the desired cash for the customer. The customer retrieves both the card and the cash from the ATM, in step 4, and leaves with the bag of groceries, and maybe a little extra cash to spare.

Note that card-issuing bank C needs terminal-owning bank A in order to provide cash payment for its good customer and depositor, D_c. The ATM deployer is equally dependent on card issuer; indispensable to him is bank A's customer base D_c. Without that base, his terminals will stand unused. The terminal-owning bank A needs the merchant, M, with his valuable space and checkout clerks. Bank A also hopes to gain the merchant's deposits and other banking business. The merchant hopes the ATM, with its money-producing skills, will generate additional retail business.

All around, in payments systems we see a complex web of interdependence. Without some critical mass of both card base and ATM's, or terminals where the card can be used, no one may find the venture profitable. You can't have a successful ball team without the winning players and the venture capital needed to make the team work as a whole. Equally important are the loyal team fans who buy the tickets and soda and cheer at the park; it is they who provide the necessary cash flow to compensate owners and the adrenaline to spur the players on. In a loose arrangement such as ball team, or electronic net, are embedded also the seeds for discontent.

The Questions Today

Internal strife is compounded by two concurrent developments: first, the rapid evolution of EFT mechanisms, from credit card to ATM and now more exotic new payments forms; and, second, the expansion of DI "banking" fraternity from the classic bank to much broader money-creating groups—savings and loans, for example—with a different way of doing business. Behind the scenes, system members successfully resolved some very thorny questions in a number of creative ways. Other questions remain unresolved and sources of corrosive open conflict, as follows:

1. How may system services best be priced "upstream" at the wholesale joint venture level? That is, what forms of compensation should be used so that system members performing special services for other system members may continue happily to do so?

First is the "interchange fee," a form of internal reimbursement from one member to another, when it receives important and costly services from the other, such as customer ATM use. The interchange fee also passes between members in a credit card system, in this case from the merchant's bank to the cardholder's bank that provides the collection services.

Switching and some other minor system fees, second, go directly to the system, to cover system services performed for all.

Third, the card-issuing bank works out a satisfactory pricing arrangement with its customer, usually as part of a broader banking relationship. No charge is normally made when the customer uses an ATM owned by his own bank because in that case the ATM is the low-cost substitute for the live teller; the customer deposits provide the implicit payment for cash availability, as always in a paper-based system. However, when the customer uses an ATM owned by another bank, the growing practice is for the customer's bank to levy a "foreign" fee. This charge, fixed in advance and uniform for all foreign ("not-on-us") ATM's, will cover all or part of the interchange fee compensation paid by card issuer to ATM owner.

Last is the arrangement between merchant and the merchant's bank, when an ATM is placed in, say, a grocery store or casino. The question of who bears the cost of terminal deployment in a setting that utilizes merchant employees and space is a hotly debated topic today within the payments arena (Felgran, 1985; Felgran and Ferguson, 1986; Kutler, 1988). The presence of in-house ATM's can help sell groceries or lubricate slot machines. But the merchant's bank may consider the deposits and other banking business generated by the merchant in deciding who should pay (or conversely be compensated) for terminal deployment. In similar manner, negotiations between the card issuer and ATM deploying bank will normally include the whole banking relationship; a broad ATM net may attract more business and generate more "core" deposits for the card-issuing bank.

The payor and payee banks in the paper-based system recognize this fact of interdependence well; indeed payee banks normally charge little or nothing for preparing deposited paper for collection, in the expectation that other banks will return the favor. Of course, in a paper-based system, if payee banks see their customer base become unbalanced, they will seek to correct the situation by attracting deposits against which the system costs can be defrayed by minimum balances or fees. In fact, banks for other reasons usually strive to enhance deposit base in order to enhance available loan funds. For card-issuing banks, pricing of the whole structure of fees for electronic services may be seen as one mode of interbank competition for deposits, hence profits. But ATM deployers do not necessarily have depositor needs to worry about predominantly in their quest for profits.

2. What is the proper sharing of internal costs between joint venture partners in providing electronic payments systems to the public?

The system divides into cardholder base and terminal base, often provided by someone other than the card issuer (again see figure 8–3). As we have just seen, an interchange fee is paid by cardissuing bank to ATM owner when cardholders use the foreign ATM terminal, i.e., one not owned by card-issuing bank. The interchange fee represents both price for services performed (question 1) and cost for services received (question 2). Given this dual role of the interchange fee, and where system balance is lacking, joint venture partners can have very different views of the proper compensation. It all depends upon which side of the equation they happen predominantly to fall.

In credit card transactions, the flow is reversed: the interchange fee is always paid by the merchant's bank to the card-issuing bank, in compensation for its billing and other costs, including any "free float" granted the prompt billpayer who may escape interest charges.[6] In on-line point of sale (POS) transactions, the interchange fees could flow in either direction: the merchant gains access to the customer's funds immediately, but the card-issuing bank hopes to secure the merchant's deposit business. Hence, there is considerable negotiation, and often the merchant decides to install the hardware himself.

3. Even more difficult, how can system members best establish the mutual sharing of responsibilities within the system—i.e., customer education, handling of complaints, software problems, retooling to handle the most up-to-date system software? How do the rules about these questions differ from time-honored principles as established in a paper-based system?

Again, the more lopsided the system balance as between providers of the two sides of the transaction, the greater the potential for internal strains and dissention. Also, as is obvious, the greater the system options for joint venture members, the more the potential for internal strife. If I, as card issuer, have the choice of moving out from regional system A into regional system B, or into either of national systems 1 and 2, then I am going to be more feisty than if I am glued irrevocably to the only game in town, the local clearinghouse or the regional Fed. This point illustrates full well the benefits of competition, helpful to consumers but not system harmony.

4. On the other side of the coin, what may be the relative nonprice (collateral) benefits for participants? How does one best measure these in the interests of system harmony, from the short-run or long-run perspective?

Proper hammering out of rules considers the ancillary business generated by a well-functioning ATM net, or the loss of business if you don't go along with other innovators. For the biggest banks, such as Citicorp or First Chicago, bank prestige is normally a plus along with the perceived ability to forge nationwide banking links to span the statewide branching barriers. Many now stress card individuality and product differentiation in TV ads: "we're not just VISA, we're Citicorp VISA." The thousands of small community banks must keep pace with the times in order to satisfy customer depositors. Banks of necessity look at the bottom line in terms of all the intangibles because, in the end, they translate into more "core" deposits and a bigger share of the financial pie nationwide.

Customers appreciate a money access medium that enables them to get cash in a variety of far-flung places. The bank's logo at the top of the card is a reminder of the issuer bank who supplies the many options. But the so-called foreign terminals, run and financed by others, are very helpful in broadening the card acceptability and promoting the proper customer image across state lines for the card-issuing bank. It is helpful to depositors that Crestar bank interconnects with terminals (owned by others) all over the Washington area, through the MOST system, and around the country through its national links. My card provides generalized money access, night or day, it provides wide money acceptability, hence satisfies the first textbook definition of a good money form.

Merchants and their banks gain, too, from the extra business generated by the presence of ATM's to spew out cash quickly in the middle of the night to hungry or thirsty patrons of, say, the 7-Eleven stores.

5. What happens, finally, when the system lacks balance? Does the era of rugged individualism by a few who want to "do their own thing," those with different profits orientation, take something stabilizing away from payments modes as we comfortably know them?

Economic choice is, of course, a good thing. System members are free to focus their system business emphasis heavily on one side or the other, card issuer or ATM deployer, depending on their optimal business strategy. However, system imbalance can breed internal conflict if partners focus their attention too narrowly. In the paper system, this problem did not naturally arise since it was just assumed that if you accepted deposits for your own deposit customers you were also willing to handle and clear the paper for customers of other banks (see Henderson, 1987; Moore, 1987; Budd and Lipis, 1973). Discrepancies were expected generally to balance out in the end.

Balance can and often does exist in an electronic system, too. When the same bank both holds the customer account and also owns the terminals, there is, of course, no interchange fee; nor is there any foreign fee paid to an outsider for running the terminal for use by depositors. Similarly, when system banks have an approximately equal distribution between their cardholder base and ATM terminals, there will be fewer problems of unequal flows between different parties to the joint venture. Just about as much money will be flowing in on interchange fee receipts as flowing out on interchange fee payments. On this score at least, there won't be too much to quarrel about.

This picture of member symmetry is not, however, the way the electronic world works much of the time. Consider the plight of a DI such as First Texas Savings that is primarily an ATM deployer but has little or no ATM card base. This institution would like very much to enjoy a higher inter-change fee which will, of course, be paid by the card-issuer banks. But predominantly card-issuer banks of First Texas' system, PULSE, may have a double problem. True, they need the strategic deployment of money machines in order to attain acceptability of the card they issue as a money-securing device. If they pay what the ATM deployer asks in order to provide their cardholder with access to this convenience, however, they may see their profits from the card-issuing business dwindle sharply. What to do?

Some members may threaten to leave the system rather than pay the higher interchange costs. But fewer members in the system means fewer card issuers and fewer cards, hence less incentive for terminal deployment in handy places; that, so the argument goes, can easily reduce the value of the regional card further to card-issuing banks and their customers alike. Or, higher interchange costs may force the embattled card issuers to raise foreign fees for use of the "not-on-us" ATM's. However, rather than pay the higher foreign fees, cardholders may just revert back to the bank-owned ATM's, a sorry scenario for the system. The absence of substitution possibilities—referred to as "perfect complementarity"—means that the success of each contributor to the final product (money dispensing or card service) depends uniquely on the actions of all other members. Everyone must play ball together; each member usually recognizes the unique interdependence.

Sometimes this recognition is not enough. Where private solutions are not possible, parties may call upon the courts or Antitrust Division to resolve conflicts. Although an internal shift in position by present Assistant Attorney General James Rill is possible (see Bell and Herfert, 1990; Rill, 1990), a 1985 speech given by Charles Rule is the latest official Antitrust Division position on EFT sharing in retail consumer markets. In suggesting their possible pro-competitive benefits, and the lack of high barriers to ATM system entry, Rule implied that the Antitrust Division would not often intervene to resolve system-sharing questions.[7] Indeed it has not done so publicly, since that speech was delivered.

The void has left it necessary for the private bar, or State Attorneys General, to resolve the rising number of private disputes in electronic banking. A foremost legal scholar in electronic banking, former Assistant Attorney General Donald Baker, notes that there is little decided case law regarding shared systems (Baker, 1989b, p. 3; 1989c). The legal precedents are limited. Of great importance is *NaBanco v. Visa* (1984), which challenged the interchange fee set by VISA in the credit card arena. Also important was 1988 arbitration, *First Texas v. Financial Interchange*, involving the setting of interchange fees in an ATM environment. However, in the latter case the arbitrator reached legal conclusions about electronic markets almost diametrically opposite to *NaBanco* and handed down a decision that neither side wanted.[8] The legal uncertainties and conflicts continue to fester here and elsewhere.

The First Texas-Financial Interchange (PULSE) Arbitration

The Dispute: Background

The arbitrator was Professor Thomas Kauper, former Assistant Attorney General for Antitrust. It was his task to look at the complex ATM pricing and system interchange fee disputes between First Texas and the PULSE system, and to resolve matters within a three-month period including a week of testimony (Baker, 1989a, pp. 5, 13–14*ff.*).[9]

PULSE is a nonprofit joint venture, founded in 1981 by seven Texas bank holding companies to provide a link between the automated teller machines of system members. At the time of the case, PULSE served over 1,800 member banks and was one of the five largest regional networks in the nation. Claimant First Texas Savings Association was a member of the PULSE system since 1983 when it requested entry for itself and its then competing ATM network, "MoneyMaker." PULSE members had some misgivings about this arrangement but eventually acceded in the face of threatened suit. The law concerning compulsory access in these cases is difficult.[10] Entry was arranged without any legal test.

The 1987–88 dispute arose when First Texas objected to a proposed cut in interchange fees. First Texas' displeasure was understandable since its focus was on putting out ATM's, not building up its cardholder base. First Texas, therefore, had more to lose than to gain from the proposed cut. It asked for a legal resolution and agreed to binding arbitration as the cheaper and faster alternative to court action. Implementation of the new lower interchange fee was delayed, pending the outcome of the test.

The Arguments

In its legal brief to the arbitrator, First Texas disputed the network's right to set interchange fees. When PULSE attempted to lower such fees to meet the competition it perceived from the national networks, First Texas (a net deployer of terminals) charged that the PULSE board was acting as a "buyer's cartel." In seeking the fee cut, PULSE was, it was claimed,

exercising market power in product markets construed by claimant as
ATM switching and cash dispensing, in Texas.[11]

First Texas had proposed a new pricing plan called the "free market"
approach. The idea was that each money machine owner could decide the
charge for use of its terminals by cardholders. However, the defendant,
PULSE, objected strenuously on grounds of cost, customer inconveni-
ences, and uncertainty. PULSE also pointed out that First Texas' allega-
tion that PULSE held market power was circular. It was true that, with the
addition of MoneyMaker, PULSE was switching 95 percent of all inter-
processor ATM transactions in Texas. But had First Texas (with its local
ATM net MoneyMaker) not forceably insisted upon entry into PULSE
in the first place, PULSE would have had strong competition from
MoneyMaker. PULSE also argued that ATM's competed with other
modes of cash access; and that the system had the problem of meeting the
competition of the national ATM switching systems such as CIRRUS and
PLUS who generally charged lower interchange fees on switched transactions. Some important PULSE members had stated their intention to drop
membership in that system in favor of lower cost national systems if the
proposed interchange cuts were not implemented.

Thus banks that were card issuers, net, had a focus based on the view
from their side of the fence. However, First Texas' motives were affected
by its lopsided way of doing business. In March 1988, First Texas operated
862 ATM's. Only 180 were on the premises of a financial institution. Most
were placed in 7-Eleven stores. First Texas ATM's, including those
positioned in 7-Eleven stores, accounted for one-third of all PULSE
transactions. But its cardholders accounted for less than 5 percent of all
PULSE-switched transactions. First Texas' deployment strategy, while
unique, had not been very profitable. Based on low use per terminal,
whether deployment was efficient was subject to question. Of course,
consumers liked having ATM's in convenience stores for use at odd hours;
their personal "consumer welfare" was enhanced. Whether this fact served
consumer welfare generally was, however, the question in the arbitration
proceedings. What was certain was that many difficulties in implementing
the scheme would be met by card issuers who held the customer's bank
account and were responsible for the final depositor billing and education.

The Opinion

Professor Thomas E. Kauper's opinion, of August 19, 1988, started from
the premise that:

... PULSE is not what it once was. Changes in its membership have brought an imbalance between buyers and sellers which in turn creates antitrust risks and imposes new duties. A greater degree of care is required than before.... Claimant's case is of necessity built largely on economic theory. It cannot establish precisely what would occur under the "free market" approach.[12]

On the "wholesale" market question, the arbitrator determined that PULSE was the dominant ATM switching network in Texas. On the "retail" market issue he concluded that ATM's are themselves a relevant, if fragile, market for antitrust purposes. This seems fairly close to the opposite conclusion from that reached with respect to credit cards in *NaBanco*. Kauper then conducted a rule of reason analysis of the PULSE interchange fee arrangement. He found that a uniform fee was permissible under the antitrust laws, but only if a method could be provided for ATM deployers individually to set the surcharges and rebates for use of their ATM's.

PULSE accordingly was directed to reinstate the (higher) "interim" fee schedule in effect prior to May 1988. Moreover, PULSE was prohibited from making any further changes in its interchange fees until (1) it adopted a policy permitting the imposition of surcharges and the granting of rebates by ATM owners to test the market for unsatisfied demand, and (2) the level of any interchange fee was determined in accordance with appropriate cost-based procedures.[13] It is a "split the baby" decision. PULSE is not required to scrap its present system. The ATM owner is free to set the fee for its ATM usage. If the owner sets such a surcharge, the consumer will be informed of per transaction cost by computer message at the money machine. If the consumer decides the transaction is worth the cost, he instructs the money machine to conclude the transaction. The charge then goes through the PULSE system software, eventually to be billed through the regular depositor statement at end of month.

The Impact of the Decision

Subsequent events have made it impossible to test the practical effects of the Kauper decision. A lot of water has flowed under the dam since the 1988 arbitration. First, the "troubled bank" status of claimant First Texas would lead to its arranged merger with the California-based Gibraltar Financial. Some leading members of PULSE—for example, MCorp and First Federal—have also been merged by regulators subsequent to the PULSE decision. PULSE itself continues to flourish in good health. In accordance with Kauper's order, PULSE proceeded to institute the variable pricing approach for any terminal deployers who wanted to try it. There have been, however, no takers.[14] Claimant First Texas is under new, and more cautious, management. Meanwhile, the focus of interest has shifted to the pending Valley Bank litigation, in a quite different part of the country.

In March 1989, Valley Bank of Nevada filed suit in the U.S. District Court of Southern Nevada against both PLUS and VISA, with which PLUS has strong ties, on charges of conspiracy to fix prices.[15] Valley wanted to charge customers of other banks in the PLUS system whatever it chose, for use of a Valley ATM within the state. However, the PLUS national network (of which Valley Bank is a member) prohibits its members from charging customers of other members an individually set posted fee on the ATM site. Valley thought the PLUS 50-cent interchange fee was inadequate to cover Valley's ATM costs. But system management was adamant.

In mid-1989 the State of Nevada passed an act making it illegal for any electronic system, such as PLUS, to prevent ATM pricing at the ATM deployer's discretion, within Nevada.[16] Valley National promptly proceeded to charge a flat $1.00 rate in merchant establishments, such as hotels, airports, and casinos. PLUS and VISA (now partially merged) sought an expedited court review of the Nevada state's 1989 legislation.

Once again, the present pricing mode for electronic services was on the line. The conflict was, finally, settled on grounds of commercial interests. In September 1990 the Ninth Circuit Appellate Court found in favor of appellee Valley Bank for, among other reasons, "legitimate state interests" including promotion of tourism and gaming within the state of Nevada.[17]

The Future: The Law and Markets

The Role of the Law

Problem areas for resolution in banking, such as whether a particular merger is anticompetitive, always have been plentiful. Evident also have been occasional allegations of Sherman Act violations such as price collusion or restrictive deals.[18] But the PULSE and PLUS problems have been of a different order. The older run-of-the-mill situations mostly reflected disputes or difficulties between market participants who were not within the same organizational structure. What is unusual in the present milieu is the conflict *within* the organization, or within the confines of the legally configured joint venture. Still more important is the basic nature of the dispute, the manner of *pricing* the new money services for others of the pioneering new schemes to emulate. To the extent that members perceive the Antitrust Division as having little real willingness to sue, they are unlikely to see the advantage of pursuing internal Division Business Review procedures.[19] The private bar must steer the resolution through the appropriate District (and eventually Appellate) Courts, at great private expense aided by economic experts working under time and cost pressures.

Furthermore, the within-system strife will likely become more not less important in future years, for several reasons. First, the new technology suggests an increase in joint ventures, or other forms of specific sharing arrangements. Second, the present confusion as to what the law allows fosters new litigation as members seek to clarify issues through the judicial route. Third, the existing EFT joint ventures are likely to seek to expand their scope.

At issue was the legality of the broadest proposed joint venture of them all, ENTREE. Driven by Antitrust Division inaction, the State Attorneys General moved to help fill the void. In mid-1989 14 of the State Attorneys General, with New York at the lead, legally challenged whether point-of-sale could be offered by ENTREE. ENTREE, the joint creature of the already powerful VISA/PLUS and MasterCard/CIRRUS systems, would have the effect, they alleged, of stifling potential competition and new entry in the offer of point-of-sale.[20] The suit was settled in May 1990 with an agreement by VISA and MasterCard to drop all plans to offer the joint ENTREE; in return the right of the two credit card companies to retain their dominant ownership in the ATM nets PLUS and CIRRUS would not be challenged.

The legitimate demands of widest money acceptability, through encompassing system links, may further increase the numbers of necessary partners, with their divergent views. Of necessity, the old payments modes and standardized "rules of the game" must break down. The partners are not all banks, as in days of yore, with their generally more homogeneous outlook. Indeed, bankers privately worry that they might lose control of the payments system altogether.[21] Novel and personally rewarding pricing schemes seem certain to receive continued attention by mavericks, until the issues at question are resolved definitively, with broader focus. "Friendly" consolidation also continues between major regional systems.[22]

Legal decisions, therefore, are and will be powerfully important in molding the money and payments schemes of the future and defining the parameters whereby they can operate. This trend, however, raises several troublesome questions. Will EFT systems increasingly have to get approval for new, but internally contested, ideas from courts or arbitrators? Is this a step up, or down, from problem-solving techniques of old, in the '20s or as recently as the '70s? There remains the difficult question of satisfactory implementation, and/or enforcement, of those pricing schemes crafted under legal duress or mandated by the courts, as temporary or permanent solutions. The practical difficulties with AT&T divestiture haunt us yet. One point seems perfectly clear. It is not conducive to long-run stable payments system functioning for some key players to be at opposite ends of a courtroom table. It is also costly for everyone, as the Texas PULSE experience indicated.[23]

At question is the role of the Fed, then, with its expertise in the payments field and its Congressional mandate as payments guardian. The role of the Antitrust Division is also clouded by the lack of any clear signals from the Division, since the past distant 1985 Rule speech, as to how electronic banking disputes might best be resolved. It is hoped that market solutions, in a competitive world, will render unnecessary any regulatory or antitrust interference. But will they?

The Role of Markets

1. A perfectly competitive solution, it is true, can leave little for any regulator or judge of the future to do. More firms, bank and nonbank alike, will compete with one another head-on in innovative product markets. Relative ease of entry negates the possibility of any monopoly profits. (An example is the sharp decline in merchant discounts since the late '70s when VISA's rule against duality was eliminated.) Technology will reduce dramatically the cost of producing and delivering the new money and payments services. In a model of perfect competition, consumers will benefit fully from the new technology through lower prices and higher quality financial services at retail. If small banks and thrifts lack the necessary capital and expertise to "go it alone," they can share in the new electronic systems or buy or rent essential components without restrictions. No one will be left out of the electronic services net, or overcharged, whether he be a customer of the big city supplier or the little local bank.[24]

The presence of competition is not, however, easy to evaluate here. The joint venture in banking functions through complex market interplay. It affects many layers of market interactions downstream from the top (the nerve center in the shape of the joint venture) through intermediate users (distributors, the bank and nonbank sellers) down to the final user at retail. We see a gradual shift over the past two decades from money and banking services supplied in largely proprietary fashion (figure 8–2), to those provided electronically and funnelled down through the joint venture to the broad consumer base (figure 8–3). In the new electronic payments form, not only clearing and settlement are shared modes, as of old. More functions characteristically regarded as one-on-one banking services, such as cash withdrawal and deposits, can and do go through the joint ventures with their numerous partners. More shared "banking" and nonfinancial functions may follow. Examples are simple loan and investment services, discount brokerage, home banking, or smart card use through the joint net.

At present, we are in the very good situation where new and old payments forms coexist. The consumer can choose still from the old paper and the new plastic (or electronic) technology. The retail banking functions are split between those served by computerized joint venture systems and those still served by the local depository institution downstream. Based upon juxtaposition of the old and new technology, the customer's local banking needs can be met from suppliers in different geographic regions and different levels of the payments stream: the upstream computer-based system, the local DI "boutique," the regional financial supermarket.

Obviously, consumers have more choices where old and new payments technologies coexist than in a world where electronics, offered in a single mode, supplants altogether the old-fashioned paper mode. The flip side of the picture is that internal disagreements are more likely to arise, too. Of course, the market, with its threat of system annihilation to warring partners, typically provides the spur to amicable settlement of internal difficulties. Solutions evolve from mutual recognition that all partners have more to gain by sticking together than by parting, for that would mean each going his own diverse and costly way. In retrospect, this practical glue helped cement the old payments arrangements. It continues to be power-fully important, in the new.

2. After stating this pretty story, let's play devil's advocate. Is it possible that market power or a regulated public utility is instead in the cards? The scale economies may be such that further joining of systems, through partial or total consolidations, is indeed the most efficient way to go. But if a shared system becomes so dominant or successful that membership affords a major competitive advantage and there is no other method of obtaining it, an "essential facility" problem may arise. It becomes easier to "piggyback" on the existing system than to enter *de novo*. Under threat of antitrust suit, leading regional systems have generally been kind to those who demand entry. Exclusion of nontraditional competitors was chal-lenged in a 1987 suit by Household Bank against CIRRUS and a 1988

complaint directed against MoneyStation. Both cases were dropped when CIRRUS and, later, Money Station admitted Household Bank.[25] The precedent nonetheless seems clear. Successful joint ventures may breed forced sharing, hence the possibility of engineered market power or claims thereof.

On the other hand, as shown by contradictory opinions in PULSE and NaBANCO, the problem of identifying markets here is so complex that market power may be difficult to delineate.[26] Assuming such power really exists, conflict resolution may take one of several forms. First, the dominant group may hammer out rules to its liking, and require other members to accept them. Exit by dissidents may be difficult if the unified national system is the only game in town; nor will they want to leave. Allegations of monopolization can continue to be made by disadvantaged members, but there will be more reluctance to go to courts if dissatisfied members see themselves as having no other place to turn. Alternatively, a regulated private utility type of solution may evolve, in response to perceived market failures or crises which became unacceptable to the public at large and to Congress. Then government will be back into the electronic funds transfers scene, perhaps to a greater extent than before.

3. This dismal extreme seems most unlikely to appear on the horizon, however. For the near-term, the most realistic outcome will probably be mixed. A perfectly competitive outcome seems unlikely, given the great scale economies inherent in EFT and the presence of "bottleneck" entry provisions in antitrust doctrine. Nor is it probable that monopoly or a public utility type regulated mode will become the chosen format in the United States at any time in the near future. Given dynamic changes in technology, other opportunities may be available for the disgruntled or disadvantaged, which can blunt the eruption of sustained market power or the ability of any one seller to maintain prices over the competitive level for long periods. Regional, national, perhaps international systems can coexist and compete effectively for some segments of the electronic business.

The irony is that in this mixed system the potential for strife requiring eventual legal resolution is probably greater than in either perfect competition or regulated monopoly. In the case of perfect competition, there are no monopolization questions for courts to consider. Where true monopoly exists, the unhappy participants have nowhere else to turn. Perhaps they cannot afford the costs and burdens of court action. Banks within clearing houses, who perceived themselves treated as second class citizens by clearing house rules, seldom brought the matter to court.[27] They were afraid, perhaps, of being thrown out from the only private clearing game in town. Of course, the Fed's presence as clearer of last resort helped in preventing market power excesses. The Antitrust Division also listened to any patently egregious problems with a sensitive ear.

Today, much responsibility falls on courts and arbitrators. The difficulty is that individual judges have no continuing real presence here nor any conciliatory role to fend off festering complaints. Worse, they may not understand fully all the diverse payments problems or may accept too readily a persuasive and, on the surface, attractive economic theory.

The Money User: The Future Tradeoffs

The final buyer of money and banking services at retail is very much affected by the present vigorous interplay of market forces and the law. He (or she) generally doesn't know it, though. He has neither focused on the issues nor seen them explained. The Fed and regulators, for their part, are preoccupied with other serious matters. And academics don't often find payments issues particularly appealing. The end results seem obscure, the consumer stakes far removed from what suppliers and courts decide many layers up in the distribution chain. However, this present disinterest, for whatever reason, may come back to haunt everyone, including the vendors. It appears that the application of the new technology to payments has created many thorny problems that the private sector will have to work out if this technology is to supplant the old payments approach. But if the problems are intractable, presumably the old payments approach is superior in some respects. That dilemma poses many questions, answered by each of us according to our peculiar economic theory "religion."

The Payments Issues

The more central banking-oriented among us would argue that the money, and payments, issues require a careful examination of the following:

1. The acceptability of money as a medium of exchange, or, to use the new legal terminology, the availability to consumers of "no-hassle" cash at terminals at a certain cost, whatever the time of day or location;
2. The stability and cohesiveness of payments modes, to permit consumer planning, a subset of point 1 above;
3. The retention of elements of certainty within the system, in order to

avoid needless transactions costs, or the circuitous routing of payments or payors under circumstances similar to the circuitous
meandering of checks in the early nonpar clearing example;

4. The presence of optimal money and payments price and quality
    options, as consistent with the market, a goal in at least partial
    conflict with points one through three above, and the focus of the
    current legal decisions;

5. The minimizing of payments risk elements, the responsibility ulti-
    mately of Fed and/or U.S. Treasury when things go wrong, and
    again a goal somewhat in conflict with the others.

While payments theory looks at money acceptability and risk as a
whole, the thrust of microeconomic theory is the notion of "consumer
welfare" for society as a whole and for consumers individually.[28] Payments
theory considers all the interconnecting links and points of system weak-
ness and strength, as they impact back to consumer satisfaction with
electronic modes as a substitute for paper clearing modes. But the micro
answers for consumers may come out somewhat differently. No one has
arrived as yet at a satisfactory synthesis of the two highly regarded, yet
divergent, theories. The "grand unified field theory" (GUTS) is elusive
here, as in physics.[29]

Payments versus Micro Theory: The Conflicts

No one argues that users of instant money should not be prepared to pay
for it. There is general agreement that the service should, in some manner,
be unbundled and costed out. However, we see a real problem when so
many firms provide some part of the service. The card-issuing banks now
unbundle in one way, through fixed and predictable charges (foreign fees).
The presence of uniform foreign fees, often shown only in fine print in a
mailing to cardholder, is subject to much controversy. One argument in
their favor is their certainty. The customer need not be greeted with
unpleasant surprises at the ATM when cash is needed. The argument
presented by plaintiffs, on the other hand, is that consumer welfare
requires that the firms who install the terminals should make the decision
about what to charge, consistent with demand. Arguments of both kinds
were made in PULSE, but neither were fully persuasive so that clean
judgments could be made.

We are simply looking through opposite ends of the glass. How does
one reconcile the two points of view? Does arbitration by a noneconomist

(PULSE) or expedited decision by a judge (Valley National Bank) suffice? Is the Fed, which normally was consulted in such matters, being pushed aside in favor of legal solutions in an era of deregulation?

The Ambiguous Consumer Welfare Concept

Even within the strict microeconomic focus, we see plenty of room for honest disagreement. Behind consumer welfare questions lie the issues of aggregate demand and the way it is fashioned from the individual demand curves of consumers. Behind "dead-weight triangles" or consumer surplus are all the economic tastes and preferences underlying those user demand curves. Money users each have some unique array of preferences for a particular electronic product, say, instant cash at ATM's, which combine both return (satisfaction) and cost (price), all tempered by available wealth (budget constraints).

Money may be thought to have utility just as any other type of commodity. The individual consumer demand curve is constructed from all those points where the marginal rate of substitution between satisfaction and cost exactly equals market price. Market demand curves for money services aggregate those of all the individual consumers. Even for any one money seeker, they may vary considerably depending upon buyer mood and occupation at the time. As between money users in the aggregate, we may see a considerable range both of demand level and variability. At issue here are the following general observations gleaned from standard micro theory:

1. One must beware of any distortion from focus on the needs of a peculiarly unique subset of consumer user, such as buyers at 7-Eleven stores at odd hours of the night or devotees of gambling casinos. The latter especially may be a peculiarly unstable group, especially when the temporal utility of money is factored in. At issue is the stability of money demand for consumers as a whole as compared with the stability of demand for a subset of consumers, i.e., possible risk lovers at gambling tables. A pricing system esteemed by one group at 1 o'clock in the morning, and ostensibly confirmed by consumer survey at that time and place, may not be suitable for the bulk of more risk-averse consumers.[30] Such a pricing scheme may, however, yield more profit for ATM deployers, especially if the appropriate market concept is not perfect competition but rather a model of spatially differentiated imperfect competition.

2. Of major importance is the true nature of the electronic money

model: perfect or imperfect competition. In the latter case, what appears to be welfare-enhancing on first blush may rather be a case of third-degree price discrimination. Given imperfect competition, that can have the unwelcome effect, for consumers at least, of enabling producers by a system of "surpluses and rebates" to tap off some consumer surplus efficiently. Also, we need to disaggregate the consumer demand function to learn the whole story. Some consumers may benefit, while others lose from the strategy, depending on strength of market demand and the perceived value of the money user's time.

This has always been an ambiguous area for economists. The founders of welfare economics, Alfred Marshall, A.C. Pigou, and later Joan Robinson, recognized these ambiguities early on. They foresaw difficulties in postulating any cleanly cut welfare assertions (Robinson, 1933; Pigou, 1932, pp. 284–285, 288–289). Like bank branches before them, ATM deployers may compete in spatially differentiated, not perfectly competitive, markets, on a basis of location rather more than price. The consumer demand curve in that case is not horizontal but downward sloping. Some market power may be present. Price does not necessarily equal marginal cost but may be above competitive levels, after normal producer profits are earned; equated instead are marginal revenue and marginal cost. Producer surplus may result, given the presence of at least some market power in spatially differentiated markets for ATM services.[31]

3. Finally, just as in the case of the Exxon Alaskan oil spill, there may be negative externalities, some susceptible to careful economic assessment, some not. Payments risk may be one, but this seems less of a problem at retail than wholesale since money cashing is backed by deposits; we do not see any potential "unwind" situation or systemic risk.[32] Customer confusion or shoe leather wear-and-tear could be a problem, but one not susceptible to rational economic judgments. The situation at retail is unlikely to lead to any rapid-fire payments shocks. Any slow disruption of present payments modes seems, however, a proper matter of Fed monitoring if payments balance or efficiency seems on the brink.

What are the social ethics and policy questions here? May more ATM's at gambling casinos or race tracks raise the personal bankruptcy rates, or heighten divorce rates when "risk lovers" explain the circumstances of bank account drains to hapless spouses in broad daylight? What use is made of any excess profits earned by gambling operators or their banks by the new strategy? Do we see a transfer of wealth from poor gamblers and their families to the mob? Fanciful questions such as these are not the unique province of the economist, nor are they likely to become so.

In a more serious vein, the question remains of whether those who stress the benefits of "consumer welfare" have adequately considered money transfer reliability or payments systems cohesiveness. As full-fledged system members, mavericks have the power to cause expensive legal battles and disrupt the system. Or, the rebels may provide needed reforms, which require careful consideration. The present pricing modes in the end may prove quite unsuitable to the demands of the new payments technology. The point is that rather dramatic retail payments changes are on the horizon, for good or ill, and very few people are even aware of them.

This chapter has looked at some conflicts and problems faced by sellers of the new money technology. Stressed also was the importance of the manner of their resolution, in shaping the way electronic payments and money will ultimately evolve. There are no easy answers and much work to be done. A more careful and nonbiased synthesis of the consumer welfare and payments theory that the courts must consider is of highest priority. The question of competitive versus spatially differentiated markets requires further analysis. The present fragmented approach may distort the appropriate issues for concern including money and payments needs of the final user.

The market should, and has, molded the character of payments system evolution. However, important market failures have been present, too. These have led to some festering conflicts. We seriously question whether the ad hoc and divided manner of present-day conflict resolution is in the public interest. The legal system is struggling to cope, but in a matter involving so obviously a public good we think a more visible public presence would be a good idea, at least until Congress sees fit to provide more definitive guidance.

Acknowledgments

I appreciate very much the help of Stephen Rhoades, Alan Berger, James Woodson, Dianne Martin, and Richard Solomon in preparation of this chapter. I also want to express my intellectual debt to Donald Baker and Karen Grimm, with whom I served as expert witness on the PULSE arbitration.

Notes

1. Among the biggest, IBM and Sears Roebuck & Co. have created the new joint venture for home banking, Prodigy, available since October 1988. At year-end 1989, it purportedly reached 170,000 homes in 21 markets across the country.

2. Figure 8–1 is adapted from the pioneering work of Henderson (1987) and Humphrey and Berger (1990). The economic issues were first analyzed by Flannery and Jaffee (1973), Phillips (1964, 1979), Eisenmenger, Munnell, and Weiss (1974), and Henderson (1987). The seminal work on law of EFT is Baker (1974) and Penney and Baker (1980). For the economics and law of mergers, in historical and philosophical sweep, see Rhoades (1983).

3. These questions were discussed also by E. Solomon, *Affidavit*, PULSE Arbitration (April 21, 1988), paragraphs 7–13.

4. For a more complete description of the new vendors, see Solomon (1990).

5. See the definitive work of Baker and Brandel (1988) for the antitrust law of joint ventures (21–1 through 21–37), and for electronic payments practice and legal theory. The concept of cooperation and conflict is analyzed there in 23.91*ff*.

6. For more specifics on credit card flows, and the concept of interchange fee based on *percentage* of ticket item, see Solomon (1987, pp. 215–217; POS tends to follow the same mode. ATM interchange fees are, in contrast, a specified amount *per item* irrespective of size of ATM withdrawal.

7. Rule (1985), reprinted in Baker and Brandel (1988) as Appendix F.

8. *National Bancard Corp. (NaBANCO) v. VISA USA, Inc.* 596 F. Supp. 1231 (S.D. Fla. 1984), *aff'd*, 779 F.2d 592 (11th Cir.), *cert. denied*, 479 U.S. 923 (1986). See Baker and Brandel (1988, 23.07 [5][a]).

9. See In the Matter of the Arbitration between First Texas Savings Ass'n and Financial Interchange, Inc., 55 Antitrust & Trade Reg. Rep. ("ATRR") 340, 352–55 (August 25, 1988) (hereinafter "PULSE")

10. See Baker (1989a); Response of Financial Interchange, Inc. to Claims and Supporting Memorandum of First Texas Savings Association, Submission to Thomas E. Kauper in Accordance with Final Arbitration Agreement, April 23, 1988, pp. 97–108.

11. Claimant alleged that under the current regime, an ATM operator lacks the ability to offer low price, high volume machines, and higher price, low volume machines, with loss of consumer convenience. Claimant also alleged competitive injury in the fact that a uniform rate fails to reimburse ATM owners for quality improvements consumers might find attractive on some ATM's (e.g., lights in high crime areas). Claimant's initial submission was filed on March 30, 1988. The hearing was in Houston, Texas, from May 31–June 4, 1988.

12. Arbitrator's Opinion, PULSE, pp. 80–82. See Baker (1989c).

13. Arbitrator's Opinion, PULSE, p. 84. In adopting such a procedure, Arbitrator noted, PULSE will be able to proceed in a manner least likely to damage bank-depositor relationships and PULSE at large.

14. According to Yvette Kantrow in the *American Banker*, April 19 and 25, 1989.

15. *Valley Bank of Nevada v. PLUS and VISA* (U.S. District Court for Southern Nevada), March 1989. Defendants are charged with conspiring to fix prices in violation of antitrust laws.

16. Kantrow in the *American Banker*, October 4, 1989.

17. See *Valley Bank of Nevada v. PLUS System, Inc.*, (U.S. Court of Appeals for the Ninth Circuit), Filed September 11, 1990, especially pp. 10970 and 10982–10987.

18. The first Sherman Act case in banking was in 1963 when a Minnesota clearing house association was indicted for fixing prices of services. See *United States v. Northwestern Nat'l Bank*, 1964, Trade Case. 71,020 (D. Minn. 1964). The seminal work on banking markets and collusion is Phillips (1964). See H. and R. Duffy, *Bank Administration* (September 1989), for consolidations in the card industry; Rhoades (fall 1989), for the performance effects of billion dollar bank acquisitions.

19. See, for example, letter from Thomas E. Kauper to Francis R. Kirkman and Allan N.

Littman re Business Review Clearance for NBI Membership Rules (October 7, 1975) and letter from Donald I. Baker, assistant attorney general, Antitrust Division, to William B. Brandt, Nebraska Bankers Ass'n (March 7, 1977). For full explanation, see Baker and Brendel (1988, 23.02[1]).

20. *Wall Street Journal*, July 27, 1989, p. B7. Bankers had urged MasterCard and VISA to accept an offer from the attorneys general to settle the federal antitrust suit filed against them. See the *American Banker*, October 2, 1989.

21. Pollock, "Automated Banker," *Bankers Monthly* (January 1989), p. 33.

22. Again, the case law is somewhat limited (see Grimm, 1990). A system merger was challenged in 1988 in a private suit by New Jersey's Treasury Network to block Philadelphia National Bank's acquisition of Mellon Bank's competing CashStream network. The case was dismissed, however, on the ground that plaintiff had failed to show antitrust injury. *The Treasurer, Inc. v. Philadelphia National Bank*, 682 F. Supp. 269 (D.N.J.), aff'd mem., (2d Cir. 1988). See Baker (April 1989, p. 14); Kutler, *American Banker* (December 21, 1988); and Kantrow, *American Banker* (March 1 and 2, 1989, and April 25, 1989).

23. According to *Bank Network News* (October 11, 1989), Scott Engel (the former president of claimant First Texas) notes the two sides agreed to split the $2 million in legal fees accumulated before arbitrator Kauper reached his decision. "I don't know if that dispute touched off this current wave of EFT litigation, but $2 million is a lot of money to spend," declared Engle (p. 1).

24. For fuller explanation, see Federal Reserve Bank of Atlanta (1984) and Solomon (1985).

25. *Household Bank F.S.B. v. Cirrus Sys. Inc.*, No 87C2353 (ND Ill. filed March 1987). The question is whether the shared system is an "essential facility" so critical to those in the business that all competitors should be given equitable access to it. See Baker (April 1989b, pp. 7-8), and Baker and Brandel (1989, 25.01[1] and 23.07[1]).

26. In NaBANCO, the court found broadly that the product market was payment systems, i.e., "all payment services used in retail sales guarantee cards." See Baker and Brandel (1988, 21.03[1][a] and NaBANCO at 1259. In PULSE, the wholesale market, however, was defined narrowly as "network switching" and the retail "fragile" market also narrowly defined as being ATM services to consumers (PULSE, 55 ATRR, pp. 352-355 and 356).

27. The Minneapolis price-fixing cases were the exception. See note 18, but the cases were settled *nolo contendere*.

28. See Henderson (1987) and Moore (1987) for payments theory; for IO theory, Rhoades (1983), Schmalansee (1981), Posner (1976), Scherer (1980).

29. For the non-physicists among us, see P. Davies, *Superforce* (1984), p. 117.

30. See Whitehead (1984) and *Fed. Res. Bull.* (February 1986, March 1987) for impartial and carefully crafted surveys of retail EFT use. However, in PULSE a survey was shaped for the arbitration, and prepared for claimant's attorneys Fulbright and Jaworski, April 1988. Valley Bank reportedly spent $300,000 in fall 1988 on a seven-week consumer research program, again directed for specific use at trial; conducted by a subsidiary of Booz-Allen, it found that consumers at gambling tables and elsewhere in Nevada would like to see more widespread ATM's, even if they must pay more (Kantrow, *American Banker*, April 25, 1989).

31. See Lind (1988), Schmallansee (1981), Salop affidavit (PULSE, 1988). Lind notes that claimant's pricing plan would set up a system of monopolistic competition in ATM's (paragraphs 40-44). The height and slope of the demand curve will depend on the location and price of other ATM's and other alternatives for access to cash. The profit-maximizing ATM owner will choose a price and output combination at a point where marginal cost equals

marginal revenue. The ATM owner will only operate if P* is above ATC*, yielding short-run monopoly profits. In the long run, monopoly profits would be eliminated by entry by competitors who would install ATMs nearby. The concept of spatially differentiated markets was discussed also by Benson at the Federal Reserve Bank of Chicago, *Proceedings of a Conference on Bank Structure and Competition* (1980, pp. 60–85) and Greenhut and associates and Salop in Chicago FRB *Proceedings* (1977, pp. 255–259).

32. Humphrey (1984) provides the seminal work on systemic risk. See also Faulhaber, Phillips, and Santomero (1990).

References

Baker, Donald I. 1989a. *Antitrust Aspects of Shared Systems*, Third Annual Institute on the Legal Aspects of Interstate Consumer Financial Services, Grand Hyatt New York, New York, March 16.

Baker, Donald I. 1989b. *Antitrust Risks to Shared Electronic Banking Networks*, ABA Antitrust Section Spring Meeting, Grand Hyatt Hotel, Washington, D.C., April 5.

Baker, Donald I. 1989c "Antitrust Challenges in Electronic Banking Networks." *Antitrust* (Fall/Winter).

Baker, Donald I., and Roland E. Brandel. 1988. *The Law of Electronic Fund Transfer Systems*. Boston: Warren, Gorham & Lamont.

Bell, Robert B., and John A. Herfort. 1990. "Justice, FTC Signal Tougher Merger Enforcement Standards." *Antitrust* (Summer).

Duprey, James N., and Clarence W. Nelson. 1986. "A Visible Hand: The Fed's Involvement in the Check Payments System." Federal Reserve Bank of Minneapolis, *Quarterly Review* (Spring).

1990 EFT Network Data Book. 1989. Chicago: Bank Network News, October.

Eisenmenger, Robert, Alicia Munnell, and Steven Weiss. 1974. "Pricing and the Role of the Federal Reserve in an Electronic Funds Transfer System." Boston Federal Reserve Bank, *Proceedings of the Conference on EFT*.

Electronic Funds Transfer Association. 1990. "Leaving Behind the Past to Enter a New Millennium." *EFT Report* Vol. 13, No. 1, Washington, D.C.

Elliehausen, Gregory E. and John D. Wolken. 1990. *Financial Service Markets for Small and Medium-Sized Business*. Washington, D.C.: Board of Governors of the Federal Reserve System, April.

Faulhaber, Gerald R., Almarin Phillips, and Anthony Santomero. 1990. "Payment Risk, Network Risk and the Role of the Fed." In David B. Humphrey, ed., Boston: Kluwer Academic Publishers. *The U.S. Payment System: Efficiency, Risk and the Role of the Federal Reserve System*.

Federal Reserve Bank of Atlanta. 1984. "Crumbling Walls." King and Whitehead, eds. *Economic Review* (May).

Felgran, Steven D. 1985. "From ATM to POS Networks: Branching, Access, and Pricing." *New England Economic Review* (May/June).

Felgran, Steven D. and R. Edward Ferguson. 1986. "The Evolution of Retail EFT Networks." *New England Economic Review* (July/August).

Flannery, Mark J., and Dwight M. Jaffee. 1973. *The Economic Implications of an Electronic Monetary Transfer System*. Lexington, MA: Lexington Books.

Geller, Henry. 1987. "Telecommunications Policy Issues: The New Money Delivery Modes." In E. Solomon, ed., *Electronic Funds Transfers and Payments: The Public Policy Issues*. Boston: Kluwer.

Gorton, Gary. 1984. "Private Clearinghouses and the Origins of Central Banking." Federal Reserve Bank of Philadelphia, *Business Review* (January/February).

Grimm, Karen. 1990. *Antitrust Issues Presented by Shared Electronic Banking Networks*. Prepared for the ABA National Institute, Consumer Financial Services in the 1990s (March 2–3).

Hannan, Timothy H. 1989. "The Impact of Technology Adoption on Market Structure." *Restat*, forthcoming, Working Paper, Federal Reserve Board of Governors, May.

Henderson, Paul B., Jr. 1987. "Modern Money." In E. Solomon, ed., *Electronic Funds Transfers and Payments: The Public Policy Issues*. Boston: Kluwer, pp. 17–38.

Humphrey, David B. 1984. *The U.S. Payments System: Costs, Pricing, Competition and Risk*. New York: New York University.

Humphrey, David B., and Allen N. Berger. 1990. "Market Failure and Resource Use: Economic Incentives to Use Different Payment Instruments." In David B. Humphrey, ed., *The U.S. Payment System: Efficiency, Risk, and the Role of the Federal Reserve System*. Boston: Kluwer, pp. 45–73.

Kutler, Jeffrey. 1988. *American Banker* (December 21).

Lind, Robert C. 1988. *Affidavit*, Submission of PULSE to Arbitrator, April 22.

Moore, Linda K.S. 1987. "Payments and the Economic Transactions Chain." In E. Solomon, ed., *Electronic Funds Transfers and Payments: The Public Policy Issues*. Boston: Kluwer, pp. 39–62.

Penny, N., and D. Baker. 1980. *The Law of Electronic Fund Transfer Systems*. Boston: Gorham Lamont Publishing.

Phillips, Almarin. 1964. "Competition, Confusion, and Commercial Banking." *Journal of Finance* 19, 32–45.

Phillips, Almarin. 1979. "Implications of the New Payments Technology for Monetary Policy." In F.R. Edwards, ed., *Issues in Financial Regulations*. New York: McGraw-Hill.

Phillips, Almarin. 1987. "The New Money and the Old Monopoly Problem." In E. Solomon, ed., *Electronic Funds Transfers and Payments*: The Public Policy Issues. Boston: Kluwer, pp. 193–210.

Pigou, A.C. 1932. *The Economics of Welfare*, 4th ed. London: Macmillan.

Rhoades, Stephen. 1983. *Power, Empire Building and Mergers*. Lexington, MA: Lexington Books.

Rhoades, Stephen. 1989. *Billion Dollar Bank Acquisitions: A Note on the Performance Effects*. Board of Governors of the Federal Reserve System (Fall).

Rill, James F. 1990. "Report from Official Washington: Merger Enforcement at the Antitrust Division." *Antitrust L.J.* 59, 1.

Robinson, Joan. 1933. *The Economics of Imperfect Competition*. London: Macmillan.

Rule, Charles F. 1985. *Antitrust Analysis of Joint Ventures in the Banking Industry*. Remarks before the Federal Bar Association, Washington, D.C., May.

Scherer, F.M. 1980. *Industrial Market Structure and Economic Performance*. Chicago: Rand McNally.

Salop, Stephen. 1988. *Affidavit*, PULSE arbitration (March).

Schmalansee, Richard. "Output and Welfare Implications of Monopolistic Third Degree Price Discrimination." *American Economic Review* 71 (May).

Solomon, Elinor H. 1985. "The Dynamics of Banking Antitrust: The New Technology, The Product Realignment." *The Antitrust Bulletin* 30 (Fall), 537–581.

Solomon, Elinor H. 1987. "EFT: A Consumer's View." In E. Solomon, ed., *Electronic Funds Transfers and Payments: The Public Policy Issues*. Boston: Kluwer, pp. 211–238.

Solomon, Elinor H. 1988. *Affidavit*, PULSE Arbitration, April 21.

Solomon, Elinor H. 1990. *Financial Sector Innovation: The Consumer Impact*. Presentation for the First Conference on Networks and Society. Tokyo, Japan: The Institute for Posts and Telecommunications Policy, March 16.

The Nilson Report. 1988 and 1989. Los Angeles: HSN Consultants, Inc.

Whitehead, David. 1984. "Firms Involved in ATM, POS, and Home Banking: A Survey." Federal Reserve Bank of Atlanta, *Economic Review* 69 (July/August).

9 THE LESS-CASH/LESS-CHECK SOCIETY: BANKING IN THE INFORMATION AGE

C. Dianne Martin and Fred Weingarten

Structural Changes in the Banking System

Unlike the medieval goldsmith who kept valuables in large strong boxes, modern commercial banks have been described as "department stores of finance" because of the wide variety of services they offer. Typical bank services include not only safeguarding money and valuables, but transferring funds, making loans, providing trust services, preparing payrolls for local companies and providing consumer credit. Banking has become an information-processing service industry (Austin et al., 1985).

Perhaps the oldest function of banks is to safeguard assets. In the past banks were primarily depository institutions that provided a secure vault to hold gold, money certificates, and other valuables. With the advent of checks in 1865, this role expanded to include the function of a clearing house. Correspondent balances were established and maintained through the shipment of gold and, later, currency between banks. Checks were discounted to cover the cost of the transfer of actual assets from one bank to another. With the creation of the Federal Reserve System in 1913 the clearing house function became centralized, which brought more stability to the banking system by lowering risk and eliminating the practice of

Solomon, E.H., (ed.), *Electronic Money Flows.*

discounting checks. In effect, checks became just as viable as tender as were gold and currency.

During the early 1960s another form of exchange, the consumer credit card, was made available to the general public. After brief periods of adaptation, both checks and credit cards gained wide acceptance from the public. Although the operations necessary to sustain checks and credit cards became highly automated, they still generated an enormous volume of paperwork that threatened to overwhelm the payments system by the late 1960s. Sophisticated telecommunications technology came to be viewed as the solution to this problem. As a result, the structure of the banking system has once again changed dramatically over the past 20 years with the installation of a number of nationwide automated clearing houses (ACH's) that use electronic funds transfer (EFT) systems. The use of electronic payments methods and automated teller machines (ATM's) has grown rapidly in the past decade ("The Use of Cash ...", 1986; Humphrey, 1984). These changes have proceeded in three stages: a proprietary phase in which banks entered the business and profited from owning and controlling the ATM's; a shared proprietary phase in which individual financial institutions connected their systems with each other and to retailers to offer cardholders more convenience and led to nationwide networks such as CIRRUS and PLUS; and a shared-industry phase in which regional and national networks began to merge and consolidate (Kutler, 1984a).

With the widespread use of EFT, banks have been transformed from depository institutions holding physical assets to information-processing centers. Money has gone from being a *tangible* entity with no intrinsic value to an *intangible* entity with no intrinsic value. At any given instant, money may be simply numbers on a spreadsheet or electrons flowing through a circuit, rather than currency or gold in a vault. Not only has money been reduced to electrons or microwaves or digital sound transmissions, but checks are rapidly succumbing to the same fate. More and more banks are using electronic check collection technology, where check images rather than the physical checks are sent for reconciliation between banks and clearing houses. Image technology has become so sophisticated that banks can obtain the payments data needed from checks quickly and cheaply without having to require the checks as documents. "In effect banks can simply transfer data around the nation or the world without any paper trace to confirm it. Electronic Data Interchange (EDI) is replacing the handling of paper" (Nadler, 1988).

With EFT the true nature of money exchange as information exchange becomes apparent. In a barter or cash system, information is exchanged by exchanging objects that represent a certain immediate value to the owners.

In a check or credit card system, information is exchanged in writing and represents the promise of future value exchange. In an EFT system, information is exchanged electronically with immediate value exchange. Thus, EFT allows the immediacy of a barter system, but there is no interchange of physical objects as in the case of a barter, cash, checks, or credit slips.

Interplay of Technology and Deregulation in the Banking System

In 1974 the Federal Reserve Board made a fateful decision. It would not get involved in building and operating a fully electronic funds transfer system for consumer payments in the United States. As a result a consistent, nationwide method for the efficient transfer of funds from consumers to retail merchants has never been implemented. Instead technology has advanced more rapidly than banking industry's ability to assimilate it. Ten years after the Fed's decision not to involve itself directly, experts in the banking industry were decrying the results:

> Fragmented in its very structure, the banking industry has approached electronic payment systems opportunities in a very confused and incoherent way. A banking industry unable to agree within itself as to the nature and promise of EFT cannot be expected to transmit the necessary messages to the marketplace and to the public. Into the breach have stepped a number of outside firms expert in the technology and its capabilities ... units of GE, ADP, McDonnel Douglas, and ... eventually even AT&T ... individually and collectively have demonstrated that they can wrest at least a measure of control over the payments systems from the depository institutions who once owned them exclusively. The rivalry for payment systems access and control has been intensifying. For almost two full decades, the banks have been losing their grip on the payment system, advanced technology, and their future. They have been told so by officials of the Federal Reserve System, by their trade associations, by outside experts ..., and by internal critics .... those who run the vast majority of the nation's financial institutions would rather not be bothered with payments system and technology matters ... But new entrants into the once protected domain of banking have financial and technological resources that banks ... have been unable or unwilling to confront directly [Kutler, 1984b].

The multiplicity of electronic networks reflects the underlying fragmentation and fractionalization that plague the industry. Those who call for centralization of networks are accused of being anticapitalistic. Somewhere between chaos and communism lies a middle ground that the banking industry must garner, or their competitors will take over the payments function entirely. It is clear that something is needed which is bigger and more cohesive and coherent than the fragmented EFT networks currently in existence (Kutler, 1984b).

Although most bank managements have recognized the need to upgrade operating systems to participate in an on-line payment system, many have overlooked the need to manage and coordinate the various EFT products that will be provided either directly or through third parties. This represents one of the most serious weaknesses in commercial banking today. It is incumbent upon bank management to increase productivity and decrease vulnerability through strategic, futuristic electronic banking plans.

> No one facet of electronic banking can be effectively utilized individually ... unless it is integrated into overall bank operations. The fragmented approach to electronic banking ... has produced serious counterproductive results such as competing networks and misdirected applications of resources ... [it has] stifled increase to productivity [Hanley et al., 1984].

This narrow emphasis has contributed to accelerated efforts by major retailers to seize the opportunity to control an increasingly large portion of the payments system. The eventual effect will be to transform the payments system from one using banking services to one dominated by retail systems capable of charging banks for the services provided. (Trigaux, 1984b) One positive result from the consumers' point of view is that households now have significant opportunities to change the methods they use to pay for expenditures.

Coinciding with the increased incentives for expansion of electronic funds transfer in the banking industry in the United States were two critical factors: the deregulation of the banking industry with the passage of the Depository Institution Deregulation and Monetary Control Act (MCA) of 1980 and the deregulation of the communications industry with the federally mandated divestitive of AT&T. Experts differed on whether technology or deregulation has been most responsible for change in the banking industry: "The single most influential force for change in payment systems has been deregulation ... 30- and 40-year old regulations are no longer applicable in today's changing and increasingly competitive environment" (Carmody, 1988). And: "It is difficult to determine which is the chicken and egg for change during the past 10 years in banking—deregulation or technology—since both derive impetus from each other" (Svigals, 1988). If we recognize the "fundamental truth [that] information is power ... technology is affecting the power of large organizations and upsetting regulatory functions and checks and balances in the system" (Burnham, 1983). At any rate, the powerful combination of the deregulation of two major industries and the speed of technological innovation began a process that has fundamentally restructured the U.S. payments system. All of these factors have made the development of a rational, unified national payments system an almost impossible task.

Technological Infrastructure of EFT

In order to understand fully the technical problems inherent in EFT, it is first necessary to understand the underlying technology that encompasses EFT. EFT technology is essentially the technology of networks and telecommunications. Today's networks consist of transmission systems (microwave radio, specialized microwave radio, dedicated lines, fiber optic communication, satellite communications, mobile radio and cellular phones), cables (copper wire, coaxial and fiber optic), radio links (terrestrial and satellite), switching systems (physical communication lines, switching boxes and computers), and other equipment providing a complex mix of services (voice, data, graphics, text, and video) through a variety of specialized interconnected networks (Defending Secrets, Sharing Data, OTA, 1987). Figure 9–1 shows the complexity of modern communications networks.

Over the past 20 years the improvement of technology in several areas has facilitated the development of EFT. Integrated circuitry has improved by a factor of 10 every two or three years to increase speed and reliability and decrease costs. Electronic building blocks such as laser scanners, bar code readers, ATM devices, plastic cards with magnetic strips, point of sale (POS) checkout scanners, and remote controllers that combine telecommunications interfaces with terminal management and applications support have been developed. There has also been significant progress made in the systems management software needed to support the expansion of networks with large numbers of nodes. The development of sophisticated data base/data communications and network architecture software has provided the tools needed to hold the systems together. In the areas where standards have been developed, such as with the nationwide implementation of the Universal Product Code, additional progress has been made in facilitating electronic transactions.

One result of the improvement in telecommunications technology has been the enormous expansion of the national wire transfer networks, such as Fedwire, CHIPS, SWIFT, which now handle a daily volume of 1.2 trillion transactions in the United States alone. Their routine use demonstrates a broad acceptance by members of the banking industry who

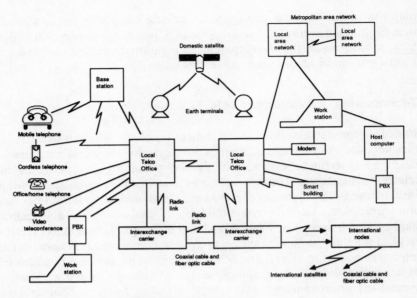

Figure 9–1.   The Communications Network
Source: *Defending Secrets, Sharing Data*, Office of Technology Assessment, 1987, p. 30.

generally view the systems as reliable and secure (Svigals, 1988). In addition, four significant changes have occurred in communications systems during the past decade that directly relate to EFT: digitally coded data, incorporation of intelligence into networks, exponential growth in electronic transactions, and the privatization of the phone and banking industries.

Digitally Coded Data

Early communications media were intended to carry sound. They carried analog data coded in wave form and reconstructed it at other end. Now all information is converted to a stream of discrete numbers encoded as discrete pulses (bits). Data in this form provide more efficient, accurate, and reliable transmission. All information looks the same to the network. Computer data, voice, video, electronic mail, and facsimile images all travel over channels as streams of information bits. Unlike analog coding which required separate medium for each communication device, digital encoding uses a common format to form a single communication network. "There is now a movement toward a worldwide digital network which will convert of all types of data to digital form in order to increase the accessibility of network capabilities, enhance the variety of services available and lower the costs of service" (*Defending Secrets, Sharing Data*, OTA, 1987).

Intelligent Networks

Since digital data is a form directly usable by computers, digital transmission has allowed the computer to be "embedded" in the communication network itself. Computers control the flow of information as it moves from point to point through the network. Such computers can also modify the form and even the content of the information and decide which information to archive. Even the so-called "signalling" information, the information generated by the system that describes the communication and establishes the path from sender to receiver, is itself now stored and transmitted around the network in digital form. This intelligence capability opens up a wide variety of new services and modes of operation and changes the way in which old ones can be delivered. It vastly increases the ability of the network to collect and retain information about the messages that flow through it and has important implications related to the privacy and security of the data.

Exponential Growth of Electronic Transactions

Most everyday transactions of life now can be captured and communicated electronically. Examples include banking at ATM's that are connected with the central computer system of the bank, often through a network that services multiple banks and bank cards; the routine processing of credit card sales on automated readers at the store so that the reader and check for credit availability and record sales on a remote computer serving that card; and the selling of items over cable television by use of the telephone. Business is now moving toward Electronic Data Exchange (EDI) through which most commercial transactions among firms, such as orders, invoices, and payments, can move electronically using no paper. Currently, most transactions involve the exchange of funds and the automation of sales transactions; soon, however, networks will carry more of the textual material of commerce, like bids, offers, acceptances, and contracts. Virtually everything that exists on paper and moves physically will probably move electronically in the future.

Privatization of Communications Networks

Deregulation and competition make the ownership and control of communication networks very complex. A simple transaction may start at a terminal owned by the originator, pass through a local network, then a private or public switched network, a long distance line, and another sequence of regional and local networks at the other end until it arrives at the receiving terminal. In some applications, the message may have been diverted to a computerized information service offered by someone else. ". . . questions such as where the message is located, which legal jurisdiction it occupies, and who is responsible for it can be difficult, even impossible, . . . to resolve" (Weingarten, 1988).

With the improved computer and communications technologies now available, EFT is at a crossroads. The goal of making the ACH and EFT systems fully automated can now be realized in the next decade. All transactions originating from New York are rapidly being converted into all electronic media. Some experts feel that this is the "first opportunity since mass-market EFT began in early 1970s to prove that all electronic is cheaper and more efficient than a mix of paper and paperless communications" (Kutler, 1987).

Technological Problems Related to EFT

The technology itself, while offering a smorgasbord of new possibilities for the payments system, also carries with it a set of vital new issues and problems. Over the centuries during which the banking system has evolved, many policies and procedures have been developed to cope with information on paper. But, these policies and procedures may not work in the same way when information is in the form of electronic signals and when it can flow halfway around the world in split seconds rather than the several days that paper takes to make the same trip. Some of these issues are mainly technological in nature. Other questions, "information issues," relate more directly to the nature of the "stuff" that flows through the technology. Still others, "social questions," relate to the behavior of institutions and individuals that use it. We will describe a few of each in this chapter, starting with technological issues.

Security of Computer and Communications Systems

The increasing dependence on information technology is creating a need to improve the confidentiality and integrity of electronic information, i.e., its security, so that computer and communications systems are less vulnerable to intentional and accidental error or misuse. "Information must increasingly be viewed as a strategic asset .... bankers have always been extremely conscious of physical security—vaults, guards, teller stations ... but data security has met with less enthusiastic response" (Rogers, 1984). Communications networks have become vital for many purposes, ranging from making interbank and government transfers to running national electric power and communications grids. There is every indication that dependence on them will increase, and both the volume and importance of information transmitted will increase. So far little has been done to improve the security of public communications systems which were designed for efficiency and reliability rather than security.

The current security concerns related to communications networks include controls on access, alteration and duplication of electronic data; ease of retrievability and searchability; verification of accuracy and origin; means for auditing or reconstructing transactions; and, more recently protection of the anonymity of the parties in a transaction. Businesses are also concerned about possible misuse of networks by insiders, competitors, and hackers. There is always a tradeoff between security and cost. To be useful for business purposes, security measures must be practical, efficient, and not exorbitantly expensive.

There are a number of serious vulnerabilities to communications networks that are still unresolved. With the rapid proliferation of ground-based or terrestrial microwave radio since the 1940s and satellite communications since the 1960s, interception of data has become easier because signals are available over wide geographic areas. Telephone lines can still be relatively easily tapped. Local area networks (LAN's) have received little security attention and are used to link together many of the computer-based systems. The same technology used to create them can be used to rapidly sort through signals in search of specific numbers, words, or voices. Computer systems are vulnerable to electrical failures, programming error, hardware failure, and deliberate abuse. Typical vulnerabilities to computer systems are illustrated in figure 9–2.

These vulnerabilities raise great concerns for banking systems as they become increasingly more interconnected over public networks in order to extend service more directly to their customers. As some recent events with network "viruses," "worms," and the like illustrate, public systems

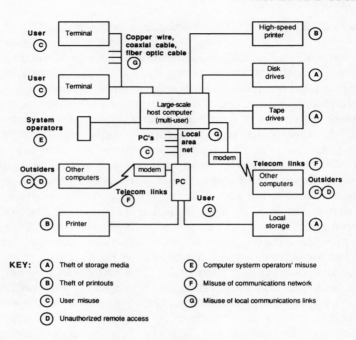

Figure 9–2. Typical Vulnerabilities of a Computer System
Source: *Defending Secrets, Sharing Data.* Office of Technology Assessment, 1987, p. 46.

provide conduits through which some try to gain unauthorized access to private systems. Whether the motive be theft, sabotage, simple curiosity, or a desire to beat the system, this type of intrusion will continue to be a significant threat to communication-based services. The major disadvantage of public networks is that they can never be fully protected.

On the other hand, the new technologies have also brought some new safeguards. For example, optic fiber lines used for long distance lines requires far more sophisticated techniques to intercept than the traditional copper wires. However, even with fiber optic systems, copper wires are often used for local connections creating a vulnerability to the system at that point. Other engineering features used for reliability and efficiency such as signal compression, spread-spectrum techniques, channel demand assignment techniques, and packet switching also complicate interception. The increased volume of transmission data will in itself make it more difficult to obtain the information of direct interest in a timely, complete,

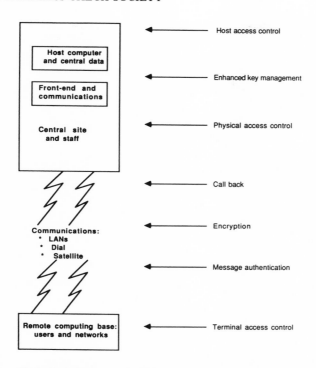

Figure 9–3. Technical Safeguards for Computer Systems
Source: *Personal Identification News*, Washington, D.C., Warfel & Miller, Inc., 1986.

and understandable context. Typical computer system safeguards such as encryption, key management, personal identification and user verification, access control software, audit trails, administrative and procedural measures, and communications linkage safeguards are shown in figure 9–3. *"It must be noted, however, that adversaries with sufficient resources can be expected to readily surmount most of these obstacles"* (*Defending Secrets, Sharing Data*, OTA, 1987, emphasis added).

All of the security concerns about communications networks and computer systems are directly related to EFT. "Hand in hand with efficiencies gained from EFT, is a growing threat of EFT crime ... increased losses striking the credit card industry could foreshadow crime problems for ... expanding retail and wholesale EFT payment systems" (Trigaux, 1984b). For example, credit card losses from fraud went from 4 cents per transaction in 1979 to 8 cents per transaction in 1982. Access to major wholesale

EFT networks widened significantly with banking deregulation in 1980. The increased access to Fedwire from 5,500 Fed members to 19,900 commercial and thrift institutions was seen by some as a potential invitation to crime. Criminal laws in many cases still fail to address the unique elements of EFT crimes because "physical property" language in statutes does not clearly cover funds movement by electronic pulses (Trigaux, 1984b; Whiting, 1984).

Standardization of Data Encryption and Transfer Protocols

One question that has arisen related to security of computer and communications systems is the extent to which the federal government should provide technology to secure communications of users in the private and public sector. As technology continues to improve, the value of information carried on these networks will dramatically increase. By the turn of the century, most payments will be exchanged in electronic form between financial institutions and among their customers. Other commercial transactions such as bids, offers, acceptances, and even contracts will be negotiated and even "signed" electronically. Phone lines already carry a wide variety of commercial information of value, such as financial information, engineering designs, formulas, production schedules, and marketing plans. Using channels that are legally defined as private, but that only have some minimal technical protection, would be insufficient. Commercial users will need access to more sophisticated techniques for protecting their information assets. Protection is not the only requirement. To engage in commercial transactions electronically, we need methods for authenticating sources, "signing" and dating documents, and "sealing" messages. These technologies are, for the most part, some form of encryption, that is, transforming data in such a way as to be unreadable until they are decoded with a "key."

If a market for something exists, we usually expect that firms will appear to meet the need without the need for government intervention. In this case, however, the federal government is already deeply involved in policies that affect the ability both of firms to develop safeguards and of users to deploy them. In area of communication security, the government has expertise gained to protect military and diplomatic communications security that may be hard to duplicate in private sector. Also, standardization and certification is necessary. If information systems must interconnect easily, then security techniques that encode information need to be compatible. If users know the connection well in advance and that it will not change from day to day, then a locally chosen, idiosyncratic technology satisfies their needs. But if users must interact with any number of terminals, owned by different organizations, in order to establish a link at any time, the coding technique must be predictable and known. In addition, since encryption involves an extremely sophisticated technology, most consumers have no practical way to evaluate the level of protection offered by any device.

These concerns suggest that standardization and certification to assure level of protection are necessary at the federal level. For this reason the Computer Security Act of 1987 put the responsibility for private and civil sector security in the hands of National Institute of Standards and Technology (NIST, formerly the NBS). The Data Encryption Standard (DES) developed by the National Security Agency (NSA) has been made available for private use to provide a standardized method for protecting electronic data through encryption.

Interconnectivity and Standardization of Systems

In addition to the standardization of data protocols, there is also the concern about standardization between the many systems themselves. These days applications are seldom installed "turkey," designed to operate independently on a single system provided by a single vendor. Rather, they are layered on top of other existing technologies and services, provided by different companies. Even a simple corporate voice telephone network serving points in several states is now composed of a combination of privately owned local networks, public switched phone lines operated by a local company, interstate services offered by another, more regional services from still another phone company, and, finally, another local network. The equipment tied on the ends of these lines may be made by different companies and designed to do different tasks. Of course, all of this technology must connect together physically and electronically for the network. Distributed data applications can be even more complex. The technology must be compatible at much higher levels of data transfer; in a sense, the technologies must speak the same language.

Finally the poor user also has a problem. Unless all of these technologies and services look similar and behave in similar ways, users have the impossible task of mastering all the different types of interfaces. As the consumer electronics industry is learning painfully, predictability and ease of use is crucial, no matter how many desirable features a piece of technology may have.

All of this need for interconnectivity, coupled with the existence of multiple providers, means that standards are a major problem for both service suppliers and users in the banking industry. The term sometimes used is "interoperability." The difficulty in achieving it is threefold:

1. Agreeing on standards raises antitrust concerns, since features that some might want to standardize, are to others competitive advantages. The federal government worries.
2. Premature or careless setting of technical standards could unduly inhibit technological development. Engineers and designers worry.
3. Standards are usually set by industry producers and providers, not users. So, customers worry.

Even with all those cautions in mind, however, it is difficult to see how a sophisticated information infrastructure of the future with all of the important applications, including financial services, can evolve without a great deal of attention being paid to both interconnectivity and standards.

Societal Problems Related to EFT

"The cashless, checkless all-electronic society has been dawning for so long that one might believe that the banking industry's sun has become stuck. Today, no less than a decade ago, we still look to a new day to dawn for the payments system" (Garsson, 1984). During the 1960s proponents of EFT dreamed of a "cashless" society that would be cheaper and more efficient, machine-intensive rather than labor-intensive. However, the paper system turned out not to be as expensive as projections and was actually cheaper than EFT. An FDIC (Federal Deposit Insurance Corporation) study found that bank earnings during the first decade of EFT were inversely related to installation of EFT. A major reason for the early problems with EFT was the restrictiveness of banking laws prior to deregulation. For example, an ATM was considered a "branch" of a bank and subject to inappropriate regulations. Another problem with EFT, however, turned out to be the less than enthusiastic response of the public to the idea of a checkless, cashless society. "The technology for EFT is light years ahead of both marketing and acceptance" (Nadler, 1988).

Public Acceptance of a Paperless World

There are many reason about why checks continue to survive. It took many years for banks to persuade people to use checks, making it now difficult to persuade them to use something else. Check handling has become more efficient and inexpensive. Bankers themselves had mixed feelings about EFT and missed opportunities to eliminate checks with new types of accounts such as NOW accounts, in which interest could have been used as an incentive to do away with checks. The public has become used to the float. Some use EFT to increase the speed of incoming funds by having paychecks electronically deposited, but maintain control over the speed of outgoing funds by using checks for payments.

The experience of the past 10 years suggest that Americans will give up their paper slowly, and only after they have been thoroughly convinced that they will benefit along with banks from payment alternatives. Despite the almost universally held belief that electronics are cheaper, the banking industry has been unable to move customers into the electronic age. There has been some success with ATM's, but still only 33 percent of banking customers use them. The result has been an increased number of transactions, with two ATM transactions replacing one paper transaction. Customers are not opposed to ATM's or EFT, but they just don't see the need or benefit. In spite of the fact that consumers continue to reject electronic payment systems in favor of paper, banks persist in marketing point of sale debit transactions and home banking by microcomputer. When people use paper, banks are truncating the paper trail with electronic images of checks. With six types of float, check handling is becoming too unwieldy. It has been suggested that banks change the pricing structure to make electronic banking free and charge for paper (Garsson, 1984).

Acceptance of electronic payments systems and ATM's is related to the overall technological literacy of the public. As experience with microcomputers in the workplace has shown, many people are put off by the nonhuman, impersonal nature of technology. In some cases, an actual fear of technology or computerphobia has been documented, even among college-educated professionals (Zoltan and Chapanis, 1982). Conversion to an all-electronic, integrated payments system is an evolutionary process which some financial experts believe is finally starting to take place as young, educated, computer literate, and more affluent people, who are more likely to use ATM's and electronic payments, begin to utilize the system. "Suburban families and families whose paychecks or social security checks are deposited automatically are more likely to have ATM cards, possibly an indication of greater financial sophistication" ("The Use of Cash ...", 1986).

Indications over the past decade as to what kind of people are most likely to use ATM and EFT systems raise again the issue of equity that drew concern in the early 1980s. There were concerns then that some segments of society who traditionally mistrusted and often did not use the banking system would become economically disenfranchised in all-electronic system. Provisions for universal accessibility and alternative payment forms (such as cash!) must eventually be dealt with by the banking system if a truly all-electronic, integrated payments system is to be realized in a democratic society. And not all of the reluctance to rush toward an all-electronic system has been on the part of the public. While the Treasury has been pushing for less paper in the handling of federal payments, the Federal Reserve has been more cautious, and the Post Office has been decidedly unenthusiastic. The regulatory powers of Federal Reserve to control the money supply would be weakened. "Indeed if the only available medium of exchange is 'electronic' money, there may be absolutely nothing left to regulate" (Logsdon, 1980). Similarly, since 65 percent of all first class mail consists of financial transactions, the use of an all-electronic payments systems would severely undercut Post Office operations.

Individual Privacy

In 1920 Justice Brandeis delineated a legal concept for privacy: "[privacy is] the right to be let alone .... [it] is the most comprehensive of rights and the right most valued by civilized man" (Logsdon, 1980). With the increased use of computer data bases for record-keeping and computer networks for transactions, the right to privacy has been severely strained.

One way to put the privacy issue in perspective is to examine the dramatic changes in record-keeping that have taken place in the United States in the last 100 years. When comparing records that documented an American life then and now, we find that 100 years ago the few records that existed kept track of births, deaths, marriages, land boundaries, and ownership. Few school records were kept, and 75 percent of the population was self-employed. There was no insurance, few government benefits, no driver's licenses, and no medical records. Today, less than 5 percent of the population is self-employed, 66 percent have life insurance, 90 percent have health insurance, 95 percent have social security account, and 60 million students are enrolled in schools and colleges. Records are kept by government agencies such as the Internal Revenue Service, Social Security, Selective Service, welfare, and motor vehicle agencies. Private companies keep millions of medical, insurance, and credit records.

Solzhenitsyn provided a chilling metaphor for all of this record-keeping in *Cancer Ward* (1968) when he stated:

> ... as every man goes though life he fills in a number of forms for the record, each containing a number of questions.... There are thus hundreds of little threads radiating from every man, millions in all. If these threads were suddenly to become visible, the whole sky would look like a spider's web ... They are not visible ... but every man ... permanently aware of his own invisible threads, naturally develops a respect for the people who manipulate the treads.

Burnham (1983) stated:

> The most important change is that the computer has mass-produced what has come to be called 'transactional information,' a new category of information that automatically documents the daily lives of almost every person in the U.S. ... the time, location, and amount of phone calls, bank deposits and withdrawals, purchases, driving records, etc. In past, before the computer, transactional information answering these kinds of questions was almost never collected.... [if it was], it was not easily available for inspection. With the computerized filing systems now available, larger organizations of our society can easily collect and store this kind of information .... they can combine it with automated dossiers containing the traditional kinds of information .... there is one more important development made possible by the computer: the incredible maze of electronic highways that can move the new and old information about the country in a matter of seconds at an astoundingly low cost.

So far the impact of information technology on privacy has been concentrated on computerized data bases. Now the concurrent revolution in communications technology will necessitate the protection of personal communication channels as well. With the changes in the basic technology underlying telephonics to fiber optics, satellites, and digital transmission, the protection of telephone and mail transmissions have been eroded or eliminated. Some new media such as electronic mail are not protected at all. The reliance on technology raises the privacy stakes for individuals as more transactions are transmitted electronically. Personal privacy is not the only reason for the interest in protecting confidentiality of communications. The increased reliance of government, business, and other social institutions on electronic communication means that all of these users are increasingly vulnerable to unauthorized intrusions. The costs of such intrusions could be high, such as the collapse of financial markets, the blacking out of the electrical power distribution grid, or the failure of the air traffic control system.

The connection between EFT and concerns about privacy are obvious. Computerized records detailing the finances of private citizens have the potential for great abuse in the wrong hands. Paul Armer, former president of the Association of Computing Machinery (ACM), viewed EFT as the greatest threat to privacy of any use of technology with the potential to be the most effective tool for social control (Armer, 1975). Margaret Atwood in her 1985 bestseller, *The Handmaid's Tale*, also saw the inherent danger in EFT in her futuristic story of the land of Gilead taken over by religious fanatics. In one day all women are fired from their jobs, and the heroine discovers that, when attempting to buy a pack of cigarettes at the corner store, her Compunumber is longer valid, thus preventing her from making any purchases.

> When I got to the corner store, the usual woman wasn't there. Instead there was a man.... He was punching my number in.... Sorry, he said. This numbers's not valid. That's ridiculous, I said.... I've got thousands in my account. I just got my statement two days ago. Try it again. It's not valid, he repeated obstinately. See that red light? Means it's not valid. You must have made a mistake, I said. Try it again.... This time I watched his fingers on each number, and checked the number that came up in the window. It was my number all right, but there was the red light again. See? he said again, still with that smile, as if he knew some private joke he wasn't going to tell me. Later, a friend tells her: Tried getting anything on your Compucard today? Yes, I said.... They've frozen them, she said.... Any account with an F[female] on it instead of an M[male]. All they had to do is push a few buttons. We're cut off.... Women can't own property anymore. It's a new law.... They had to do it that way, the Compucounts and the jobs both at once ... [Atwood, 1985, pp. 227–234].

Concerned legislators resisted attempts to create a national data base in the 1960s and passed the Privacy Act of 1974. This act was originally written to cover information handling practices by federal, state, and local governments as well as private industry, but it was pared down to cover the federal government only. This act recognized that ordinary people were being affected by the "collection maintenance, use the dissemination of personal information by federal agencies and that the use of computers and sophisticated information technology, while essential to the efficient operations of government, has greatly magnified the harm to individual privacy that can occur" (*Federal Register*, 1977).

In spite of the Privacy Act, however, the widespread use of computerized data bases, electronic record searches and matching, and computer networking is leading rapidly to the creation of a de facto national data base containing personal information on most Americans. Though the national data base was not authorized by specific legislation, widespread use of data linkages has led, in practice, to creation of such a data base. Use of the social security number as an electronic national identifier has facilitated the development of this data base. A national data base is actively being created, although in a piecemeal fashion, primarily among federal and state agencies, with some private sector involvement by employers, credit agencies, and banks. Figure 9–4 illustrates how the connected web of information alluded to by Solzhenitsyn is rapidly becoming reality (Smith, 1989).

A significant step toward a national data base was the establishment of the State Income Eligibility Verification System (SIEVS) required by the 1984 Deficit Reduction Act (DEFRA) and used to verify information provided by welfare clients during application process. SIEVS contains wage and benefit data from the state wage information collection agencies, wage benefit and other income data from the Social Security Administration, and unearned income data from the IRS. The proposed electronic issuance and redemption systems for eligibility benefit programs would also be significant components of a de facto national data base, but they would significantly change its nature. Most of the present data linkages occur within the public sector. If issuance and redemption of public assistance were added, it would involve private sector providers, such as doctors, insurers, and food stores. These private linkages would provide information on the health problems and buying habits of millions of Americans, increasing the potential for government "study" (surveillance?) of these patterns (*Electronic Records and Individual Privacy*, OTA, 1986).

Another legislative solution to the privacy problems raised by the new technologies was the enactment of the Electronic Communications Privacy Act (ECPA) of 1986. It attempted to provide a legal protection for the privacy of electronic communications at the same time that it recognized three disparate concerns: the concern of criminal justice agencies that their investigations not be unduly hampered, the concern of ham radio operators and CB scanners to keep their right to monitor public airwaves, and the concern over whether to sanction private interception of cable satellite signals. "Common carrier technology and the tradition of privacy has moved into competition with broadcast technology and the tradition of open waves" (Weingarten, 1988). The technical advances in communication systems described earlier have muddied the distinctions between common carrier and broadcast technology. For many years, for example,

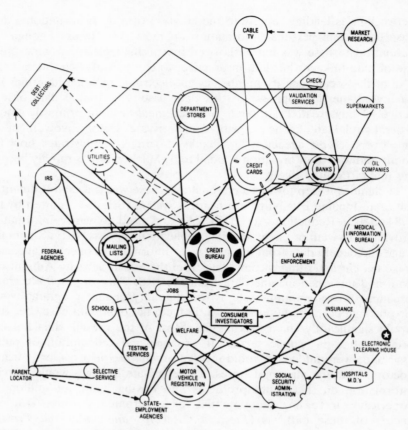

Figure 9–4.   De Facto National Data Base
Source: Reprinted from *Privacy Journal*, Washington, D.C., June 1989.

the telephone system used microwaves for long distance carriage of voice. Microwaves operate as beams along a line and are not useful for broadcast. Now, some cordless phones broadcast in an FM spectrum and some cellular telephone channels operate in television frequencies. Satellites are hybrid, carrying both telephone and television programming simultaneously. The ECPA strove for balance—it expanded legal protection to a wide variety of new electronic applications such as private networks, electronic mail, and transactional information, both stored in a system and in transit. However, the technology involved is such a moving target that the law can barely keep pace with the new problems that arise. Like the Privacy Act before it, it is doubtful whether the ECPA will remain as the final word on legislative solutions to the privacy problem.

One technological solution to the privacy problem has been proposed specifically to counteract the vulnerability of payment transactions in computer systems and communication paths to intrusion. Several sophisticated computer protocols have been developed to protect the privacy and maintain the security of individuals and organizations in automated payment transactions. These "privacy protected payment" protocols allow the bank to collect information about the individuals through their payments by creating a coded used-money list in which the identity of the payers during payment is kept anonymous. The objective is to protect the privacy of the transaction while ensuring the validity of money used (Floch, 1988; Stol, 1988). Privacy protected payment systems are still being developed and tested.

The use of such protocols requires enormous memory capacity and high-speed computing capabilities not currently available or economically feasible for most banks at this time. Another suggestion to protect privacy involves the notification of individuals whenever information is collected or disseminated about them. This also raises the issue of the costs of privacy. Several experts have noted that society may not be willing to pay the economic cost involved to insure privacy. "Always compelling information gatherers to give notice that they are collecting information could become a tremendous burden to the government as well as to private enterprise" (Mylott, 1984). "The proposers of [privacy] regulation often seem to assume that the added costs will be borne by the credit bureaus, presumably out of their profits. This is nonsense. If the credit bureaus are to stay in business, the added costs must be passed along to the consumer—credit will become more expensive" (Armer, 1975). The costs related to protecting privacy are due to three things: manual and technological controls on operating procedures, the access rights of subjects, and the usage control by subjects. In discussing the possibility of establishing a government agency to monitor privacy, Logsdon (1980) noted that a similar watchdog bureau that monitored wages and prices during World War II started out with a staff of less than 50 people, and by war's end had grown to an army of bureaucrats numbering 17,000!

Potential for Computer Surveillance

Implied in the concern for privacy is the implication that ordinary citizens should be free from the fear of having their lives under any form of surveillance by government agencies or private companies. In the past the lack of real-time storage and retrieval capabilities limited the government's ability to perform surveillance to highly selective cases performed manually by investigative agencies. However, new technology has created new opportunities for monitoring. Telephone systems transmit digitally coded data over intelligent networks using switches that are now digital computers and can do far more than switch messages. They can recognize patterns, process information, store it for later use, and print out reports detailing activity on the network. A switch can be used to monitor phone usage automatically and selectively. Many of the local switches are now owned and operated by the private firm, not the phone company. A striking recent example of this was the use of a university-owned, computer-controlled telephone to track the source of obscene phone calls made to local daycare providers from the university president's own private phone line (Davis and Sanchez, 1990).

In his 1967 book, *Privacy and Freedom*, Westin warned that with the growth of computerized record-keeping, the improvements in information-processing capabilities, and the linking of data bases across networks, the use of computers to perform widespread surveillance would become easily possible.

> As information-recording processes have become cheaper and more efficient, the government's appetite for data has intensified and been accompanied by a predilection toward centralization and collation of file material .... technological improvements in information-handling capability have been followed by a tendency to engage in more extensive manipulation and analysis of recorded data. This in turn has motivated the collection of data pertaining to a larger number of variables, which results in more personal information being extracted from individuals (Miller, 1971).

For example, another data base that can be viewed as part of the national data base is the IRS Debtor Master File which was also authorized under DEFRA. This file was created using information from data bases of a number of federal agencies and was to aid in the administering of tax refunds to collect on delinquent federal debts, such as student loans, which are located using computer matching against other files. John Shattuck of the American Civil liberties Union has stated (1984) that:

> Computer matching is an attractive investigative technique. It appears to permit law enforcement officials to instantaneously root out all instances of wrongdoing of a particular kind ... it constitutes a general surveillance system that supposedly can detect and deter misconduct where ever it is used ... the rapid and unchecked growth of computer matching leads inexorably to the creation of a de

facto National Data System in which personal data are widely and routinely shared at all levels of government and in the private sector.

Historically, the government has always claimed the right to intrude on individual privacy when the public interest is great enough. Richard Kusserow, Inspector General of Health and Human Services, defends the government's use of computer matching (1984):

> The overall objective is to expand the cost-effective use of computer matching techniques that prevent and detect fraud abuse and erroneous payments, and at the same time, to protect the rights and privacy of individuals.

This information appetite is not only restricted to government. Businesses and other organizations also gather information about individuals. The distinction between private and government data collection is less important than the exercise of power. Record-keeping is primarily an administrative function and should not constitute surveillance. It becomes so when information is used to influence decisions affecting particular individuals. The existence of computer data banks opens up the possibility of extension and refinement of data surveillance methods, such as the pooling or matching of data from previously scattered files and the more extensive use, extraction, and processing of data in many different ways to serve a variety of uses, other than original intent for data (Miller, 1971).

> Government agencies are more and more relying on the private sector to provide sensitive personal individual information about American citizens instead of gathering the information themselves.... [This trend] threatens individual privacy by diminishing the control individuals have over information about themselves ... the government is relying on several data gathering outfits notorious for their sloppy information collection ... the demarcation between government action in which there is constitutional protection for citizens and commercial activity where there are no such protections, has become irretrievably blurred ... the increased linkage of ... data collection tends to diminish the quality of information in each sector, because applicants start falsifying information or withholding it, when they fear that information that they provide will sooner or later be used for a purpose other than the one for which it was collected [Smith, R.E., 1984].

Of particular relevance to the EFT discussion is the fact that only a few states have limits on what a bank can disclose to state, local, or private investigators or to commercial companies.

> The data keepers say we have nothing to fear, that they are scrupulous about protecting our records. They insist, too, that they have no use for dossiers on individuals, and use the detail available only to target broad markets and to

know the "hot buttons" that make those markets respond ... but the world changes. Events occur and movements swell that cause people to sacrifice the rights of their peers ... imagine the big marketing databases put to use in other times ... by less trustworthy souls. What, for instance, might health insurers do with the subscription lists of gay publications ... [Larson, 1989]?

Governance and the Sovereignty of Nations

Do powerful transnational businesses, using global networks, make the concept of "national sovereignty" obsolete? Since the mid-1800s the scale of technology and the scope of its impacts have changed American life with national transportation, manufacturing, and communications systems. These changes have tended to broaden the role of central government and to diminish the roles of state and local governments. Just as the development of a national transportation and communication system during the last century expanded federal government, technology is expanding the theater of commerce and politics to global dimensions. In the process it is diminishing the degree which any nation, including the United States, may act as an autonomous sovereign. Large-scale enterprises force issues from the local to national to international level. In particular, global communications networks are contracting federal government power by interlocking national economics, facilitating transnational business, and increasing the necessity of political economic cooperation among nations. The worldwide nature of today's technology-oriented problems, such as pollution, depletion of natural resources, global drug traffic, and intercontinental weaponry, all combine to force cooperative actions in the international arena and the surrender of some national sovereignty.

Transnational enterprise is subtly but significantly different from post-WWII multinational cooperation. New transportation and communication technologies have allowed transnational corporations to shift operations between countries depending upon contingencies such as labor costs, resources, and political and economic climate. These developments have increased the power of the transnational corporation as economies of scale have allowed the internationalization and vertical integration of their markets. Deregulation of the international monetary system, rapid movement of investment funds around the world, trading of stock on foreign exchanges and international corporate ownership and mergers make transnational businesses even more independent of national politics and interests (*Science, Technology and the Constitution*, OTA, 1987). If the "coin of the realm" for nations is replaced with a single international electronic currency in the coming decade, the lines of sovereignty will be further blurred.

Conclusions

In this chapter we have indicated some of the policy issues raised by the use of new information technologies in banking and finance. But, the futurist's job is never over. One of the frustrations in thinking about the effects of technological change is that it never stops changing, and it is usually breathtakingly rapid. Computer performance has doubled every two years since the end of World War II, and no one sees any slowing down in the foreseeable future. No other technology in history comes close to such a sustained rate of change and refinement. Even conservative assessment suggests that by the end of the century, the commercially available technology will include: (1) supercomputers capable of performing trillions of arithmetic and logical operations per second; (2) a universal very high capacity digital communications network serving both offices and homes; (3) home and office personal computers with very high resolution displays and with the computing capacity of today's supercomputers; (4) computer software that duplicates human reasoning and decision-making in tightly structured and limited domains of knowledge; and (5) libraries and imaging systems that contain in electronic form most important information and records—data, books, pictures, films, and sounds.

If the generations of technical applications developed over the last decade have raised a number of serious questions, we can only begin to perceive dimly the impacts of the generations to come. Entire modes of doing business will change radically, and the legal, political, and corporate systems based on the centuries-old print medium will have to adapt. At best, we have only begun to think of the opportunities, confront the problems, and pose the solutions.

Note

1. During the writing of this chapter, C. Dianne Martin was with The George Washington University and Fred Weingarten was with the Office of Technology Assessment, U.S. Congress.

212   MONEY AND SOCIETY

References

Armer, Paul. 1975. "The Individual: His Privacy, Self Image and Obsolescence."
    Computers and People (June), 18–23.
Atwood, Margaret. 1985. *The Handmaid's Tale*. New York: Fawcett Crest.
"A Step Toward a Paperless World." 1987. *ABA Banking Journal* 79:2 (February),
    56.
"A 'Utility' to Handle Fund Transfers." 1987. *American Banker* 152:21 (January
    30), 1.
Austin, Douglas V., Donald R. Hakala, and Thomas J. Scampani. 1985. *Modern
    Banking: A Practical Guide to Managing Deregulated Financial Institutions*.
    Boston, MA: Bankers Publishing Co., pp. 37–38, 315–320.
Benton, J., and W. Boucher. 1989. "EFT/POS Predictions and Reflections." *EFT
    Today* 2:1 (January/February), 21–23.
Burnham, David. 1983. *The Rise of the Computer State*. New York: Random
    House, ch. 3.
Carmody, Liam. 1988. "EFT: Emerging Trends of the 1990's." *EFT Today*
    (preview ed.), 9–11.
Cole, S. 1987. "A Sleeping Electronic Banking Giant Begins to Stir." *Bank
    Marketing* 10:10 (October), 32–33.
"Consumers Reject Electronic Payment Systems in Favor of Paper." 1988. *Bank/
    Financial Services Marketing* 22:2 (July), 7–8.
Davis, Patricia, and Rene Sanchez. 1990. "Obscene Phone Calls Are Traced to AU
    President." *The Washington Post* 1987. (April 25), 1, 24.
Defending Secrets, Sharing Data. 1987. Washington, D.C.: Office of Technology
    Assessment (OTA), U.S. Congress.
Duffy, J. 1988. "Global Approach Argued to Protect Consumer in Electronic
    Banking." *American Banker* 153:138 (July 18), 2.
*Electronic Delivery of Public Assistance Benefits: Technology Options and Policy
    Issues*. 1988. Washington, D.C.: Office of Technology Assessment (OTA), U.S.
    Congress.
"Electronic Delivery Systems in the 1990s—What Bankers Can Expect." 1987.
    Bank Administration 63:12 (December), 24–26.
Electronic Records and Individual Privacy. 1986. Washington, D.C.: Office of
    Technology Assessment (OTA), U.S. Congress.
Farrel, R. 1989. "Why Hasn't EFT Caught On?" *EFT Today* 2:9 (May), 2.
Federal Register: Protecting Your Right to Privacy. 1977. Washington, D.C.: U.S.
    Government Printing Office.
Floch, J. 1988. "Privacy Protected Payments: An Implementation of a Transaction
    System." *Norges Tecniske Hoegskole*. Trondheim, Norway: Royal Norweigian
    Council for Scientific and Industrial Research, December.
Fried, Charles. 1970. *An Anatomy of Values: Problems of Personal and Social
    Choice*. Cambridge, MA: Harvard University Press, ch. IX.

"Funds Transfer: Some Privacy Concerns." 1984. *Revolving Credit/Funds Transfer Letter* (June 29), 5–7.

Garsson, Robert M. 1984. "Electronic Society—What's Holding It Up?" *American Banker* 149:96 (May 15), 18–21.

Hanley, Thomas H., Carla A. D'Arista, and Neil A. Mitchell. 1984. "Electronic Banking—Key to the Future If Properly Planned and Integrated." *American Banker* 149:100 (May 21), 4–6.

Hoar, T. 1984. "Auditing in the Electronic Banking Era." *Bankers' Magazine* 167:3 (May/June), 27–32.

Hogg, P., and G. Horkota. 1989. "Banking on Telecommunications." *Canadian Banker* 96:3 (May/June), 18–24.

Howard, A.E. Dick. 1985. "Privacy and Automony in American Law." In Lewis H. Lapham, ed., *High Technology and Human Freedom*. Washington, D.C.: Smithsonian Institution Press, pp. 33–40.

Humphrey, David B. 1984. *The U.S. Payments System: Costs, Pricing, Competition and Risk*. New York: Salomon Brothers Center for the Study of Financial Institutions.

Kantrow, Yvette. 1987. "Treasury Pushing for Less Paper." *American Banker* 152:250 (December 23), 10.

Kantrow, Yvette. 1988. "Going from Paper to Electronics." *American Banker* 153:200 (October 12), 8.

Kantrow, Yvette. 1989. "Electronic Check Hangling Seen for 90s." *American Banker* 153:76 (April 10), 6.

Kling, Rob. 1976. "EFTS Social and Technical Issues." *Computers and Society* (Fall), 309.

Kling, Rob. 1978. "Value Conflicts and Social Choice in Electronic Funds Transfer Systems Developments." *ICS Technical Report No. 112*, University of California at Irvine, April 24.

Kusserow, Richard P. 1984. "The Government Needs Computer Matching to Root Out Waste and Fraud." *AEDS Monitor* (September/October), 12–14.

Kutler, Jeffrey. 1984a. "Industry 'Mess' Hurts EFT Profress." *American Banker* 152:48 (March 11), 8–9.

Kutler, Jeffrey. 1984b. "The Technology Gap in the Banking Industry." *American Banker* 149:243 (December 10), 20–22.

Kutler, Jeffrey. 1987. "1990 Goal—Making EFT System Fully Automated." *American Banker* 152:234 December 1, 3.

Lanza, J. 1989. "Funds Transfer at Crossroads: Managing a Mature Product." *Bankers' Magazine* 172:2 (March/April), 52–56.

Larkin, J. 1988. "Cooperation Needed to Stave Off International EFT Cartel." *Payment Systems Newsletter* 8:24 (December 30), 4–5.

Larson, Erik. 1989. "What Sort of CAR-RT-SORT Am I?" *Harper's Magazine* (July), 65–69.

Logsdon, Tom. 1980. *Computers & Social Controversy*. Rockville, MD: Computer Science Press, pp. 123–150, 307–330.

Miller, D. 1984. "Beware of the 'Hacker' Attack." *ABA Banking Journal* 76:11 (November), 50.

Miller, Arthur R. 1971. *The Assault on Privacy: Data Banks and Dossiers*. Ann Arbor, MI: University of Michigan Press.

Mowshowitz, Abbe. 1976. *The Conquest of Will: Information Processing in Human Affairs*. Reading, MA: Addison Wesley, pp. 146–183.

Mylott, Thomas R., III. 1984. *Computer Law for Computer Professionals*. Englewood Cliffs, NJ: Prentice-Hall, pp. 102–108.

Nadler, Paul S. 1988. "Will the Sun Ever Rise on a Checkless Society?" *American Banker* 153:105 (March 31), 4.

"Privacy Act of 1974." 1976. *Federal Reserve Bulletin* (June), 521–536.

Rogers, C. 1984. "Tips on Staying Afloat in the Age of Information." *American Banker* 149:135 (June 10), 4.

Science, Technology and the Constitution: Background Paper. 1987. Washington, DC: Office of Technology Assessment (OTA), U.S. Congress.

Shattuck, John. 1984. "Computer Matching is a Serious Threat to Individual Rights." *AEDS Monitor* (September/October), 9–11.

Smith, B. 1984. "The Future of Banking—A Technological Renaissance." *Financial Computing* (November/December), 57.

Smith, Robert Ellis. 1984. "1984: Civil Liberties and the National Security State." Testimony before the House Judiciary Committee, Subcommittee on Courts, Civil Liberties and the Administration of Justice, April 5.

Smith, Robert Ellis. 1989. "'The Knee Bone Connected to the Thigh Bone.'" *Privacy Journal* 15:8 (June), 4–5.

Solzhenitsyn, Alexander. 1968. *Cancer Ward*. New York: Modern Library.

Stol, N. 1988. "Privacy Protected Payments: A Possible Structure for Real Implementation." *Norges Tecniske Hoegskole*. Trondheim, Norway: Royal Norweigian Council for Scientific and Industrial Research, February.

Svigals, Jerome. 1988. "EFT Technology Evolution: The Next 10 Years." *EFT Today* 1:6 (August/September), 9–11.

Tracey, B. 1986. "Finding the Key to Unlock EFT." *Computers in Banking* 3:12 (December), 64.

"The Banks Great Struggle to Master a Tangle of Data." 1984. *Business Week* (December 10), 106.

"The Use of Cash and Transaction Accounts by American Families." 1986. Federal Reserve Board (FRB) Publication.

Trigaux. Robert. 1984a. "EFT Crime Potential is Great, Says Justice Study." *American Banker* 149:36 (February 21), 2,8.

Trigaux, Robert. 1984b. "Court Approves Bank Entry into Data Processing (Citicorp)." *American Banker* 149:195 (October 3), 1.

Weingarten, Fred W. 1988. "Communications Technology: New Challenges to Privacy." *John Marshall Law Review* 21:4 (Summer), 735–753.

Westin, Alan F. 1967a. "Legal Safeguards to Insure Privacy in a Computer Society." *Communications of the ACM* 10, 533–537.

Westin, Alan F. 1967b. *Privacy and Freedom*. New York: Atheneum.
Westin, Alan F. 1973. "Databanks in a Free Society: A Summary of the Project on Computer Databanks." *Computers and Automation* 22 (January), 18–22.
Whiting, N. 1984. "Taking the 'Byte' Out of Computer Crime." *Supervisory Magazine* 29:9 (September), 29–32.
Zoltan, E., and A. Chapanis. 1982. "What Do Professional Persons Think About Computers?" *Behaviour and Information Technology* 1, 55–68.

Index